R £6-95

New Studies in the Philosophy of Religion

General Editor: W.D. Hudson, Reader in Moral Philosophy,
University of Exeter

This series of monographs includes studies of all the main problems in the philosophy of religion. It will be of particular interest to those who study this subject in universites or colleges. The philosophical problems connected with religious belief are not, however, a subject of concern only to specialists; they arise in one form or another for all intelligent men when confronted by the appeals or the claims of religion.

The general approach of this series is from the standpoint of contemporary analytical philosophy, and the monographs are written by a distinguished team of philosophers, all of whom now teach, or have recently taught, in British or American universities. Each author has been commissioned to analyse some aspect of religious belief; to set forth clearly and concisely the philosophical problems which arise from it; to take into account the solutions which classical or contemporary philosophers have offered; and to present his own critical assessment of how religious belief now stands in the light of these problems and their proposed solutions.

In the main it is theism with which these monographs deal, because that is the type of religious belief with which readers are most likely to be familiar, but other forms of religion are not ignored. Some of the authors are religious believers and some are not, but it is not their primary aim to write polemically, much less dogmatically, for or against religion. Rather, they set themselves to clarify the nature of religious belief in the light of modern philosophy by bringing into focus the questions about it which a reasonable man as such has to ask. How is talk of God like, and how unlike, other universes of discourse in which men engage, such as science, art or morality? Is this talk of God self-consistent? Does it accord with other rational beliefs which we hold about man or the world which he inhabits? It is questions such as these which this series will help the reader to answer for himself.

New Studies in the Philosophy of Religion
General Editor: W. Donald Hudson

OTHER TITLES

Wittgenstein and Religious Belief

W. DONALD HUDSON
Reader in Moral Philosophy, University of Exeter

© W. Donald Hudson 1975

First published 1975 by
THE MACMILLAN PRESS LTD
London and Basingstoke
Associated companies in New York
Dublin Melbourne Johannesburg and Madras

SBN 333 10261 4

Printed in Great Britain by
UNWIN BROTHERS LTD.
Woking

Contents

Abbreviations

BBB   *The Blue and Brown Books* (Oxford, 1960).

LRB   *Lectures and Conversations on Aesthetics, Psychology and Religious Belief*, edited by Cyril Barrett (Oxford, 1966).

OC   *On Certainty*, edited by G.E.M. Anscombe and G.H. von Wright, translated by Denis Paul and G.E.M. Anscombe (Oxford, 1974).

PG   *Philosophical Grammar* edited by Rush Rhees, translated by Anthony Kenny (Oxford, 1974).

PI   *Philosophical Investigations*, translated by G.E.M. Anscombe (Oxford, 1958).

PR   *Philosophical Remarks*, edited by Rush Rhees, translated by Raymond Hargreaves and Roger White (Oxford, 1975).

RFGB   'Remarks on Frazer's *Golden Bough*', *The Human World*, May 1971.

T   *Tractatus Logico-Philosophicus*, translated by D.F. Pears and B.F. McGuinness (London, 1963).

WWK   *Ludwig Wittgenstein und der Wiener Kreis*, shorthand notes recorded by F. Waismann, edited by B.F. McGuinness (Oxford, 1967).

Acknowledgements

I am grateful to Basil Blackwell Ltd for permission to reproduce extracts from *Lectures and Conversations on Aesthetics, Psychology and Religious Belief* (ed. C. Barrett, 1966). Although quotations from other books are not long enough to require formal permission, I am no less grateful to the authors, editors and publishers concerned for making this material available. I should also like to express my thanks to Mrs E. Ridgeon for secretarial help of various kinds in the production of this book.

W.D.H.

1 The Man

In this book I shall be concerned with how religious belief appears in the light of Wittgenstein's philosophy. First I will try to give as clear an account as I can of both his earlier and his later thought. Then I shall describe how he evidently saw religion at three stages of his intellectual pilgrimage and discuss the philosophical questions to which his views about it give rise. Before doing this, however, it may be of interest to say something about the man himself and his personal attitude to religion.[1]

Ludwig Wittgenstein's early environment was one of wealth and culture. Born in Vienna on 26 April 1889, he was the youngest of seven or eight surviving children born to Karl and Leopoldine Wittgenstein. He spent his childhood in his family's palatial Viennese home and on its country estates. Karl Wittgenstein was a very rich iron and steel magnate. Though he appears to have been of Jewish descent, there is some uncertainty about his precise ancestry. The Nazis classified him as of mixed Jewish blood and left his fortune intact. His son Ludwig in due course inherited a considerable part of it, but he gave it away to other members of the family. Bertrand Russell says he did this on the ground that money is only a nuisance to a philosopher. Norman Malcolm thinks it was because he did not want to have friends for the sake of his money. Both Wittgenstein's parents were cultured persons with strong artistic interests. Music was their particular passion and they passed this on to their children. One of them, Paul, became a concert pianist and after he lost his right arm, Ravel wrote his famous *Concerto for the Left Hand* especially for him. Ludwig Wittgenstein himself in his youth cherished the ambition of becoming a professional conductor and remained a very accomplished musician throughout his life. He had absolute pitch and was said to know whole symphonies by heart. He would quote Schopenhauer's

1

remark 'Music is a world in itself' when trying to express all music meant to him. Not only musicians, but many of the leading thinkers and writers of *fin de siècle* Vienna were close friends of Wittgenstein's parents and used to visit his boyhood home. The ideas current among them at that time seem to have influenced Wittgenstein deeply, as we shall see when we come to consider his views about the mystical.

Until the age of fourteen Wittgenstein was educated by private tutors at home and then he went to school in Linz. After Linz, he proceeded to the *Technische Hochschule* in Berlin—Charlottenburg to study engineering, no doubt with the intention of entering his father's business in due course. Then, in 1908, he came to England to do research. During the next few years, he passed rapidly from one interest to another. First he was concerned with aeronautics. After conducting some experiments at the Kite Flying Upper Atmosphere Station in Derbyshire he went to Manchester University and started to design a jet reaction propellor. The design of this propellor raised mathematical problems and thus Wittgenstein's interest turned to pure mathematics. Then he started to think about the philosophy of that subject. Gottlob Frege and Bertrand Russell were acknowledged authorities on mathematical philosophy, and Wittgenstein, having read their works, visited Frege in Germany and went to study with Russell in Cambridge. His early progress in philosophy was spectacular. Towards the end of his first term at Cambridge in 1912, he said to Russell: 'Am I a complete idiot or not? If I am, I shall be an aeronaut; but if not, a philosopher.' Russell suggested that he should write a paper on some philosophical subject during the vacation. When he showed it to Russell, at the beginning of the new term, the latter read one sentence and then said, 'No. You must not become an aeronaut!' Getting to know Wittgenstein, Russell has said, was one of the most exciting intellectual adventures of his life. Another illustrious Cambridge philosopher of that time, G.E. Moore, has written in similar vein: 'When I did get to know [Wittgenstein] I soon came to feel that he was much cleverer at philosophy than I was. ... with a much better insight into the sort of inquiry which was really important and best worth pursuing, and into the best method of pursuing such inquiries.' Wittgenstein

2

quickly absorbed all that Russell and Moore had to teach him and was soon discussing philosophical questions with them on equal terms.

When war broke out in 1914, Wittgenstein volunteered for the Austrian army and eventually became an artillery officer, serving with distinction on the eastern and southern fronts. Throughout the war he continued to think about logical and philosophical problems, recording his conclusions in notebooks which he kept in his knapsack. Whilst on leave in August 1918, he completed his first book which is now known as *Tractatus Logico-Philosophicus.* Once published, it was quickly recognised in the philosophical world to be a remarkable piece of work and, as we shall see, it had a profound effect, particularly on the Vienna circle of logical positivists. Some years later, on his return to Cambridge, Wittgenstein submitted it for the Ph.D., his examiners being Russell and Moore. After what must have been a unique *viva voce* examination, Moore is said to have submitted a report containing the sentence, 'It is my personal opinion that Mr. Wittgenstein's thesis is a work of genius; but, be that as it may, it is certainly well up to the standard required for the Cambridge degree of Doctor of Philosophy'!

In November 1918, two days after the Armistice, Wittgenstein was taken prisoner by the Italians and spent some months in a camp near Monte Cassino. On his release he went for one year to a teacher training college in Vienna and then worked as a village schoolmaster in Lower Austria from 1920 to 1926. These have often been spoken of as 'the lost years' in Wittgenstein's life because so little has been known of them, but recently Professor W.W. Bartley visited the villages in which Wittgenstein taught, and gleaned from those of his old pupils who still lived there many fascinating recollections of what Wittgenstein did and said. These are presented in Bartley's *Wittgenstein* (London, 1973). I shall have more to say about them below (pp. 97–104). Unhappily Wittgenstein was temperamentally unsuited to school teaching and eventually gave it up in despair. Returning to Vienna, he spent some months working as an assistant gardener in a monastery; and then occupied himself for two years building a mansion for one of his sisters in Vienna. It is interesting to know that, even after his return to Cambridge, he still had

3

himself listed in the *Wiener Adreβbuch*, i.e. the Viennese City Directory, as 'Dr. Ludwig Wittgenstein, occupation: architect', and was described as a resident of the city who lived with his sister Hermine and his brother Paul at the Palais Wittgenstein, Argentinier—strasse, 16. He stayed in Cambridge during the three eight-week terms, but spent at least half of each year in Vienna. After the *Anschluss* he had to give up his Viennese passport and choose between German and British nationality. He chose British.

Wittgenstein had not lost touch altogether with his Cambridge friends during his schoolmastering days. F.P. Ramsey, the brilliant mathematician, who had helped to translate the *Tractatus* and who though only twenty years of age had written a remarkable review of the book in *Mind*, came to see him twice and, at Ramsey's instigation, Wittgenstein visited England in 1925. Eventually, he resumed serious philosophical work and early in 1929 he returned to Cambridge. It was in the following June that he was awarded his Ph.D. He was made a Fellow of Trinity College in 1930. Wittgenstein had already begun to work out the main lines of his later philosophy. Some of his writings from this period concern the philosophy of mathematics. It was to these that Russell referred when, in 1930, he reported to the Council of Trinity College, which was considering the award of a grant to Wittgenstein, in these words: 'The theories contained in this new work of Wittgenstein are novel, very original, and indubitably important. Whether they are true, I do not know. As a logician, who likes simplicity, I should wish to think that they are not, but from what I have read of them I am sure that he ought to have an opportunity to work them out, since when completed they may easily prove to constitute a whole new philosophy.' These were prophetic words, but subsequently Russell became extremely antipathetic towards Wittgenstein's later thought and in the obituary which he wrote for *Mind* 1951 he remarks curtly: 'Of the development of his opinions after 1919 I cannot speak.'

At Cambridge, Wittgenstein became something of a legend. He dressed very casually and sat loosely to all conventions. His rooms were furnished with the utmost austerity: in the bedroom a canvas cot; in the sitting-room one armchair, two canvas chairs, a wooden chair, a table and a fireproof safe, in

4

which he kept his manuscripts and notebooks, together with an old-fashioned iron oil-stove in the centre of the room. For adornments, he had the framed silhouette of one of his ancestors and sometimes some flowers, but nothing else. A pile of chairs was kept on the landing outside for the use of those who came to his class on Fridays or Saturdays from 5 to 7 p.m. He lectured without script or notes of any kind but not without careful preparation. G.E. Moore attended many of his lectures and Wittgenstein would deliver most of his remarks directly to Moore when he was there. He spoke rapidly, gesticulated freely, and moved about the room as he spoke. But if he ran into difficulties, he would signal for silence and spend comparatively long periods in reflection before continuing. Questions would often be addressed by him to individuals and he was hard on them if their replies struck him as foolish. But he was even harder on himself and would sometimes exclaim loudly and repeatedly 'What a fool you have for a teacher!' After the lecture, he would often go to the cinema for relaxation, sitting very close to the screen and munching a meat-pie. This was said to be the only way in which he could take his mind off the problems of philosophy.

Though he spent much of his time in conversation with friends and enjoyed long walks in their company, Wittgenstein did not find academic life congenial. He frequently expressed contempt for his colleagues in Cambridge and for professional philosophers generally. Even Moore and Russell were not free from his disdain. He remarked once to F.R. Leavis: 'Moore? — he shows you how far a man can go who has absolutely no intelligence whatever.' And in a letter to Paul Engelmann dated 8 May 1920 he said that he could not bring himself to have the *Tractatus* published with Russell's introduction which looked 'even more impossible' in translation than it had done in the original. Subsequently he changed his mind about this. Only once did he dine at high table in Trinity and then he came away with his hands over his ears, protesting that the slick, point-scoring conversation of the dons sickened him. Not only was it insincere but they did not even enjoy it! He preferred the conversation of his bed-maker! After that, it is said, if ever he ate in Hall, he asked to be served on a card table below the level of high

5

table. When someone told him that the 'Joint Session', i.e. the annual get-together of professional philosophers, would be held the following July in Cambridge, he replied: 'To me it is just as if you had told me that there will be bubonic plague in Cambridge next summer. I am very glad to know and I shall make sure to be in London!' He did so. Sometimes he tried to stop pupils reading for their degrees, affirming that they could not take philosophy seriously so long as they were doing so. He actively discouraged the promising ones from becoming academic philosophers — and particularly from marrying other philosophers! Karl Britton (one of his pupils) tells us that Wittgenstein once said to him that, if he must become a teacher of philosophy, he ought to do something else first. 'I ventured the suggestion that I might become a journalist' says Britton, 'and at this he was both angry and alarmed. I must at all costs do a real job and not a second-hand one; he would much rather have heard that I intended to become a thief!' It may well have been the necessity which lecturers, journalists, and suchlike, are under to write or talk even when they have nothing to say which aroused his aversion. When told of a research student who had decided not to write his thesis because he felt that he had nothing new to say, Wittgenstein exclaimed, 'For that action alone they should give him his Ph.D.!'

The history of philosophy was a subject about which Wittgenstein said that he knew little. But this was not said in humility. Of Hume, for example, he once remarked that he had himself thought so much more deeply about the problems with which Hume deals that he had no patience to read him. He used to tell his pupils that, if they took a book seriously, it would puzzle them so much that, after the first few pages, they would throw it across the room and start thinking for themselves. But he admired some authors, e.g. Plato, Augustine, Kirkegaard, especially the latter. And, in his later years, at any rate, he was not arrogant about his own work. When a friend suggested that what eventually became *Philosophical Investigations* should be called *Philosophy*, he replied, 'How could I take a word like that which has meant so much in the history of mankind; as if my writings were anything more than a small fragment of philosophy?'

His Cambridge Fellowship lasted until 1936, and during

6

these years Wittgenstein not only lectured but wrote volu-
minously. One of the shorthand-typists, to whom Wittgenstein dictated his works, has recorded that each day for a
week he brought her a selection of vitamin tablets, saying
that she would need them if she was to keep up with him! He
certainly drove himself extremely hard. Apart from the
Tractatus and one paper entitled 'Some Remarks on Logical
Form' (*Proc. Arist. Soc. Suppl. Vol. 1929*), none of his
writings were published in his lifetime.

After his Fellowship terminated he spent almost a year
away from Cambridge in a house in Norway, where he began
the *Investigations*. In 1939, on Moore's resignation, Wittgenstein was elected to the latter's chair at Cambridge. But war
broke out almost immediately and he took a job as a porter
at Guy's Hospital and then worked in Newcastle, making
ointments. He came back to Cambridge after the war, but
resigned his chair in 1947, subsequently visiting Ireland and
the United States. On 29 April 1951, he died in Cambridge.

Like most remarkable men Wittgenstein could make
widely differing impressions on people according to the
circumstances in which they met him, or the intimacy with
which they knew him. F.R. Leavis, for instance, was
outraged, when he first encountered Wittgenstein at a
tea-party one Sunday afternoon in Cambridge, by the ex-
cessively rude manner in which he expressed contempt for
the efforts of a young man who had just responded to an
invitation to sing one of Schubert's songs. Though they had
not been introduced, Leavis followed Wittgenstein out of the
room and chided him for his disgraceful conduct. 'But I
thought him foolish!' said Wittgenstein in surprise. Angrily
retorting that this was no excuse, Leavis waved aside
Wittgenstein's rejoinder that they ought to become better
acquainted and stalked away. But eventually he did come to
know Wittgenstein and his opinion changed. He recently
described Wittgenstein as 'a complete human being, subtle,
self-critical and un-self-exalting', 'a centre of life, sentience
and human responsibility'. Though some who knew Wittgenstein slightly testify only to his arrogance and austerity, those
who knew him longest and most intimately, were impressed
by other qualities. M.O'C. Drury says: 'During the twenty
years that I knew him he was the most warm-hearted,

generous and loyal friend anyone could wish to have.'
Despite their differing opinions of him, however, all those
who came into intellectual contact with him, however briefly
or remotely, were immediately impressed by the intensity of
his commitment to philosophy. 'We have never *seen* a man
thinking before!' some Swansea students are reported to have
said after they first heard Wittgenstein discussing philosophy.
The price of genius is often that its possessor must live on the
brink of mental illness and some of those who knew him best
say that Wittgenstein did so throughout his life. His passion
for philosophy was the kind of passion which more frequently induces despair than elation. He worked at the subject
with a kind of anguish, feeling each intellectual difficulty as
an intolerable burden. Neurotically, he worried lest he would
die before he had solved the problem. He appears to have
been completely without any desire for public acclaim. Only
the problems interested him, not the honours which sometimes accrue to distinguished academics. His intellectual
integrity made a profound impression on his pupils. Karl
Britton, for instance, writes: 'Wittgenstein's absolutely single-
minded devotion to the investigation of philosophical problems, his high seriousness and absolute honesty — these
came to be one of the most important 'absolutes' in my life. I
well remember thinking: What would it be like to be really
disillusioned with philosophy? It would be to think that
Wittgenstein's attempt was not worth while; that it is not
worth while trying to think things out to the bitter end — as
Wittgenstein was trying to do. Wittgenstein made us think it
was worth while, and it has always seemed to me very bizarre
that his philosophy should be regarded by some as trivi-
alising, or not taking philosophy seriously enough.' This
characterised him to the last. A short time before his death
he said to his friend Drury, 'Drury, whatever becomes of you,
don't stop thinking.'

Wittgenstein's family had embraced Christianity and both
his father and grandfather had been prominent Viennese
Protestants. His mother was a Roman Catholic, however, and
it was in her church that Wittgenstein had been baptised and
subsequently instructed in the Christian religion. He became
very contemptuous of it in his youth but changed his attitude
when he was a young man. Malcolm records a conversation in

which Wittgenstein told him that at the age of twenty-one he had seen a play in Vienna during which one of the characters expressed the thought that no matter what happened in the world, nothing bad could happen to him. In this thought of being independent of circumstance Wittgenstein said that he had seen the possibility of religion and had dropped his attitude of hostility towards it. Bertrand Russell in his obituary notice remarks on the change in Wittgenstein's attitude to Christianity and says: 'The only thing he ever told me about this was that once in a village in Galicia during the war (1914—18) he found a bookshop containing only one book, which was Tolstoy, on the Gospels. He bought the book, and, according to him, it influenced him profoundly.' This book is generally believed to have been that translated in English under the title *The Gospel in Brief*. Wittgenstein spent so much time reading it that he is said to have become known to those serving with him as 'the man with the Gospels.'

Throughout his adult life Wittgenstein's attitude to religion was anything but that of a hostile positivist critic. He always gave his own religion during his wartime service as 'Roman Catholic'. Amongst his closest friends and most appreciated pupils he happily numbered many christians. It is said that when he encountered the rituals of organized religion he observed them without demur. He never spoke derisorily about Christianity, or its priests and pastors. When other philosophers expressed contempt for religious beliefs, Wittgenstein on occasion rebuked them. At his death he was given a Roman Catholic burial.

Wittgenstein, however, was not a religious believer. Referring once to two of his pupils who had become Roman Catholics, he said: 'I could not possibly bring myself to believe all the things that they believe.' Malcolm, to whom he made this remark, seems to think that it was wistful rather than disparaging but, so far as I am aware, Wittgenstein never gave any unambiguous indication that he would have liked to be able to count himself a believer. So far as the *Tractatus* is taken to represent his main ideas, we could perhaps bring ourselves to believe that he saw himself as one who had discovered that Christianity cannot be put into words and who therefore expressed his adherence to it in the only

9

possible way, namely by consciously modelling his life on that of Christ (see below p. 103). But from what he said in his lectures on religious belief and from the lack of anything in his life which could be described as religious worship, it seems clear that he saw himself quite unambiguously as an unbeliever.

Nevertheless, Malcolm's remark that although Wittgenstein was not 'a religious person' he had in him 'the *possibility* of religion' is not without point. Dr. H.H. Farmer's analysis of religious experience as compounded of the experiences of 'ultimate demand' and 'final succour' comes to mind. If these are the elements of religion, then Wittgenstein does seem to have had their possibility within him. As for final succour, I have already referred to the impression made on him by the play in Vienna. It is in line with this that when he was giving examples of religious experience in his famous lecture called 'Ethics', he said that sometimes he had the feeling that he was absolutely safe, whatever happened. And again, to the same effect we may recall that, while walking with some frightened schoolchildren through the woods late at night, he is said to have gone from one to the other bidding them 'think only about God' (cf. below p. 103). As for the experience of ultimate demand, Wittgenstein once said that a meaning can be given to immortality, if one conceives of moral obligations which are so binding that not even death could release one from them (see below p. 163). He himself had, from time to time, a morbid sense of his own unworthiness. Self-reproach echoes through his letters to his friend, Paul Engelmann: 'I have had a most miserable time lately ... the result of my own baseness and rottenness' 'I have been morally dead for more than a year!' 'I have had a very miserable time lately, and am still afraid the devil will come and take me one day. I am not joking!', and so on. He spoke frequently of suicide, not only to Engelmann but to Russell. He would call on the latter late at night and say that he was about to take his life and then sit in silence. Some of this may have been a pose deserving the gentle fun which Russell pokes at it: 'On one ... evening, after an hour or two of dead silence, I said to him "Wittgenstein, are you thinking about logic or about your sins?," "Both", he said, and reverted to silence.' But few men can have been more sincerely haunted by the thought that they lived under

10

some sort of Judgment. In his *Lectures on Religious Belief* it is belief in a Last Judgment which he discusses at greatest length. Though he could not say to himself the precise things which believers in such a Judgment are wont to say, theirs was a frame of mind with which he could quite evidently sympathise.

It may be added, I think, that Wittgenstein understood what it is like to experience other related religious emotions or attitudes, such as those of adoration, wonder, and dedication. As an example of what it is to feel adoration, we may recall the simple story of how, on a visit to Swansea, he once encountered an old christian who claimed that Jesus Christ was the greatest of philosophers. In response to this Wittgenstein tried to explain that Jesus Christ was not a philosopher in his sense at all. But afterwards he said that he understood why the old man wanted Jesus Christ to be greatest of everything. As for wonder, we have Wittgenstein's own word for it, in the lecture 'Ethics', that besides experiencing the feeling of absolute safety, he also sometimes had a certain experience which could only be described as wondering at the existence of the world; and he took this as an example of the kind of experience which religious believers have. If it strikes us that this example is too sophisticated to be typical of most religious believers, we should perhaps recall Wittgenstein's remark that, in order to understand religious experience, one must have a certain 'obtuseness'. Wonder at the existence of the world, as Wittgenstein conceived of it (see below p. 80), is inexpressible in words. It is not an intellectual attainment but a stance of gratitude and joy before all there is. A philosopher may feel such an emotion but the wayfaring man and the fool, no less. As for dedication, one evening shortly before his death, Wittgenstein quoted to a friend the inscription which Bach wrote on the title page of his *Little Organ Book*: 'To the glory of the most high God, and that my neighbour may be benefited thereby.' Pointing to his own pile of manuscripts he said, 'That is what I would have liked to have been able to say about my own work.'

After an illness which he had known for some time to be fatal, he was eventually told that he had only a few days to live. 'Good', he said. Before losing consciousness his last

11

remark was 'Tell them I've had a wonderful life!' Malcolm comments gracefully: 'When I think of his profound pessimism, the intensity of his mental and moral suffering, the relentless way in which he drove his intellect, his need for love together with the harshness that repelled love, I am inclined to believe that his life was fiercely unhappy. Yet at the end he himself exclaimed that it had been "wonderful". To me this seems a mysterious and strangely moving utterance.'

2 Wittgenstein's Philosophy

In order to understand what Wittgenstein had to say about religious belief it is necessary to know something of his philosophy as a whole and in this chapter I will attempt to give a short account of its main features.

It has been widely held that there are really two Wittgensteins, the earlier and the later. There are grounds for thinking that Wittgenstein himself took such a view. In the preface (dated 1918) to his *Tractatus Logico-Philosophicus* he claimed that it provided the final solution on all essential points to the problems of philosophy,[1] but in his preface (dated 1945) to *Philosophical Investigations* he attributed grave mistakes to the *Tractatus* and said that the new ideas in the *Investigations'* could be seen in the right light only by contrast with and against the background of' his old way of thinking.[2] Undoubtedly there are important differences between his early and late work, but recently commentators have been disposed to emphasise the similarities rather than the differences.[3] The remark from the preface to the *Investigations*, quoted a moment ago, has been taken by some to mean no more than that his new way of thinking was intended to preserve and develop what was good in the old.[4] Something of both the differences and similarities between Wittgenstein's earlier and later thinking will become apparent as we proceed; but it is important for our purposes, I think, to bring into focus right from the start two general features which characterise his philosophy as a whole.

The first of these is his attempt throughout to show what can, and what cannot, be said. The problem of *meaning* was always with him. When is language meaningful, and when meaningless? His claim to know the answer to this question became, it is true, less sweeping and simplistic as his work proceeded. In the *Tractatus*, he felt assured that he could circle the whole of language, drawing what he called 'a limit

13

...to the expression of thoughts'.[5] The necessary and sufficient conditions of intelligibility, that is to say, seemed perfectly plain to him; they applied to language as a whole and divided at a stroke everything which it makes sense to say from everything which it does not. But in his later writings — the *Blue and Brown Books*, the *Investigations*, etc. — he was content, without defining the limits of meaning for language as a whole, to plot the boundaries of intelligibility which separate one kind of discourse from another. On his earlier view, there is one kind of thing, and one only, which can be said: to depart from it is to talk nonsense. On his later, there are many different kinds of thing which can be said, but the danger always exists of getting them mixed up with each other and so landing oneself in error or confusion. Although his attention thus turned from the external limits to the internal subdivisions of language his concern throughout was with the question of what it is for language to have meaning.

A second important feature of his philosophy is perhaps less obvious though, I think, no less all-pervading. In both his early and late work he was trying to arrive, through an analysis of the meaning which language has, at an understanding of the nature of reality. Throughout the *Tractatus*, he argues, in effect, that because there is a certain character which language must have in order to be meaningful so, corresponding to this, there is by implication a certain character which reality must have; and when we come to the *Investigations* we find him contending that it is grammar, or the use to which language is put, which determines 'what kind of object anything is' (PI,373). Both points of view will be explained and discussed below. For the moment I simply point out that Wittgenstein's account of meaning, however it may have changed or developed, always carried with it certain ontological implications. To say, as superficial critics of his method of philosophising sometimes do, that it is about nothing but words is quite mistaken. It should be seen rather as an effort to penetrate by means of a critique of language to an understanding of reality. This is not to deny, of course, that Wittgenstein regarded philosophy as a second-order, rather than a first-order, discipline; that is, as concerned with doctrines of logical form rather than of

14

metaphysical truth in the traditional sense. But there is nonetheless always a connexion between his analysis of language and his conception of reality. Many problems of interpretation arise concerning this connexion. Wittgenstein at times seems to hold views which, on the surface at least, are incompatible. For instance, how are we to reconcile two views which seem to be evident in the *Tractatus*: namely, the view on the one hand that what cannot be put into words does not exist with, on the other hand, the view that there exist mystical things which cannot be put into words? Or again, when we are thinking of the relationship between grammar and the kind of object anything is, how are we to bring into harmony two stand-points both of which seem to be adopted in the *Investigations*: the one, that language is not derived from the world of objects but somehow constitutes it as rules constitute games; the other that our language-games would lose their point or purpose if the laws of nature changed independently of them? However troublesome such questions as these may be, the fact that they are central to the interpretation of Wittgenstein, supports my contention that one of his main concerns throught was to clarify the nature of reality from a consideration of language.

Amongst the earliest remarks which Wittgenstein wrote in his *Notebooks* are some which, interpreted with care, summarise what I have been saying about these two general features of his philosophy. In September 1913, for instance, he wrote, 'Philosophy... consists of logic and metaphysics, the former its basis';[6] and in August 1916: 'My work has extended from the foundations of logic to the nature of the world.'[7] Logic I interpret here as the science of intelligibility, of what it would, or would not, make sense to say. Metaphysics I take to mean, not the study of some postulated supra-sensible world additional to the world which empirical science explores, but an investigation into how the conception or conceptions of objective reality, inherent in the things which people say, are constructed. Wittgenstein arrived at metaphysical conclusions about the nature of reality from a logical analysis of the concept of meaning in both his early and his late work.

I. WITTGENSTEIN'S EARLY THOUGHT

Publication of the Tractatus

The *Tractatus Logico-Philosophicus*, in which Wittgenstein gave a definitive expression to what is commonly called his 'picture theory' of meaning, is now a philosophical classic. He completed it whilst he was on active service with the Austrian army and, during the summer of 1918, whilst on leave, tried unsuccessfully to find a publisher. On returning to the front he was taken prisoner by the Italians and held captive until August 1919. After his release, five different publishers resisted his renewed attempts to get the book into print, so eventually he despaired and put the typescript into the hands of Bertrand Russell in the hope that he would have more success in getting it published. Russell went to China about that time but his representative offered the *Tractatus* first to the Cambridge University Press, by which it was rejected, and then, since it was short enough to be considered as an article, to a few learned journals. Eventually, Wilhelm Ostwald, editor of the journal *Annalen der Naturphilosophie*, accepted it on condition that Russell wrote an introduction to it. With this introduction it appeared during the autumn of 1921 under the title 'Logisch-Philosophische Abhandlung.' Negotiations were then begun with C.K. Ogden, editor of the series called 'The International Library of Psychology, Philosophy and Scientific Method', to bring out an edition in which the German text and an English translation would be printed side by side. This edition appeared in book form in 1922, F.P. Ramsey, Wittgenstein's Cambridge friend, having prepared the English translation. G.E. Moore suggested the title *Tractatus Logico-Philosophicus* (on the analogy of Spinoza's *Tractatus Theologico-Politicus*) for the English–German edition, and it was accepted after an alternative proposal, viz. *Philosophic Logic*, put up by Ogden, had been rejected by Wittgenstein. The latter considered *Tractatus Logico-Philosophicus*, though 'not ideal', to have 'something like the right meaning'; but of the alternative suggestion he declared that he had no idea what it meant since 'there is no such thing as philosophic logic.[8]

Recently some of the correspondence involving Wittgenstein, Ogden, Russell and Ramsey, about the negotiations leading to the publication of the *Tractatus* has been

16

published. In places it makes ironic reading. For example, there is a letter from Ramsey to Wittgenstein, dated 15 September 1924, in which, having said that Ogden has asked him, whilst in Vienna, to collect from Wittgenstein any corrections which he might wish to make to the text 'in case there should be a second edition', Ramsey quickly remarks, in parenthesis, '(This is not really likely)'! Later on he drives the gloomy warning home again: 'But it isn't worth while taking much trouble about it yet as a second edition is unlikely.'![9]

The *Tractatus* is a notoriously difficult book to understand. In Wittgenstein's opinion, all the leading philosophers of his day misunderstood it to varying degrees — Frege, Russell, Moore and, most of all, the Logical Positivists. It certainly makes great demands upon any reader and there is still much controversy amongst philosophers as to the correct interpretation of certain passages within it. However, it is undoubtedly one of the most important philosopical works to appear in our age.

Origins of the Picture Theory

G.H. von Wright[10] has put on record a conversation in which Wittgenstein recounted how the picture theory of meaning first suggested itself to him. He was serving in the trenches on the East Front at the time but even so had been greatly preoccupied with the problem of what gives propositions their significance. In a magazine which he was reading, he saw a schematic picture which showed the possible sequence of events in a motoring accident. It occurred to him that the picture served as a proposition describing a possible state of affairs. If pictures could serve as propositions, why should not propositions serve as pictures? Indeed is not that precisely what significant propositions *must* do? One of the earliest formulations of the picture theory is an entry in Wittgenstein's *Notebooks*, dated 29 September 1914, which reads 'In the proposition a world is as it were put together experimentally. (As when in the law-court in Paris a motor-car accident is represented by means of dolls, etc.)'[11] Presumably, this entry is connected with the magazine picture, but if so, the date of the entry makes it impossible for Wittgenstein to have been on the eastern front when he

17

read this magazine.[12] Wherever and whenever he saw it, the magazine picture no doubt stimulated his thoughts. But it seems likely that the germ of the picture theory had been in his mind for some time, having been planted there by a thinker who anticipated some of his ideas on this subject. Heinrich Hertz in his *Principles of Mechanics* (English translation, London and New York, 1899) propounded a picture theory of meaning with particular reference to the language of mechanics; and Wittgenstein certainly knew of this because he explicitly mentions Hertz, when referring to 'dynamical models' as pictures of reality (4.04). Hertz restricted the application of the theory to the language of mechanics, whereas Wittgenstein applied it to language as a whole; but there can be little doubt, especially in view of Wittgenstein's early training as an engineer, that he had long been familiar with Hertz's work and that it influenced him when his own picture theory was taking shape.

Wittgenstein's picture theory was an exercise in armchair logic. He analysed the concept of a picture and then deduced from this what reality must be like in order to be a pictur*able* entity and what language must be like in order to be a pictur*ing* entity. It did not upset him at all that his conclusions were not empirically testable. His starting point was the presumption that 'a proposition is a picture of reality' (4.01). The question which he wished to answer was: if the significance of propositions consists in the fact that they are pictures, what then follows concerning the nature of reality and language respectively? Wittgenstein's picture theory is a paradigm case of establishing ontological conclusions from purely conceptual premises. From a postulate about *meaning* — namely, that it is essentially picturing — he deduced a metaphysic both of language and of reality. The picture theory is not a simple matter to understand or explain. In the space available I will do my best to make its meaning clear.

Two Features of a Picture

As Wittgenstein used the word and as it is normally used, 'picture' is a relational term in the sense that if anything, P, is a picture, then there must be something other than P — call this S — *of which* P is a picture. Wittgenstein was concerned

18

to discover what must (logically) by true of P and S respectively for P to be a picture of S. He conceived not only of representational paintings or drawings as pictures, but of schematic drawings, three-dimensional models, musical scores and gramophone records. But although his analysis of the concept of a picture would apply to any of these, the thought uppermost in his mind was always the application of his analysis to language conceived as a picturing entity. He was intent upon showing that the concepts of a picture and of a proposition respectively are such that propositions can be conceived as pictures of reality; and that it is only when we so conceive of them that we see clearly how they come to have meaning.

There are two features which, it evidently seemed to Wittgenstein, must be allowed for in any analysis of what it is for P to be a picture of S. One is that P *must* be a *determinate* picture, if it is to be a picture at all: that is to say, there must be some reason(s) why P is a picture of S and not of anything else. The other feature is that P *may* be an *experimental* picture: that is to say, S, which P pictures, could be a state of affairs which is not yet known to exist or one which, on investigation, will turn out not to exist.

Wittgenstein has these two features very much in mind when he invites us to think of propositions as pictures. For instance, he says: 'Everything that can be put into words can be put clearly.' (4.116b; of. Preface p.3); which is to say that if language has meaning at all that meaning must be determinate. Again, as we have already noted, he says: 'In the proposition a world is as it were put together experimentally' (Notebooks 1914—16, 29.ix.14.): in other words, propositions make sense irrespective of their truth or falsity. We shall see as we proceed that Wittgenstein's picture theory can be regarded as an attempt to provide a theory of the meaning of propositions which takes full account of these two features: the requirement that they be determinate and the possibility that they should be experimental.

Objects and States of Affairs
A picture, on Wittgenstein's view of the matter, is a state (or states) of affairs which represents a state (or states) of affairs. It is important to see what is meant by a state of affairs first,

19

if we are going to see how he provided for determinateness and experimentation in pictures.

'A state of affairs', he says, 'is a combination of objects' (2.01). We will return to 'objects' in a moment but first we must note certain distinctions concerning combinations of them. Two such distinctions are basic: they are respectively that (i) between the atomic (or elementary) and the molecular (or complex), and that (ii) between the possible and the impossible. States of affairs *may be either elementary or complex. Sachverhalt*, here translated 'state of affairs', was Wittgenstein's word for an atomic or elementary combination of objects. All such elementary 'states of affairs' are 'independent of one another' (2.061), in the sense that the existence, or non-existence, of any of them neither entails nor excludes the existence of any other(s) of them (cf.1.21). *Sachlage*, translated here 'situation', is a term which Wittgenstein used to refer to complex states of affairs as well as elementary ones. Wittgenstein offered no examples of atomic or elementary states of affairs, but *if* 'It is red' and 'It is blue' described atomic states of affairs, then either their conjunction, or their disjunction, would describe a situation — i.e. either 'It is red and blue' or 'It is red or blue.' (The latter is equivalent to 'It is not not red and not blue': i.e. the disjunction is molecular in that it can be constructed out of atomic statements by conjunction and negation.) All 'states of affairs' and 'situations' *must be possible* combinations of objects. Each object has what Wittgenstein calls a 'form', i.e. 'the possibility of its occurring in states of affairs' (2.0141). What is possible is evident only by contrast with what is impossible, and so Wittgenstein is saying that, for each object, there are combinations which are possible and others which would not be. Wittgenstein offered no examples of objects but *if* a note of music were an object, a possible state of affairs would be for it to be loud; an impossible, for it to be red. 'Possible' and 'impossible' in this connexion are used in a logical sense. The 'form' of an object is a matter of what it is logically possible for the object to be or do in conjunction with other objects.

A state of affairs may be possible though the statement which describes it is false. The statement 'The flag of Britain is red, white and green' is false but not self-contradictory.

20

There is nothing in the several elements of the state of affairs which this sentence describes, nor in the way they are combined, which puts it on a par with 'This note is red'. It could be the case that Britain's flag was red, white and green, but in fact it is not. Wittgenstein employed the word *Tatsache*, translated here by 'fact', to mean what is expressed by a true statement. This introduces a further important distinction into the discussion of states of affairs, namely that between the *actual* and the *putative*. States of affairs may obtain in reality; or they may exist only in the imagination. But, when Wittgenstein speaks, as he does sometimes, of what pictures represent as 'facts' (cf. 2.1.), we must not infer that he thought all pictures must be true ones. This runs counter to his basic idea that pictures may put a world together experimentally. It was certainly no part of his analysis of a picture to deny that some significant pictures are false ones. His view was quite clearly that, in order to be meaningful, a picture must depict a logically possible state of affairs; and that, as such, it may be either true or false according to whether or not it agrees with the facts which make up the world (2.223).

Wittgenstein differentiated between a *positive* and a *negative* fact. The former is a state of affairs which exists, and the latter one which does not (2.06b). For examples, take 'The cat is on the mat' which states a positive fact; and 'The dog is not on the mat', which states a negative one. Both are facts concerning the world. 'For the totality of facts determines what is the case and also whatever is not the case' (1.12). To know what is, and what is not, the case is to know all there is to know about the world.

'Objects' (*Gegenständen*, sometimes called *Dingen*, or 'things') are what states of affairs consist of in the last analysis. They are the ultimate simples of reality, not divisible into parts nor reducible to anything other than themselves and so not able to come into existence or pass away. That is to say, they exist necessarily. They 'make up the substance of the world' (2.021).

As a state of affairs, a picture, like what it pictures, is a combination of objects. These elements of a picture will be different kinds of object according to the nature of the picture. Graphic paintings or drawings, thoughts and pro-

21

positions were all regarded by Wittgenstein as states of affairs which serve as pictures. In the last analysis, he evidently thought of the first kind as composed of what Max Black[13] has called 'graphemes', i.e. elements which represent their corresponding objects either by physical similarity (as in the case of representational paintings) or in some more complicatedly conventionalised way (as in the case of technical drawings, musical scores, etc.). Thoughts were regarded by Wittgenstein as, in some sense or other, psychical pictures and when asked by Russell what the constituents of thoughts are, and what their relation is to those of the pictured *Tatsache*, he replied: 'I don't know what the constituents of a thought are but I know *that* it must have such constituents which correspond to the words of Language. Again the kind of relation of the constituents of the thought and of the pictured fact is irrelevant. It would be a matter of psychology to find out.' Asked if a thought then consisted of words, Wittgenstein replied, 'No! But of psychical constituents that have the same sort of relation to reality as words. What these constituents are I don't know.'[14] Propositional pictures consist in the last analysis of names. Names are logical 'simples' (3.202): 'they cannot be dissected any further by means of a definition' (3.26). That is to say, they can only be defined ostensively, not verbally. An elementary proposition p is 'completely analysed' when we have reached these 'simple signs' of which it is composed (3.201). It is shown to be a picture of a situation S when we have shown *both* the *one-for-one* correspondence of the names, into which p can be analysed, to the objects, into which S can by analysed, *and* the connexion between *the way* in which the names of p are *combined* and *the way* in which the objects of S are *combined*. If a proposition is complex it must be analysed first into elementary propositions.

Objects which make up the substance of the world (2.021) must be logically distinguished from those combinations of themselves called states of affairs or situations which make up the world itself. 'The world is all that is the case' (1): and what is the case is 'the existence of states of affairs' (2). Objects do not exist outside states of affairs. The nature or essence of an object is its form, i.e. its possibilities of occurrence in states of affairs (2.0123b cf.2.0141). To know

22

an object is to know its nature or form, i.e. all its possible occurrences in states of affairs (2.0123a).

Wittgenstein was not all disconcerted by the fact that he could offer no examples of either objects or states of affairs. All he had set out to do was to demonstrate that they are logical necessities. We must now see that he did this by showing that if there are to be pictures which are capable of being what I have called above determinate and experimental, then there must be states of affairs and objects. This brings us to the question of how pictures have meaning.

Bedeutung and Sinn

We have seen what a state of affairs is. Now we must see how those states of affairs which we call pictures represent or portray other states of affairs. A picture, like any state of affairs, consists in the last analysis of objects combined in a certain way. What is the connexion between the objects in their combination, which constitute the picture, and the objects in their combination, which constitute the state of affairs which the picture represents?

The first step in understanding Wittgenstein's way of answering this question is to look at the distinction which he drew between two sorts of meaning which pictures must have. He says that the individual objects or elements of the picture each has *Bedeutung* which will be translated here as 'reference'. The combination of elements, i.e. the picture as a whole, has *Sinn*, which will be translated 'sense'.

The meaning (*Bedeutung*) or reference of an element in the picture, whether graphic, psychical or verbal, is the object in the depicted situation to which it refers (cf.3.203). The meaning (*Sinn*) or sense of a picture as a whole is 'a possible situation in logical space' (2.202, cf.2.221). 'Logical space' is the realm of the logically possible: it is constituted by all logically possible states of affairs, both those which make up the world as it is and those which make up the world as it might be. For a picture to have sense (*Sinn*) it must be logically possible for its elements to be put together in the way that they are.

The fact that the meaning of a picture is a matter of both *Bedeutung* and *Sinn* takes care of the requirement that its meaning should be both determinate and experimental. Since

23

each object in the picture must have reference (*Bedeutung*) to an object in the situation, this makes it logically possible to reach a point where one can say that *this* picture, P, can refer to *that* situation, S, alone. The analysis can be completed: one can say (of *all* the elements in P and *all* those in S respectively) '*This* one refers to *that* one, and no further analysis can show otherwise, because neither *this* nor *that* is further analysable'. Hence the meaning is determinate.

The fact that the picture as a whole can have sense (*Sinn*) i.e. that it can represent a possible situation in logical space, means that it is possible to construct pictures experimentally. As we have seen, Wittgenstein spoke of objects (or elements) as having 'form', i.e. certain possibilities of occurrence within states of affairs (2.0141). In accordance with these possibilities we can combine elements into pictures which may not be true ones. All pictures are experimental in the sense that their meaning is a matter logically distinct from their truth or falsity. Any proposition, say, 'John loves Mary', must (logically) be known to be meaningful before it can be known to be true or false. It is asserted, so to say, experimentally, and only then can it be verified or falsified. But if propositions — or any other pictures — had only the same kind of meaning as their individual elements, i.e. only *Bedeutung*, if in other words propositions were simply complex names, then we would be in a dilemma. For, in such case, no picture could be meaningful until it was known to be a true one; but it still could not be known to be either true or false until its meaning was known. If, for instance, the meaning of the proposition 'John loves Mary' is John's loving Mary, then, if John does not love Mary the proposition will not only be false, but meaningless. But how could we ever know whether this proposition 'John loves Mary' is true or false unless first we knew that John's loving Mary is what it meant? To define the meaning of a picture as *Bedeutung* alone would thus be self-defeating.

Meaning, which is determinate and experimental, is given to a picture by *Bedeutung* and *Sinn* in due combination. Suppose 'Smith is eating strawberries' were an elementary proposition (which it is not) and the elements of it were 'Smith', 'is eating' and 'strawberries'. If these elements had no *Bedeutungen* or references, i.e. if there were no objects —

24

Smith, the act of eating, and strawberries — corresponding to them, then the proposition would be meaningless. But, given (a) that it is logically possible for Smith to be eating strawberries and (b) that there are 'laws of projection' (4.0141) which connect the name 'Smith' with Smith, the name 'is eating' with the act of eating and the name 'strawberries' with strawberries, then 'Smith is eating strawberries' will have meaning, even before anyone knows whether or not Smith is in fact eating strawberries. So it is, says Wittgenstein, that whereas, when we come upon a *name* which we have not encountered before we *do not* understand it until its meaning (*Bedeutung*) has been explained to us, nevertheless, if we come upon a *proposition* which we have not encountered before we *can* understand its meaning (*Sinn*) without any explanation, provided only that we are familiar with the meanings (*Bedeutungen*) of the names used in it. If, for instance, 'Jacynth' were a name in this sense and I had not encountered it before, I would have to ask 'Who or what is Jacynth?' before I could understand it. But once I knew that 'Jacynth' was the name of a woman, I could understand the proposition 'Jacynth is a novelist' even though it was news to me. This is what Wittgenstein meant when he wrote 'It belongs to the essence of a proposition that it should be able to communicate a *new* sense to us' (4.027); and 'A proposition must use old expressions (i.e. names) to communicate a new sense' (4.03, parenthesis mine). This new sense may be information, true or false, which we did not have before; or it may be a conjecture which we still need to test against reality (2.222). The meaning of a proposition is always a matter of both *Bedeutung* and *Sinn*. Because its elements have objects corresponding to them, this makes it possible for the meaning to be determinate (cf. 3.23), and because these elements can be combined to represent a possible situation in logical space, this means that the meaning of a proposition can be experimental (cf.4.027).

Structure and Form

'The fact that the elements of a picture are related one another in a determinate way', said Wittgenstein 'represents that things are related in the same way' (2.15a). He called 'this connexion of its elements' the 'structure' of the picture,

25

and 'the possibility of this structure' its 'form' (2.15b). The relationship between, on the one hand, the structure and form of a picture and, on the other, the structure and form of the situation which it represents is a complex matter. It takes us to the heart of the picture theory.

The first thing to bear in mind is what 'represents' (*stellt vor*) means in 2.15a, quoted at the beginning of this sub-section. It does not mean that the picture is related to what it represents as an element of the picture is related to an object in the situation. We saw above (p. 24) what anomalies arise if a proposition is taken to be a complex name. We must hold clearly in mind that it is the 'fact' that things in the picture are related as they are which represents that things are related as they are in the situation depicted. This is the force of Wittgenstein's remark at 3.1432 with reference to propositional pictures. 'Instead of "The complex sign '*aRb*' says that *a* stands to *b* in relation R", we ought to put "*That* 'a' stands to 'b' in a certain relation says (*sagt*) that *aRb*". That is to say, the *fact that a* stands in relation R to *b* in the symbol '*aRb*' says that in the world what 'a' stands for stands in the relation which 'R' stands for to what 'b' stands for.

Max Black[15] has offered an example of how a picture fact represents a state of affairs, and it will be useful to introduce this here. He takes the following instance of a picture:

$$0 \quad +$$

and refers to it as a picture-fact. Let its meaning be defined by the following conventions or rules of projection, says Black:

(i) O stands for Russell.
(ii) + stands for Frege.
(iii) If a symbol such as 0 is immediately to the left of one such as +, this means that whatever 0 stands for admires whatever + stands for.

Given these stipulations, the picture-fact is a picture of Russell admiring Frege. It represents (cf.2.15a quoted above) that Russell and Frege are combined in the relation of

26

admiring and being admired in one state of affairs as 0 and +
are combined by the relation of being to the left of in the
picture-fact.

How precisely is such representation effected? It would
seem clearly to be the case that if a picture fact represents a
situation, then there will be both (i) an *external* and (ii) an
internal connexion between them. This, at any rate, is how
Wittgenstein appears to have seen the matter. We will
consider each kind of connexion in turn.

Take first the *external* connexion. In the above example,
the stipulations (i) to (iii) are matters of convention. It has
been arbitrarily decided that '0' stands for Russell, '+' for
Frege and being to the left of for admiring. This must have
been the kind of thing which was in Wittgenstein's mind
when he spoke of 'laws of projection' (3.11—3.13, 4.0141)
whereby a picture is connected with the situation which it
depicts. This kind of connexion between the picture and
what it represents is external in the sense that there is
nothing in the picture itself which tells you that '0' stands for
Russell, etc. Sometimes, of course, the elements of a picture
look like what they represent as '0' does not look like Russell
or being to the left of, like admiring. But even if the picture
fact in our example were a photograph in which Russell was
applauding or bowing before Frege, so that it would be the
most natural thing in the world to call the picture 'Russell
admiring Frege', nevertheless the marks on paper which are
the elements of the picture would have to be conventionally
related to the elements of the situation. Russell, after all, was
not a two-dimensional set of marks on a piece of printing
paper. This set of marks which pictures Russell must
(logically) be connected by some rule(s) or law(s) of
projection with Russell himself.

The fact that the connexion between a picture and what it
represents is in part external is evidently what Wittgenstein
had in mind at 2.173: 'A picture represents its subject *from a
position outside it*...That is why a picture represents its
subject *correctly or incorrectly*' (italics mine). The words
'from a position outside it' indicate that the convention
whereby elements of the picture in their particular combination represent the objects of the subject in theirs is
arbitrary. The words 'correctly or incorrectly', meaning truly

or falsely, call attention to the further point that until we know the content of this arbitrary convention — that *this* represents *that* — we cannot know whether or not the picture is a true one.

What now of the *internal* relation between a picture and what it depicts? I think that there are two closely related points to notice here, one concerning the *sense of a picture* and the other concerning *pictorial* and *logical form*.

In what he had to say about the sense of a picture Wittgenstein brought out that there is an internal relation between a picture and what it depicts. A picture, P, does not stand for the possible situation in logical space, S, which is its sense (*Sinn*) in the way that P's elements stand for the objects in S which are their references (*Bedeutungen*). A picture '*contains*' the possibility of the situation which it represents (2.203): or to be rather more precise, what the picture contains is the possibility of expressing its sense (3.13c). Every picture, whatever its particular way of representing reality may be, is a logical one (2.182): it expresses a possible situation in logical space. A logical picture is a thought (*Gedanke*) (3). In propositions, as indeed in all pictures, thoughts find an expression which can be perceived by the physical senses (3.1). We express a thought when we *use* a picture with a sense. What Wittgenstein says of propositions would apply to all pictures: 'The method of projection is to think of the sense of the proposition' (3.11b). That is, to use it with this sense. A state of affairs is not a picture of another state of affairs until it has projection; that is, until it is *taken for* a picture of something. So, the connection between the situation which a picture depicts and the picture itself is internal in the sense that to use the picture as a picture at all is to express the situation which is its sense.

In what he had to say about pictorial and logical form Wittgenstein attempted to explain how it is that a picture can have the sense which it has, i.e. how the internal relation between it and what it represents is constituted. He said that a picture and what it depicts 'must have something in common' (2.16); and he even spoke of this as 'something identical' (2.161). The 'something' he called *pictorial form (die Form der Abbildung)* or more fundamentally, *logical form* (*die logische Form*). By 'form', as we saw above, Wittgenstein meant the possibility of structure. His basic idea then, so far as the internal connexion of a picture and what it pictures is concerned, was that they must have possibility of structure in common. Now, it is easy to see that, if there is to be a picture at all, the elements of a picture must be able to combine as they are required to combine, in order to make the picture; and those of the situation represented must be able to combine as they are taken to combine. For example. '0' must have the possibility of being to the left of '+', just as Russell must have that of admiring Frege, if the picture-fact:

$$0 \quad +$$

is to represent Russell admiring Frege. Is this, then, the possibility of structure (i.e. the form) which they must have in common? It is conceivable that either what is taken for a picture or what it purports to picture should fail to have form, or possibility of structure. Suppose, for example, that someone proposed that '0' should stand for Russell, '+' for Frege, and *being louder than* for admiring. It would then be impossible to depict Russell admiring Frege with these materials because '0' cannot (logically) be louder than '+'. '0' and '+' are marks on paper. They can be connected by the spatial relation, being to the left of; but since they are not sounds, one cannot be louder than the other. We may, then, safely say this on the subject of the form common to a picture and what it pictures: it must be possible for the elements of a picture to combine *as they are required by the relevant laws of projection to combine*, and for the objects of the situation depicted to combine *as they are taken to do in any description of the situation*, if the one is to be a picture of the other.

But is this what Wittgenstein meant — is it *all* he meant — when he spoke of pictorial or logical form? Let us look closely at what he did say. Of pictorial form, he said: 'What a picture must have in common with reality in order to be able to depict it — correctly or incorrectly — *in the way it does*, is its pictorial form' (2.17, italics mine). This remark could, I think, be taken to mean no more than that, *given* 'the way that it (i.e. the picture) does (depict reality)' (i.e. *given* the laws of projection or the stipulations adopted in this particular case, e.g. Black's (i) — (iii) above) the picture and what it depicts must have the possibilities of structure which they are required to have in order to be that particular picture and that particular situation, otherwise there could be no picture. Given Black's stipulations (i) — (iii), we could not have the picture fact we have unless '0' were capable of being to the left of '+' and Russell were capable of admiring Frege. 'Pictorial form' on this view is simply the possibility in the picture and the pictured of there being that picture.

But although Wittgenstein goes on to speak of logical form in terms very similar to those which he has used of pictorial form there are differences which must be noted. 'What any picture, *of whatever form*, must have in common with reality, in order to be able to depict it — correctly or incorrectly — *in any way at all*, is logical form, i.e. the form of reality' (2.18, italics mine). This 'in any way at all' seems as if it must mean that in *any* picture of a situation there must be a possibility of structure, which is *identical with* that of the situation. It is not easy to see precisely what was in Wittgenstein's mind here. Two possible interpretations suggest themselves.

On one of these, to take an example, if P1 is a painting of S, and P2 is a musical representation of S, where S is a battle, then, in the last analysis P1, P2 and S must all have a common logical form. They must, that is to say, have the *same* possibilities of structure. But it is, to say the least, not immediately apparent how this could be. The relations between paint marks on the one hand, and between musical notes on the other, seem radically different; and both seem radically different from the relations between soldiers in battle. Of course, P1, P2, and S would all need to be analysed much further before their ultimate elements are revealed but the presumption of the interpretation which I am now considering is that they can all be reduced to simples which in the last analysis have the *same* possibilities of structure. We are prepared for Wittgenstein not to offer us any examples of such simples; but we are entitled to look for some reason why there must be this common logical form between a picture and reality. It does not seem to be essential to either the determinateness or the experimentation involved in picturing. Provided there are unambiguous laws of projection whereby the elements of the picture and the situation depicted are correlated one-for-one, and the methods of combination are correlated, the picture can be as determinate or experimental as you like without supposing identical form. Moreover, there seems to be a *prima facie* case against the view that the possibilities of structure of a picture and a situation could, in the ultimate, always be shown to be identical. To return to the picture fact wherein '0' is to the left of '+' and represents Russell admiring Frege, notice that 'being to the left of' is a transitive relation, whereas admiring is not. If A is to the left of B and B is to the left of C, then A is to the left of C; but if Russell admires Frege and Frege admires Wittgenstein, it does not follow that Russell admires Wittgenstein. Are we to say that, nevertheless, things which can be to the left of each other and men who can admire other men must all be reducible to elements which can be structured in a way which in the last analysis is both being to the left of and admiring? Why should we have to say this? It is what having logical form in common means on our present interpretation; but it does not seem very plausible.

On a somewhat different, and I think more plausible, interpretation, the logical form which a picture, whatever its particular way of depicting reality, must have in common with reality in order to be able to depict it in any way at all, is simply the possibility of picturing as such. Even if in the final analysis the elements of a picture are combined in a different way from those of the situation which it depicts, there must be some correspondence between the structure of the picture and that of reality for the picture to be possible. Perhaps what I have in mind here could best be explained as follows. The account which physical science gives of the physical world is no doubt highly abstract, partial, schematic. Nature is, most likely, infinitely more complex a phenomenon than science portrays. However in so far as nature chimes in with predictions deduced from scientific hypotheses, we are entitled to say that the logical structure of science and the structure of nature must be to some extent identical. In fact, the course of nature does chime in to a very considerable degree. Scientific hypotheses are very frequently corroborated when put to the test. Partial though science's

31

account of nature may be, it cannot be entirely mistaken since it so often gives rise to predictions which are fulfilled in the event. Now, it is just because of this that science can be said to give us a picture of nature. If it were not so, if nature invariably falsified scientific predictions, then it would be not only false, but meaningless, to say that it gave us a picture of nature. Common to a picture and what is pictured must be the possibility of this picture existing as such. It is not enough, in order for there to be a picture, P, of situation, S, that the elements of P, combined as they are, have been correlated by arbitrary laws of projection, with the elements of S, combined as they are. There must be something more, even if it is only the unchanging character of the situation S, which makes it logically possible for P to exist as a picture of S. If S were continously changing, then our correlations between P and S could not last long enough for P to exist as a picture of S. If the form of reality had nothing in common with the form of our pictures of it, then the latter could exist only as figments of our imagination, not as pictures of reality. This is the necessity which Wittgenstein so to say, imposes on reality through his picture theory of language. If language is to picture reality, then reality must be such that it can be talked about: from the logical structure of language we can, therefore, draw certain conclusions about the nature of reality. As we noted above, the basic move is from linguistic premises to ontological conclusions.

Language

All that I have said so far about pictures in general applies to the particular case of language. In concluding this section I will refer to two further points which Wittgenstein made about propositions. They would apply *mutatis mutandis* to any kind of picture of reality, but he refers them to propositions in particular. When we turn our attention in chapters 3 and 4 to certain criticisms of language which purports to express religious belief, we shall find that these two points are of especial importance.

One is that if a proposition is significant it is significantly negatable. To understand a proposition, Wittgenstein held, is 'to know what is the case if it is true' (4.024). But to know what is the case if the proposition 'It is raining' for example, is true, I must be able to distinguish between rain and fine; that is to say, I must know what it would be like for 'It is raining' to be false. Its negation must be significant. This is what Wittgenstein evidently meant when he wrote in his *Notebook*: 'In order for a proposition to be capable of being true, it must also be capable of being false' (5.6.15); and in the *Tractatus* 'The positive *proposition* necessarily presupposes the existence of the negative proposition and *vice versa*' (5.5151c). We shall see the relevance of this criterion of significant negatability when we consider the argument that religious beliefs are meaningless because unfalsifiable in chapter 4.

The second point about language is that which Wittgenstein described as his 'fundamental idea'. He expressed it thus: ' ... that the "logical constants" are not representatives; there can be no representatives of the *logic* of facts' (4.0312b). By 'logical constants' he meant connective words such as 'not', 'and', 'if − then', 'or'. By saying that they are not representatives he meant that they are not the names of objects. Elementary propositions are 'concatentations of names' (4.22) and contain no logical constants: that is why they are, as we noted above (p. 20), logically independent of one another, able neither to contradict nor to imply one another. Wittgenstein's reason for saying that logical constants are not the names of objects was that, if 'not', for example, named an object, then a state of affairs referred to by 'p' could not be the same as one referred to by 'not not p'. The latter would have two more objects (not, not) in it than the former. But 'not not p' is materially equivalent to, has the same truth value as, pictures the same state of affairs as, 'p'. Logical connectives constitute the logical form of propositions and so it follows that logical form as such cannot be represented. Note how Wittgenstein put it: 'Propositions can represent the whole of reality, but they cannot represent what they must have in common with reality in order to be able to represent it − logical form' (4.12). In chapter 3 we shall see how this conclusion was related to Wittgenstein's views about the mystical.

II. WITTGENSTEIN'S LATE THOUGHT
The Later Writings
Wittgenstein believed as we noted above (p. 13) that he had found in the *Tractatus* 'on all essential points the final solution of the problems' of philosophy. Further reflection led him to revise this belief. The process whereby he came to abandon the picture theory of the *Tractatus* and to adopt the views about meaning and reality which find definitive expression in the *Philosophical Investigations* was a protracted one. There is some evidence that he continued to think about the philosophy of language even in the years 1920—26 which he spent as a schoolmaster.[16] After he gave up school teaching, whilst working first as a gardener at a monastery, and then designing a Viennese mansion for his sister in collaboration with his friend Paul Engelmann, he continued to be interested in philosophical problems and had conversations with Moritz Schlick who later became famous as the founder of the Vienna Circle of Logical Positivists. Rudolf Carnap, Friedrich Waismann and Herbert Feigl also at various times participated in these conversations. Then, during March 1928, Feigl and Waismann persuaded Wittgenstein to attend a lecture by the Dutch mathematician, Brouwer, on the philosophy of mathematics. When they went to a café afterwards, says Feigl, Wittgenstein 'became extremely voluble and began sketching ideas which were the beginning of his later writings.'[17] Feigl thinks that this evening marked the return of Wittgenstein to strong philosophical interests; but it seems more likely that he had never in fact forsaken them. At all events, he was back in Cambridge as a research fellow of Trinity College by 1929.

In the decade which followed until the outbreak of war Wittgenstein wrote a great deal. Soon after his return to Cambridge he prepared a paper, 'Some Remarks on Logical Form'[18] for the Joint Session of the Artistotelian Society and the Mind Association in 1929. Although he expressed dissatisfaction with it before it was due for delivery, it is of interest because it reveals some of the grounds which he found for the beginning of his rejection of the picture theory. In the early thirties two long books, *Philosophische Bermerkungen*[19] and *Philosophische Grammatik*[20] were written and in these he explicitly rejected the logical atomism of the

Tractatus and gave a first formulation to some of the main ideas about the philosophy of language, mathematics and mind which are the staple of his later thought. Many passages in his *Philosophical Investigations*[21] and his *Remarks on the Foundations of Mathematics*[22] are extracts from, or restatements of, passages in these two earlier works. In term time Wittgenstein lectured in Cambridge. His class of 1933–34 had notes dictated to it which eventually circulated as *The Blue Book*;[23] and his class of 1934–35, notes which became known as *The Brown Book*.[24] In these volumes the concept of language-games was systematically developed. Wittgenstein spent some of the vacations of 1930–32 in Vienna having further conversations with Schlick and members of his Circle. Waismann made notes of these discussions and they have now been published under the title *Ludwig Wittgenstein und der Wiener Kreis*.[25] After his brief visit to Russia in 1935 and a year spent in a hut in Norway working on *Philosophical Investigations,* he came back to Cambridge and resumed his lecturing. Some of the pupils who attended his classes in 1938 kept and collated their notes; these have now appeared under the title *Lectures and Conversations on Aesthetics, Psychology and Religious Belief*.[26] Wittgenstein left Cambridge on the outbreak of war, returning in 1945. A selection of his writings in the period 1945–48 has been published under the title *Zettel*.[27] British academic life was never very congenial to him and after the war he seems to have found it very distasteful. He resigned his chair in 1947 and went to Ireland where he finished *Philosophical Investigations* a year later. In the closing period of his life he continued to write and some of this work has been published under the title *On Certainty*.[28]

Of these later works only the paper 'Some Remarks on Logical Form' was published during his lifetime, the remainder being published by his literary executors during the period since his death in 1951. The style of these later works is different from that of the *Tractatus*. The latter presents a highly abstract, tersely phrased, rigorously conducted argument, whereas the later writings tend to be discursive, repetitive as between one work and another, full of illustrations and composed in a conversational manner which is often more reminiscent of letters to a friend than of other philosophical treatises. This does not, of course, mean that these later works are easy to read or understand; the problems with which they deal are without exception very complicated ones. My interest will be mainly in what they reveal of Wittgenstein's reasons for abandoning the picture theory and adopting a different theory of the meaning of language and its relation to reality.

The Demise of the Picture Theory

Wittgenstein gradually abandoned the referential theory of the *Tractatus* for a theory of meaning which may conveniently be designated 'meaning as use'. Before dealing with the substance of this theory, let us note three grounds on which Wittgenstein grew dissatisfied with the *Tractatus* theory. They were (i) his recognition that propositions can form systems; (ii) his recognition of the modal component in language; and (iii) his recognition of the limits of analysis.

(i)

In the *Tractatus* Wittgenstein had said, in effect, that, if we are to get at the meaning of any piece of language we must analyse it into elementary propositions which are *logically independent* of one another and consist of elements (names) which refer one-for-one to the simples (objects) of reality. He came to see that elementary propositions may be *logically related* to one another within systems and that, in order to understand any single proposition, one must understand the whole system to which it belongs. Moreover, he came to believe that the ultimate simples or reality are not, or not merely, the one-for-one correspondents of the elements of individual propositions, but are whatever looks as if it *has* to exist in order for there to be the systems of propositions which there are (cf. PI 50).

Wittgenstein moved towards these conclusions through reflecting on propositions which describe properties admitting of gradations or degrees, such as colour or length. He argued that, whilst such propositions cannot be analysed into simpler propositions and so are elementary according to that criterion, they may nevertheless exclude one another and so are not elementary in the sense of being logically independent of one another.

36

His line of argument for the unanalysability of such propositions ran as follows. In the *Tractatus* he had taken it that, because it would be contradictory to say that a single point in a visual field had two different colours, propositions assigning particular colours or shades to such points in a visual field cannot be elementary, the reason why they cannot being that it is logically impossible for elementary propositions to contradict one another(cf. 6.3751). Given the principles of the *Tractatus* it follows that propositions assigning particular colours or shades to points in a visual field must be capable of further analysis into more elementary propositions. It was this conclusion which Wittgenstein came to reject. Suppose, he said,[29] that an entity E has two units of brightness (a property admitting of degrees or gradations) and that *b* stands for one unit of brightness. 'E($2b$)' states the fact that E has two units or degrees of brightness. How are we to analyse 'E($2b$)'? If we analyse it 'E(b) + E(b)', this says no more than 'E(b)'. If we distinguish between the units and analyse it 'E(b') + E(b'')', we assume two different units of brightness. But in this latter case, if there were some other entity which possessed only one degree of brightness, a question would arise as to which of the two — *b'* or *b''* — it was. This question would be manifestly absurd. So neither analysis is satisfactory. This *reductio* seemed to Wittgenstein to be conclusive against the view that all propositions describing properties such as colour or length which admit of gradations can be analysed into more elementary ones.

Though unanalysable, such propositions are not, Wittgenstein now realised, logically independent of one another. If I know that a point in a visual field is blue, I know not only that, but also that the point is not green, not red, not yellow, and so on. Similarly, if I know that an object is 3cm long, I know not only that, but also that it is not 4cm, 5cm, etc. long. Wittgenstein's explanation of why this is so was that, in such cases, 'a *system* of propositions is laid against reality like a ruler'[30] A ruler may be thought of as a system of propositions; it consists in effect of a set of descriptions of what it is for anything to be e.g. 1cm long, 2cm long, 3cm long, and so on to the full extent of its degrees or gradations. These descriptions are logically interrelated. In the *Tractatus*

Wittgenstein had argued that all inference rests on the form of tautology, but now he recognised that an inference can have the form 'A man is two metres tall and so he is not three metres tall' even though 'Two metres tall' is not tautologous with 'Not three metres tall'. Within a propostion-system, said Wittgenstein, one can infer from the existence of a state of affairs to the non-existence of all others which are described by the same proposition system.[31] These proposition-systems are *systems* in the sense, for instance, that I am entitled to infer 'This is not 3cm long' from 'This is 2cm long' as I would not be entitled to infer 'This is not at the North Pole' from 'This is 2cm long'. The proposition, 'This is at the North Pole' does not belong to the same system of propositions as 'This is 2cm long'. To know what does, and what does not, belong to a proposition-system, Wittgenstein said, is to know something about the logical syntax, or logical grammar, of the property with which that system deals: I know something about the logical syntax or grammar of length when I know that 'This is 2cm long' excludes 'This is 3cm long' and of colour when I know that 'This is red' excludes 'This is blue'. There are internal relations between such propositions which form part of the logical syntax of length or colour respectively.

Rules of logical syntax 'belong to the method of depicting the world,'[32] said Wittgenstein. He regarded them as providing clues to the nature of reality. 'Objects' in the technical sense of the *Tractatus* came to be thought of as whatever must necessarily exist, given a proposition-system. For example, the four primary colours, red, yellow, blue and green, are the essential elements of the colour system in the sense that all combinations of them could be written in symbols which indicated where the colour in question comes on the primary colour scale. Or again, the standard metre in Paris serves as a paradigm for the proposition-system of metric measurement: it is basic to that method of representing reality in the sense that it constitutes in the last analysis what it is to speak in metric terms of all (PI 50: cf. below p. 65).

The idea of proposition-systems contains in embryo the idea of language-games which is so prominent in Wittgenstein's later thinking about the problem of meaning. But it is not so very far removed from some of the ideas in the *Tractatus* e.g. where Wittgenstein said that, in order to know the meaning of an expression, one must know all its possibilities of combination within propositions (cf.3.311); and spoke of rules of logical grammar, or logical syntax, as governing the use of signs and giving them meaning within our language (3.325, 3.326, 3.327). It may be, therefore, that his theory of meaning as use was not so far removed from what had been in his mind when he wrote the *Tractatus* as has sometimes been supposed. Nevertheless, the idea of the *job* which is being done with words, as distinct from that of the *picture* which they are portraying, is predominant in his later thought.

(ii)

This recognition that something is always being *done* with language, even supposing the latter to picture reality, was evident in Wittgenstein's growing realisation of the importance of what may be called the modal component in sentences. The picture theory of the *Tractatus* for the most part seems to identify the sense of a proposition with the picture it represents, but at 4.022b Wittgenstein had drawn a distinction between what a proposition 'shows' and what it 'says'. 'A proposition *shows* (*zeigt*) how things stand *if* it is true. And it *says* (*sagt*) *that* they do so stand.' This distinction, once drawn, raises the question whether a proposition, if it were nothing more than a picture, could both show how things stand if it is true and say that they do so stand. Wittgenstein evidently thought so when he wrote the *Tractatus*. But could it? A picture could certainly represent things standing in such-and-such a way (cf.2.202); it would have no sense unless it could do that (2.221). But whereas that might be the whole story so far as the sense of a picture is concerned, it can hardly be the whole story so far as the sense of a proposition goes. A picture as such need not *say* anything: it can simply portray its sense, i.e. be a picture of a possible situation. But a proposition must, as such, say something, in the sense of asserting that something or other is the case. The most that can be said for a picture as the sense of a proposition is that if P is a picture of a situation S, then P may be *used in saying* how things stand. In order to say

39

this, however, we would need to add something to the sense of P, viz. something which says that P is how things stand.

The essential point here does not only apply to propositions stating facts. A picture may be used in commands, wishes, questions, and other kinds of utterance, but in every such case something is added to the picture. We could, in effect, hold up P and say not only 'P is how things stand' (indicative mood), but also 'Is P how things stand?' (interrogative), 'Let P be how things stand!' (imperative), 'Would that P were how things stand!' (optative). In each case something different is added to the picture in order to give the utterance its particular meaning. A distinction may therefore be drawn, within each of the kinds of utterance which we have mentioned, between two logical elements of which they are composed. These two elements have been variously differentiated as respectively: 'the descriptive content' and 'the modal component',[33] 'the sentence-radical' and 'the use';[34] the 'phrastic' and the 'neustic'.[35] The distinction between these two elements, variously named, may be a matter of distinct signs. For examples: '*It is the case* that P is how things stand' and '*Is it the case* that P is how things stand?', where, in each instance, the italicised words contribute the modal component (the use, the neustic) and the unitalicised words, the descriptive content (sentence-radical, phrastic) to the sentence. But this is not essential. Very commonly, the main verb contributes the modal component whilst at the same time contributing to the descriptive content of the sentence. In the four utterances instanced above, viz. 'P *is* how things stand' (indicative), '*Is* P how things stand?' (interrogative), '*Let* P *be* how things stand!' (imperative) and '*Would* that P *were* how things stand!' (optative), the verb 'to be' contributes to the common descriptive content — things standing thus — but the variations of its mood determine the differing modal components. Actions or circumstances, other than purely grammatical or linguistic ones, may contribute the modal component; for example, the tone of a speaker's voice may indicate that 'P is how things stand' is intended as a question not a statement. But, one way or another, we need to know what is being done with a picture — or as Wittgenstein put it in his later

40

criticism of the picture-theory, we need to know in what language-game a sentence is a move[36]—before it can *say* anything to us.

Wittgenstein came to see that he had been led into two mistakes by comparing language to a picture and seeing its meaning to lie simply in the representation of possible situations. On the one hand, he had failed to explain satisfactorily the modal component in propositions; and, on the other, he had paid too little attention to how the modal component can vary in meaningful utterances. Picturing is not the whole story about propositions nor are propositions the whole story about meaningful discourse.

(iii)

The *Tractatus* proceeded on the assumption that the way to arrive at the meaning of any piece of language is to analyse it into elementary propositions which consist only of names. Wittgenstein came to have doubts about this on two counts. Could such an analysis of the meaning of any piece of language in fact be effected? Even if it could would it make the meaning clear? I will deal with these in turn.

Names, according to the *Tractatus* are the simples of language and they correspond one-for-one to objects which are the simples of reality. But Wittgenstein came to see that it does not make sense to speak of an *absolute* one-for-one correspondence between the simples of language and of reality respectively because it makes no sense to speak of breaking reality down *absolutely* into its simples. Said Wittgenstein in *Philosophical Investigations*, 47:"But what are the simple constituent parts of which reality is composed? — What are the simple constituent parts of a chair? — The bits of wood of which it is made? Or the molecules, or the atoms? "Simple" means: not composite. And here the point is: in what sense 'composite'? It makes no sense to speak absolutely of the 'simple parts of a chair'. This is so because 'we use the word "composite" (and therefore the word "simple") in an enormous number of different and differently related ways" If you ask what the simple parts of a tree, for example, are, then you have to realize that 'multi-colouredness is one kind of complexity; another is, for example, that of a broken outline composed of straight bits.'

41

So, you might try to break down your visual image of the tree into the specks of colour which compose it, or into the tiny straight lines which make up its outline; but there would be no point in saying that in the one case, but not in the other, you had arrived at the absolute simples of the tree. What you take to be the simples of anything is relative to your prior decision as to what kind of complexity is in question. 'But isn't a chessboard, for instance, obviously and absolutely, composite? — You are probably thinking of the composition out of thirty-two white and thirty-two black squares. But could we not also say, for instance, that it was composed of the colours black and white and the schema of squares? And if there are quite different ways of looking at it, do you still want to say that the chessboard is absolutely "composite"? Asking "Is this object composite?" *outside* a particular language-game is like what a boy once did, who had to say whether the verbs in a certain sentence were in the active or passive voice, and who racked his brains over the question whether the verb "to sleep" meant something active or passive.' When we are asked what the simples of anything are, therefore, we must always reply 'That depends on what you understand by "composite".' But this, said Wittgenstein, 'is of course not an answer but a rejection of the question'. The attempt to get at the meaning of language by analysing it *absolutely* into simples which correspond one-for-one with the simples of reality must necessarily fail.

If, however, such an attempt were successful would that be the way to make the meaning of language clear? Wittgenstein came to see that it would not (see PI 60). Suppose I say 'My broom is in the corner'. This could conceivably be further analysed into 'My broomstick is in the corner and so is my brush, and my stick is fixed in the brush'. The analysing sentence expresses what was, as it were, hidden in the sense of the first sentence, according to the theory of meaning which Wittgenstein had developed in the *Tractatus*. But is the analysing sentence what anyone who uttered the first sentence would really mean? Wittgenstein remarks that if we asked the speaker of the first sentence if this is what he meant he would probably say that he had not thought specially of either the stick or the brush; and that would be the *right* answer because he had not meant to speak of either

42

in particular. Suppose, again, that, instead of the command 'Bring me the broom' someone said 'Bring the broomstick and the brush which is fitted to it!' Would the hearer understand the command better in this analysed form? On the contrary, he would probably be puzzled by it and say 'Do you want the broom? Why do you put it so oddly?' True, the broom is taken to pieces when the stick is separated from the brush; but it does not follow that the order to bring the broomstick also consists of corresponding parts.

The *Tractatus* had assumed that a sentence does not have meaning if it does not have an absolutely determinate sense; that is to say, if its meaning is not *exact*. Wittgenstein came to see that the quest for absolute exactness is doomed to failure (like that for absolute simplicity); and that sentences with what we might call comparatively inexact meanings can be perfectly adequate. In *Investigations* 88 he said: 'If I tell someone "Stand roughly here" – may not this explanation work perfectly? And cannot every other one fail too?' We would indeed understand perfectly what was meant if someone said 'Stand roughly here!' But now what if someone said 'Come at one o'clock exactly!' and I took it that he wanted me to time my arrival for one o'clock exactly as the most accurate chronometers would determine it under laboratory conditions, would not that be a misunderstanding? 'Inexact' is really a reproach, and 'exact' is praise, said Wittgenstein, because what is inexact attains its goal less perfectly than what is exact. Thus the point here is what we take as 'the goal'. On ordinary occasions, my meaning is not unclear because I do not give distances in terms of the smallest conceivable measurements. Something short of this may attain my goal perfectly well.

Wittgenstein came to think that the word 'meaning' is being used 'illicitly' if it is used to signify the thing which corresponds to a word. This confuses the meaning of a name with its bearer. A man may be the bearer of the name 'Smith', for instance, but if he died, we should not say that the meaning of 'Smith' had died; for if 'Smith' did cease to have meaning once its bearer had ceased to exist then it would be meaningless to say 'Smith is dead'. Suppose two men are using a tool which they call 'N' and each says 'N' when he wants the other one to bring him that tool. The tool

43

gets broken. Not knowing this, one man says to the other, 'N'. Is this meaningless because what 'N' names no longer exists? It might be: the man addressed might simply stand there not knowing what to do. But the two men could have an arrangement whereby, if a tool named by one of them is broken, the other shakes his head. 'In this way the command "N" might be said to be given a place in the language-game even when the tool no longer exists, and the sign "N" to have meaning even when its bearer ceases to exist.' (PI 41). So Wittgenstein came to the conclusion that 'for a *large* class of cases — though not for all — in which we employ the word "meaning" it can be defined thus: *the meaning of a word is its use in the language*' (PI 43: second italics mine). It is important to note the 'though not for all' here; and also the remark which immediately follows that which I have just quoted in PI 43; viz. 'And the *meaning* of a name is sometimes explained by pointing to its *bearer*.' Wittgenstein must not be taken to have said that language can never be used to name things, only that it is not exclusively so used. We must turn now to a more careful consideration of this theory of meaning as use.

Radicals and Functions

Attention has already been called to Wittgenstein's distinction between a sentence-radical and the various uses to which it may be put (see above p. 40). In a footnote in the *Investigations*[37] he draws the distinction in these terms:

> Imagine a picture representing a boxer in a particular stance. Now, this picture can be used to tell someone how he should stand, should hold himself; or how he should not hold himself; or how a particular man did stand in such-and-such a place; and so on. One might (using the language of chemistry) call this picture a sentence-radical (*Satzradikal*) . . .

Professor G.E.M. Anscombe translates *Satzradikal* by 'proposition-radical' in the English version, but I think it better to use 'sentence-radical' as Stenius does[38] because the point which Wittgenstein was making applies to commands and questions as well as to statements and, in the context, he clearly intends it to have that wider application (cf. PI 23).

Wittgenstein's mention of chemistry in the above quotation refers to the fact that there are some chemical substances consisting of two kinds of component which never occur in isolation and are known respectively as 'radicals' and 'functions'. To take an example from Stenius,[39] ordinary alcohol has the formula $C_2H_5(OH)$; C_2H_5- being the 'radical' and $-OH$, the 'function' which produces an alcohol. However, this 'radical' can combine with a different 'function', namely that signified by $-O$, to produce, not an alcohol, but an ether viz. $(C_2H_5)_2O$ or ethyl ether. By the same token, $CH_3(OH)$ is methyl alcohol, whereas $(CH_3)_2O$ is methyl ether; and $C_3H_7(OH)$ is propyl alcohol, whereas $(C_3H_7)_2O$ is propyl ether.[40] By analogy with such chemical substances Wittgenstein was claiming that there can be a set of sentences, like those about the boxer in his example, each containing two kinds of logical component which never occur in isolation, one, the 'radical', being common to all sentences in the set, and the other, the 'function', differing from sentence to sentence.

In Wittgenstein's example of the boxer, it is the mood of the verb which contributes the functional element to the sentence. The radical is the representation of a boxer in a particular stance. This radical would be used in the indicative mood to tell someone 'how a particular man did stand in such and such a place' and in the imperative, to tell someone 'how he should hold himself; or how he should not hold himself'. But Wittgenstein was only too well aware that the functional element can be much more complicated than that. The function or use of language is normally determined by factors additional to, or other than, the mood of a verb. Sentences in the same mood may be used for widely differing purposes. Take, as an example, the indicative sentence 'You will go there' and suppose it to be uttered by the following speakers in the following circumstances: (a) By an officer to a private during army manoeuvres; (b) By a friend to a man who has just said that he cannot make up his mind whether to go to such-and-such a place or not; (c) By one actor to another in the course of a play; (d) By a person who has been asked to translate 'Vous irez là'; (e) By a young man who is trying to get his girl friend to go away with him for the week-end. Giving an order (cf.(a)), is a different use of language from speculating about an event (cf.(b)); both are different from either play-acting (cf.(c)) or translating (cf.(d)); and all four of these are different from asking or pleading (cf.(e)).[41]

From considerations such as these, two points clearly emerge. One is the nature of the distinction which Wittgenstein drew between what he called *surface grammar* and *depth grammar* (cf.PI 664). The 'surface grammar' of 'You will go there' in all five of the above examples, is identical. In each case we could parse the sentence in the same way as a statement of fact. In this 'surface' sense of grammar the construction of the sentence is the same in all cases. But, as we saw, in every case from (a) to (e), 'You will go there' is used to do something other than state a fact in the future tense. It is used to order, to speculate, to play-act, to translate and to plead, respectively. Such is the 'depth grammar' of its uses in (a) to (e). In order to get at the meaning of an utterance, it is always necessary to penetrate below its surface grammar to its depth grammar.

The other point which emerges is the importance of the *context* within which an utterance is made. Until we know the context, we cannot be sure what is being said. If asked to say what 'You will go there' meant when uttered on a certain occasion we would need to know who said it, to whom, and in what circumstances. Was it an army officer to a private whilst choosing a recce party; or was it a young man to his girl friend whilst showing her a letter from the hotel to say that they had booked him a double-room? And so on. It is important not to make the mistake of supposing that examples (a) to (e) are complex uses of 'You will go there', as against a simple use, in which it merely states a fact, or putative fact. In order to know that 'You will go there' is an assertion of fact, not an order or whatever, we would need to know the context of the utterance just the same. To know, for instance, that a speaker said this to hearers who were listening to a forecast of events in some context in which the whole point of one person speaking to another was that factual information might be conveyed. We would have to see 'You will go there' as, in Wittgenstein's words, 'a *move* in the language-game' of assertion (cf.PI 22); as made by, for

46

example, a travel agent in the course of telling his customer what places will be visited on a package tour.

The notion of *language-games* dominates Wittgenstein's later philosophy. By way of definition he said: 'I shall. . . call the whole, consisting of language and the actions into which it is woven, the "language-game"' (PI 7). and he also said: '. . . the term "language-*game*" is meant to bring into prominence the fact that the *speaking* of language is part of an activity, or of a form of life.' (PI 23). These remarks accord with what I was saying just now about the need to know the circumstances in which a remark is made in order to understand it. Utterances must be located within their appropriate language-game before their significance can be appreciated. In all this the essential point which Wittgenstein was concerned to make was that the meaning of language is not, or not simply, a matter of that to which it refers, but of the *use* to which it is being put.

A Primitive Example

We can see something of what is meant by 'use' in the last quotation from the example which Wittgenstein gave of a primitive language-game:

> A is building with building stones: there are blocks, pillars, slabs and beams. B has to pass the stones and that in the order in which A needs them. For this purpose, they use a language consisting of the words "block", "pillar", "slab", "beam". A calls them out; — B brings the stone which he has learned to bring at such-and-such a call. Conceive this as a complete primitive language. (PI 2)

Certain difficulties arise in so conceiving of it, as Wittgenstein was well aware, but we need not pause to consider these because the example as it stands suffices to illustrate the essential nature of a language-game as a 'whole consisting of language and the actions into which it is woven' (PI 7). We see this if we ask: what will B need to know in order to understand what A means when he says 'Slab' etc.? He will need to know at least the following things. (i) He must be aware of what it is for 'Slab' to be the *name* of something. What conveys such awareness is training in the language-game of asking what things are called and accepting names as answers (PI 27). B cannot understand the language-game which A is playing with him as they build unless he already understands how to participate in the language-game of naming things. (ii) B must know *what* it is of which 'Slab' is the name. If, for instance, he mistakenly supposed that 'Slab' meant whiteness, then he might pick up a white slab the first time A said 'Slab', but pick up a white beam the second time A said it. Wittgenstein remarks upon the fact that 'ostensive definition can be variously interpreted in *every* case' where it occurs. (PI 28). B must have received some kind of training in the use of 'Slab', which will guard him against such misunderstanding, before he can know what A means by 'Slab'. (iii) B needs to know what to *do* when A says 'Slab'. This utterance occurs within the context of a shared building activity, conducted by A and B, and the point of the utterance cannot be grasped by B unless it is understood as part of that shared activity.

B will understand what A means only when he has received some *training in how to play* the somewhat complicated language-game which he and A are playing. He cannot be told the meaning of 'Slab' simply by being shown that to which it refers. He has to learn how to use the word in certain ways — including how to use it to picture, or refer to, that which it names — before he can grasp its meaning.

Language as a Complex
Language-games become vastly more complicated than the primitive example which we have just been considering. If we wish to place an utterance — for example an expression of religious belief — within its appropriate language-game in order to understand it, then we may well find that this language-game is one within which words are used for a variety of interrelated purposes; that some at least of these uses are constantly changing in subtle ways; and that it is difficult to define precisely how certain uses of words in this game differ from uses of the same words in other language-games. But, however hard the task may be, the only way to grasp the meaning of language is, said Wittgenstein, not to impose a theory of meaning like the picture theory upon it, but to '*look at* its use *and learn from that*' (PI 340, second

48

italics mine).

Language, as a whole, is a complex of language-games distinct from each other and yet often interdependent. They are interdependent in the way that ordering or requesting appears to be dependent on naming in the above primitive example. Some uses of language are precisely regulated as, for example, those of mathematics or natural science; some uses are harder to define precisely, as for example those of poetry or prayer. Diverse as they are, language-games run into one another in the sense that in order to grasp the use to which language is being put in one 'game', we may need to appreciate how this is like, and how it is unlike, the use to which similar language is put in other 'games'. For example, we shall see when we come to consider the bearing of Wittgenstein's late philosophy upon religious belief that a recognition of the similarities and dissimilarities between the use to which certain words are put in religious and non-religious contexts respectively illuminates the nature of religious belief and perhaps helps to solve some of the intellectual problems connected with it. The interdependence and diversity of language-games, the fact that language as a whole is dynamic and changeful, the contrast between language-games which are precise and those that are not — all this is described by Wittgenstein in terms of the following simile:

Our language can be seen as an ancient city; a maze of little streets and squares, of old and new houses, and of houses with additions from various periods; and this surrounded by a multitude of new boroughs with straight regular streets and uniform houses. (PI 18)

The most comprehensive single paragraph on the subject of language-games in Wittgenstein's later writings is however *Philosophical Investigations*, 23, which runs as follows:

But how many kinds of sentence are there? Say assertion, question, and command? — There are *countless* kinds: countless different kinds of use of what we call "symbols", "words", "sentences". And this multiplicity is not something fixed, given once for all; but new types of language,

49

new language-games, as we may say, come into existence, and others become obsolete and get forgotten.(We can get a *rough picture* of this from the changes in mathematics.)

Here the term "language-*game*" is meant to bring into prominence the fact that the speaking of a language is part of an activity, or of a form of life.

Review the multiplicity of language-games in the following examples, and in others:
Giving orders and obeying them —
Describing the appearance of an object, or giving its measurements —
Constructing an object from a description (a drawing) —
Reporting an event —
Speculating about an event —
Forming and testing a hypothesis —
Presenting the results of an experiment in tables and diagrams —
Making up a story; and reading it —
Play-acting —
Singing catches —
Guessing riddles —
Making a joke; telling it —
Solving a problem in practical arithmetic —
Translating from one language into another —
Asking, thanking, cursing, greeting, praying.
— It is interesting to compare the multiplicity of the tools in language and of the ways they are used, the multiplicity of kinds of word and sentence, with what logicians have said about the structure of language. (Including the author of the *Tractatus Logico-Philosophicus.*)

In this paragraph many of Wittgenstein's leading ideas about language-games are summarily expressed. The multiplicity and changefulness of language—games are recognised. The list of examples which he gives here is the most multifarious to be found anywhere in his writings and conveys a clear impression of how diversified language-games may be; and the fact that language-games are constantly coming into being or fading into obsolescence is clearly stated. This passage also has Wittgenstein explicitly contrasting the theory of meaning as use, which his doctrine of language-games is intended to explain and substantiate, with the picture theory which he had put forward in the *Tractatus*, and rejecting the latter as manifestly mistaken. Both Wittgenstein's favourite similes — viz. language as a *game* and language as a *tool* — are used in the course of this passage, and the connexion between language and 'forms of life' is expressly noted. On these two latter points more must be said.

Games and Tools

Are Wittgenstein's ideas of language both as a complex of *games* and as a set of *tools* consistent with one another? Let us take them in turn.

Chess was one of his favourite analogies in comparing language to a game. Just as, where chessmen are concerned, 'the meaning of a piece is its rôle in the game'(PI 563), so the meaning of any piece of language is the part which it plays in a language-game. There is a story to the effect that Wittgenstein first thought of this analogy when he saw some boys kicking a football about and it occurred to him that this is what we do with words. The feature of games which seemed to him most relevant in this analogy was the fact that they are normally played in accordance with rules. Similarly, he thought, language is used in accordance with rules and to know the meaning of any piece of language is to know the rules for its appropriate use. Of course, this is not to say that as a matter of psychological fact speakers or hearers have to think first of the rules and then use, or classify, language accordingly before they can understand what they are saying or hearing. Children of necessity must learn to speak before they can come to a study of grammar; and many people use language successfully throughout their lives without ever being capable of stating correctly the rules of its accidence or syntax. The point about rules is a logical, not a psychological, one. Just as there could not (logically) be games such as chess or football unless they were constituted by rules, so there could not (logically) be what we call language unless implicit within it there were rules which prescribe what it is appropriate to say or do and when. In Wittgenstein's primitive example, A has to learn what to say when he wants B to bring him a stone, and B has to learn what to do when A

51

says 'Slab' etc.; communication between them is possible only when they have both learned these rules. The meaning is in the rules. But just as there is a difference between players and spectators at a soccer match, so there is a difference between those who participate in a language-game and those who observe others doing so; between, say, scientists who use scientific language in pursuing their researches and philosophers of science, who reflect upon the scientists' use of language in order to discover what the logic of scientific discovery is. The working scientist does not concern himself with the problem, for example, of whether scientific reasoning is fundamentally deductive or inductive as a philosopher of science might; he just gets on with reasoning scientifically. Nevertheless, the rules of scientific reasoning are implicit in all that he does. He obeys them, even though he would find it hard, or even impossible, to say what they are. Discovering the meaning of language is like deducing from the way a game is being played what its rules must be. The fact that we can observe − possibly even play − the game before we can state what its rules are does not make it any less true that the rules constitute the game.

There is a certain finality about the rules of language. Speaking about the rules for the use of 'not', Wittgenstein said, 'without these rules the word has as yet no meaning; and if we change the rules, it now has another meaning' (PI p. 147 footnote). In *Zettel* 320 he wrote to the same effect: 'Why don't I call cookery rules arbitrary, and why am I tempted to call the rules of grammar arbitrary? Because "cooking" is defined by its end whereas "speaking" is not. That is why the use of language is in a certain sense autonomous, as cooking and washing are not. You cook badly if you are guided in your cooking by rules other than the right ones; but if you follow other rules than those of chess you are *playing another game*; and if you follow grammatical rules other than such-and-such ones, that does not mean you say something wrong, no, you are speaking of something else.'

A game may be, indeed usually is, an end in itself; but this seems clearly not to be true of a tool. A tool is for doing something; it exists to serve a purpose beyond itself. So when Wittgenstein says, 'Think of the tools in a tool-box: there is a

52

hammer, pliers, a saw, a screw driver, a rule, a glue-pot, glue, nails and screws — the functions of words are as diverse as the functions of these objects. (And in both cases there are similarities)' (PI 11), some of his readers have wondered whether he thinks it necessary for language to have a function or purpose, i.e. to make some difference in the world, before it has meaning.[42] Such a remark as 'Look at the sentence as an instrument, and at its sense as its employment' (PI 421) would suggest that he does. But there are two distinct kinds of thing at least which can be *done* with words. One is, so to say, a verbal kind of thing: we can use words to state, to warn, to evaluate, etc. where all these are different forms of verbal communication. In J.L. Austin's[43] terminology this 'verbal kind of thing' is called the 'illocutionary force' of language i.e. what we are doing *in* saying this or that; and Austin has shown how it may vary from speech-act to speech-act. The other kind of thing which can be done with words is, so to say, non-verbal: we can use words to excite, to harrass, to terrify, to uplift, etc. where all these are psychological effects produced in our hearers or even in ourselves as we speak. In Austin's terminology this is the perlocutionary force of language - what we are doing *by* saying something; and, of course, it may differ from case to case. It seems fairly clear that Wittgenstein did not regard the perlocutionary force of language as essential to its meaning. He said: 'Grammar does not tell us how language must be constructed in order to fulfil its purpose, in order to have such-and-such an effect on human beings. It only describes and in no way explains the use of signs' (PI 496). I would take this to imply that Wittgenstein thought of language as a tool-kit in the sense that he recognised the variety of the verbal jobs which we can do, the different illocutionary acts which we can perform, with words. It was the multi-functional character of language — as against his former view that the one thing language does is to picture a reality beyond itself — which he was concerned to emphasise. But this multi-functional character of language does not imply that there are extra-linguistic ends to which it must be the means. It is true, of course, that the world would be a different place if certain kinds of thing were not said: for example, human society would, no doubt, be entirely

53

different from what it is if science, or morality, or religion, were unknown universes of discourse. But this does not imply that language as a whole is a tool, or set of tools, for producing certain effects *beyond itself*.

Forms of Life

Professor P. F. Strawson in his review (*Mind* 1954) of the *Investigations* listed the idea of 'forms of life' as one of the three cardinal elements in the thought of the book; and Professor Norman Malcolm in his review (*Philosophical Review* 1954) thought it hardly possible to over-emphasise the importance in Wittgenstein's later philosophy of what he meant by a 'form of life'.

What did he mean? Nowhere does he say precisely. He speaks explicitly of hope (PI p.174) and certainty (OC 358) as forms of life in contexts where he is evidently likening them to animal attitudes. This comparison seems to divorce them from language. But I think it more enlightening to concentrate on passages where he takes 'form of life' to be not *fundamentally* different in meaning from 'language-game'. A language-game, as we have seen, is a 'whole consisting of language and the actions into which it is woven' (PI 7). Wittgenstein said that ' . . . to imagine a language means to imagine a form of life' (PI 19). And again: ' . . . the term "language-*game*" is meant to bring into prominence the fact that the *speaking* of language is part of an activity, or of a form of life' (PI 23). The first point to take, then, is that language-games are forms of life in the sense that we cannot understand language except as part of an activity which is not simply oral. Professor G. Pitcher has commented illuminatingly on a remark of Wittgenstein's with which the latter drives this point home, namely the oft-quoted 'If a lion could talk, we could not understand him' (PI p. 223). Says Pitcher, suppose a lion said 'It is now three o'clock' without paying attention to a timepiece; or suppose he said, 'Goodness, it's three o'clock, I must hurry to keep that appointment!' but made no effort to move. In every respect this lion's behaviour, let us suppose, is exactly like an ordinary lion's except for his amazing ability to speak English sentences. In such case, Pitcher remarks, 'we could not say that he has *asserted* or *stated* that it is three o'clock, even though he has

54

uttered suitable words.' And he goes on: 'We could not tell what, if anything, he has asserted for the modes of behaviour into which his use of words is woven are too radically different from our own. We could not understand him, since he does not share the relevant forms of life with us.'[44] Apart from the activities the words are meaningless. The speaking of language is part of a form of life.

But there is, I think, more to it than this. In talking of 'forms of life', Wittgenstein was calling attention to what may be described as a certain kind of *ultimacy* which language, as actually spoken by men within a community, can have. He said that forms of life are 'the given' and have 'to be accepted' (PI p. 226; cf.p. 200: 'What we have . . . to do is to *accept* the everyday language-game . . . '). The *ultimacy* of which I am speaking was, I think, to Wittgenstein's mind an ultimacy of both *intelligibility* and *justification*. The forms of life in which we participate constitute, in some final way, what for us it is intelligible and justifiable to say. There is no way of going beyond them — no sort of higher logical order to which appeal can be made — in the quest for intelligibility and justification.

Those wholes, consisting of language and the activities into which it is woven, with which we are familiar, determine what is, and what is not, *intelligible* to us. People who do not share the same forms of life as ourselves can be 'a complete enigma' to us, said Wittgenstein. Even though we had a mastery of another country's language, if its traditions were entirely strange to us, we should be at a loss to understand what its people were saying to each other (PI p. 223). And he goes on to make at this point the remark about the lion, to which I have already referred.

It is important, since our particular concern in this book is with religious belief, to note that religious speech-acts, such as those involved in praise, prayer, confession, or proclamation of faith, are unintelligible to the secular-minded in much the same way that the remarks of Wittgenstein's lion would be unintelligible to any human being. As Professor A. C. MacIntyre[45] has pointed out, a social context which is missing has to be supplied, or one which is present has to be abstracted, before a religious man can understand a completely secular man or *vice versa*. It does not suffice for the secular man orally to profess belief. A secular man who from time to time uttered sentences from the Creed such as 'I believe in God the Father Almighty', but whose general behaviour apart from this was devoid of any other manifestation of religious belief, such as acts of worship, service or advocacy, would be as puzzling to religious believers as Wittgenstein's lion would be to any human being. The religious believer could echo, concerning this secular man, Pitcher's words about the lion almost exactly: 'We cannot tell what if anything he is professing for the modes of behaviour into which his words are woven are too radically different from our own. We do not understand him, since he does not share the relevant forms of life with us.'

There is an ultimacy of *justification* as well as intelligibility. 'What people accept as a justification' said Wittgenstein, 'is shown by how they think and live' (PI 325). But he was not simply recording a psychological fact; he was indicating a logical terminus. The demand for reasons why I should say what I say reaches 'bedrock' and 'my spade is turned' (PI 217), when I come, in the last analysis, to certain forms of life. All I can say is 'This is simply what I do' (ibid.) Our belief in the uniformity of nature is a case in point. Our whole way of thinking about, and living within, nature rests upon it. 'Nothing could induce me to put my hand into a flame — although after all it is *only in the past* that I have burnt myself' (PI 472). The idea that I can meaningfully discuss whether I am, or am not, justified in believing in the uniformity of nature is ludicrous. I have no concept of 'nature' apart from the 'uniformity of nature'. Another example of a form of life which is embedded in our minds in an ultimate way is the belief that men have 'souls', i.e. are aware of themselves, act as free agents, know good from evil and beauty from ugliness, etc. This notion pervades the thought of civilised, as it did of primitive, man (cf. RFGB p. 31). Everything in our ordinary ways of talking about human beings and their behaviour seems to presuppose something of this kind. It is not that we are 'of the opinion' that human beings have souls: the agreement is 'not . . . in opinions but in form of life' (Cf. PI 241). When I am speaking of another person's experience or activity 'my attitude towards him is an attitude towards a soul. I am not of the *opinion* that he has a soul' (PI p. 178). Everything I say about other people is an expression of this attitude or form of life. It is the 'tacit presupposition' of all the language which I use about my fellow human beings. So much so, Wittgenstein thought, that to remark of another human being 'I believe that he is not an automaton', just like that, would make no sense (PI p. 178). At best, all this could mean is that this man always behaves like a human being, and not occasionally like a machine. Any idea that a human being could be conceived as an automaton (even if he were going to be so conceived of only for the idea to be rejected) is, in fact, mistaken. We can form no conception of what it would be like for a human being to be an automaton. What has to be accepted — the given — is the form of life constituted by the concept of the 'soul'. For this form of life underlies, in one way or another, everything which we normally say about human beings. We always think of men as saying things to themselves, as being responsible for their own actions, as being aware of moral or aesthetic values, and so on. (Incidentally, Wittgenstein would have said much the same things about the belief that men have bodies (cf. OC 247–8, 257, etc.).)

Tacit Presuppositions
From a recognition of the fact that certain forms of life are ultimate in our ordinary ways of thinking and talking, we may be led to ask what the presuppositions of these forms of life themselves are. Wittgenstein has it: '. . . what we do in our language-game always rests on a tacit presupposition' (PI p. 179).* He added the quizzical comment: 'Doesn't a presupposition imply a doubt? And doubt may be entirely lacking. Doubting has an end.' Then he offered this illustration; 'It is like the relation: physical object — sense-impressions. Here we have two different language-games and a complicated relation between them. — If you try to reduce their relations to a *simple* formula you go wrong' (PI pp. 179–180). The purport of all this seems to be that language-games always go down, in the last analysis, to something which is taken for granted and, at least so far as that language-game is concerned, lies beyond doubt. What is taken for granted is a certain concept (or set of concepts), or certain rules of inference, or both, which logically constitute the language-

* For justification of my interpretation of this question, see my letter in the *Times Literary Supplement*, 7 March 1975.

game in question.

Wittgenstein's example of the relation between a physical object and sense impressions is a case in point. The sense impressions, on the basis of which we talk about physical objects, are discontinuous. Now we see the chair; now it goes dark and we don't; now it comes light and we see it once again. But we speak of it as the identical chair throughout; we think of it as a continuously existing physical object though our sense-experience of it is not continuous. There are generally accepted criteria for deciding whether or not it is the same chair which we see on each occasion: e.g. Is it the same size and shape? Do we know anything which leads us to suspect that a different chair has been substituted for the original one? And so on. But even if, by these criteria it is the same chair, someone may raise a more fundamental doubt. Are we ever logically entitled to take the occurrence of the discontinuous (our sense impressions of the chair) as evidence of the existence of the continuous (the chair itself)? In the nature of the case, must not such evidence always be logically inadequate to support that which it is invoked to support? Such doubts seem to be philosophically profound, but as Strawson[46] has shown, it is possible to take quite a different view of them. He points out that 'a *condition* of our having this conceptual scheme (*sc.* that of common sense or natural science in which we speak about physical objects on the evidence of sense impressions) is the unquestioning acceptance of particular-identity in at least some cases of non-continuous observation.' Anyone who refuses to accept this, he says, ' . . . pretends to accept a conceptual scheme, but at the same time quietly rejects one of the conditions of its employment. Thus his doubts are unreal, not simply because they are logically irresoluble doubts but because they amount to the rejection of the whole conceptual scheme within which alone such doubts make sense.' Doubts about whether or not our sense impressions give us good grounds for what we say or think in terms of physical objects arise within the conceptual scheme of science or common sense, where there are generally accepted ways of resolving them, as we have already noted. But doubts which call in question the rules of inference tacitly presupposed by, and constitutive of, this whole conceptual scheme are, as Strawson says 'unreal',

58

that is, they are doubts which reject any resolution of themselves in the only place where they could be resolved, i.e. the language-game in which we speak about physical objects.

It was perhaps with such tacit presuppositions in mind that Wittgenstein insisted that there comes a point where all one can say is 'This game is played' (PI 654). We shall see the importance of this when we come to consider religious belief and unbelief. Some doubts about religion are such that they seem to put us in this dilemma: they cannot be resolved within religion because they amount to a rejection of the whole logical basis of religion; but they cannot be resolved outside religion because they have to do with that which religion, and it alone, is about. This raises the question of whether or not religious believers and unbelievers can contradict one another; we shall find that Wittgenstein regarded this question as one of the fundamental issues in the philosophy of religion.

The Bewitchment of Intelligence
In the *Investigations*, Wittgenstein speaks of philosophy as 'a battle against the bewitchment of our intelligence by means of language' (PI 109). This comes at the end of a paragraph in which he has said that philosophical problems have to be solved 'by looking into the workings of our language, and that in such a way as to make us recognise those workings: *in despite of* an urge to misunderstand them'. Philosophical problems 'are solved, not by giving new information, but by arranging what we have always known'. In another place, he says that they 'arise when language *goes on holiday*' (PI 38). And again: 'The confusions which occupy us arise when language is like an engine idling, not when it is doing work' (PI 132). The moral of all this is plain enough. To understand language, you must see it at home not on holiday — that is, conforming to the rules of its appropriate language-game; you must see it at work not idling — that is doing the job which it has to do within its appropriate language-game. Philosophical reflexion has shown a fatal tendency to generate pseudo-problems by taking language out of its appropriate context and puzzling over how, if at all, it can be made to conform to criteria of intelligibility appropriate to contexts other than its

own. 'A philosophical problem has the form: "I don't know my way about." ' (PI 123).

For example, protagonists both for and against religion sometimes treat beliefs about God as if they are, or ought to be, scientific hypotheses. Apologists for religion sometimes claim that belief in God must be accepted because there is the same sort of evidence for it as there is for any well-supported scientific theory; and apologists against religion sometimes claim that religious beliefs must be rejected because, since they are not empirically falsifiable in the way that scientific hypotheses are, they must be meaningless. Wittgenstein, as we shall see in chapter 5, considered such apologetics to be misconceived. If we look carefully at religious language and at scientific, we shall see that they work differently. We do not need new information about religion or science to see this; all we need is to go back to what we have always known about them and arrange this before our minds in such a way that the logical differences between them are manifest. Language must be brought back from its metaphysical to its everyday use. 'One must always ask oneself: is the word ever actually used in this way in the language-game which is its original home?' (PI 116).

Two kinds of confusion in particular seemed to Wittgenstein to bewitch the intelligence of the philosophicallty minded. One was the confusion between 'surface grammar' and 'depth grammar' to which some reference has already been made. The other was the temptation 'to draw some misleading analogy' (BBB p. 48) or to be held captive by a picture (PI 115).

Wittgenstein did not use the following example, but the philosophical perplexity which arose about the nature of moral intuition would be an instance of the confusion about grammar to which I have just referred. The similarity between 'This act is right' and 'This apple is red' has misled some moral philosophers into supposing that the former sentence, like the latter, predicates an observable property of a subject. Moral rightness is not a natural property and it is not observed by sight, as, on both counts, redness is. So it must be a non-natural property and there must be some faculty of moral intuition which apprehends it. Thus classical intuitionists reasoned. One of the great debates in British

60

philosophy in the seventeenth and eighteenth centuries concerned the nature of this moral intuition.[47] Was it like our sense of beauty, or like our awareness of self-evident truths? The 'moral sense' school opted for the former, and the rational intuitionists for the latter, of these alternatives. But a consideration of the 'depth grammar' of 'This act is right' and other such moral judgments shows that they do not describe so much as evaluate. They look like statements of fact but when we consider the uses to which they are put, these differ radically from those to which scientific or common sense statements of fact are put. Moral judgments are used to guide actions and choices; not simply to say how things are, but what ought to be done. Once this is grasped, the philosophical problem about what faculty in us apprehends the non-natural properties of rightness, etc. simply disappears.

As an example of what Wittgenstein meant by being held captive by a picture, he referred to St. Augustine's puzzlement about how time can be measured (BBB p. 26). As a matter of empirical fact we do measure it: we say things like 'It took half an hour', 'It is a million light-years away' and so on. Nevertheless, said Augustine in effect, because time rolls by like a stream it is not logically possible to measure it. If we lay a measuring rod against something in order to measure it, our measuring must necessarily be done in the present. So we cannot measure time past because it has flowed by and is no longer there in the present to be measured; nor, an interval in the future because it has not yet arrived in the present to be measured. Furthermore, since the present is no more than a point and a point has no measurement, the present itself cannot be measured. So past, present and future are all immeasurable. Therefore, time cannot be measured. But how can it be that time both is (empirically) and is not (logically) measurable? This dilemma arises because we are held captive by the picture of time as a rolling stream. That is, by the conception of it as a spatial phenomenon. We can take spatial measurements by laying a measuring-rod alongside things; but we cannot measure time in the same way. How do we in fact measure time? By taking certain natural events (e.g. the rising and setting of the sun) or certain artificially contrived events (e.g. the point by point unwinding of a spring) as *termini a quo* and *ad quem*. If we bear this in mind

61

St. Augustine's kind of puzzlement will be dispersed. Once we free ourselves from the misleading analogy whereby time is treated as a spatial phenomenon, i.e. as a stream, the dilemma disappears.

It is through clearing up confusions of such kinds in such ways, Wittgenstein believed, that philosophical problems are solved by being dissolved. He said 'the clarity that we are aiming at is indeed *complete* clarity. But this simply means that the philosophical problems should *completely* disappear' (PI 133).

We must not, however, draw the conclusion from what Wittgenstein said about philosophical problems that he regarded them as purely linguistic matters. True, they arise when we get lost in language, but it does not follow that to solve them is to do nothing more than clear up verbal confusions. There is a connexion between language and reality. Wittgenstein has a rather complicated conception of this connexion in his late philosophy. We must try to see what it was.

Language and Reality

Wittgenstein's conception of the relationship between language and reality in his later work is markedly different from that which he had entertained in the *Tractatus*. E. K. Specht calls the former a 'Constitution Theory' as against the latter which had been a 'Correspondence Theory'[48] In the *Tractatus*, Wittgenstein had conceived of a world of objects existing quite independently of language; of language as consisting in the last analysis of the names which we give to these objects; and of the possibilities of meaning within language as determined by what combinations of objects are possible in reality. Language, on this view, simply corresponds to, takes its shape from, reality. By contrast, in the later writings, Wittgenstein held that language is not, or not simply, a mirror of the world of objects but is somehow involved in the construction of that world. Reality, on this view, is to some degree, constituted by, takes its shape from, language.

This latter view — the 'Constitution Theory' — seems to be behind the following remark from the *Investigations*: 'Grammar tells what kind of object anything is (Theology as

62

grammar)' (PI 373). The word 'grammar' occurs frequently in Wittgenstein's later writings. It refers to the rules for the use of any given piece of language as these are determined by the latter's appropriate language-game. By 'grammar' Wittgenstein meant both these rules themselves and the observation and description of them. Specht[49] compares his use of 'grammar' to the use commonly made of the word 'logic' to refer both to the science of logical structures and to these structures themselves. The expression 'grammatical proposition' also has a special sense in Wittgenstein and is of particular interest so far as the relationship between language and reality is concerned. Specht defines what Wittgenstein meant by 'grammatical proposition' thus:

> Everything that Wittgenstein says indicates that by a grammatical proposition is to be understood a proposition that makes an assertion about an object; but it is a proposition which depends exclusively for its truth value on the rules of usage of the linguistic sign which signifies the object.[50]

Some grammatical propositions — e.g. 'A bachelor is an unmarried man' — are clearly analytic; others — such as 'One and the same surface is not blue and red at the same time'[51] — are synthetic. The former example is analytic because the expressions 'bachelor' and 'unmarried man' are synonymous; the latter example is synthetic because there are no synonyms that verbally define the colour words 'blue' and 'red'. Colour-talk, as we noted above[52] forms a system of propositions such that if I know that X is red, I know that it is not blue, not green, etc., even though 'red' does not mean 'not blue', 'not green', etc. We know that the same surface cannot be both blue and red at the same time, not from empirical observation, but from observation and description of the rules for the use of the expressions 'surface', 'coloured', 'red', 'blue'. Such knowledge seems to have been regarded by Wittgenstein as a kind of synthetic *a priori* knowledge.

The object which we call a coloured surface is, in this sense, constituted by grammar; that is to say by the rules of the language-game within which the expression 'coloured surface' is used. So long as we have that language-game coloured surfaces exist; but if we ceased to use the expression 'coloured surface' as we do, coloured surfaces as we know them would cease to exist. Friedrich Waismann has pointed out that in some languages e.g. Russian, German and Italian, colour can be described by verbs.[53] If we adopted this practice universally and exclusively then we should conceive of colour as an activity of agencies, not a property of surfaces. We should say, for example, 'The sky blues', not 'The sky is blue.' In such case, the grammatical proposition, 'One and the same surface is not blue and red at the same time' would be meaningless because there would no longer be any such thing as a coloured surface. To conceive of the blueness of the sky as the property of a surface would then be as misconceived as to think of the tolling of a bell as an aspect of its shape. However, it may well be that some such grammatical proposition as 'One and the same colouring agency cannot both blue and red at the same time' would be true by virtue of the rules for the use of 'colouring', 'agency', 'to red', and 'to blue'. If this were so, it would be a pointer to the fact that there are restrictions on what can meaningfully be said about colour, which are imposed, not by linguistic usage, but by the extra-linguistic realities of the natural world, or human psychology, or both. What we speak of as colour might well be such that two dissimilar instantiations of it never occur at an identical point in space and time; and it might well be that our modes of preception are such that, even if these instantiations did occur, we could not apprehend them. Wittgenstein recognised that language-games 'lose their point' if they are at variance with extra-linguistic reality. 'The procedure of putting a lump of cheese on a balance and fixing the price by the turn of the scale would lose its point if it frequently happened for such lumps to suddenly grow in size or shrink for no obvious reason.' (PI 142)

From the considerations which I have put forward in the last paragraph, it would appear that the relationship between language and reality — as conceived by Wittgenstein — is twofold. On the one hand, men are to some degree free to construct reality by the language which they use. But, on the other hand, the facts of nature impose some limitations on the extent of their freedom to do so. Specht[54] argues forcefully that this was Wittgenstein's view. He calls attention to the latter's remark:

> There is *one* thing of which one can neither say that it is one metre long, nor that it is not one metre long, and that is the standard metre in Paris. — But this is, of course, not to ascribe any extraordinary property to it, but only to mark its peculiar role in the language-game of measuring with a metre-rule. (PI 50)

The standard metre in Paris serves as an ontologically objective paradigm for the meaning of the word 'metre'; but once it is adopted as such, the linguistic rules for the use of the word 'metre' prescribe that there are no metres which do not conform to the definition given to this paradigm within the language-game. Metres are thus, to put it crudely, both linguistically and extra-linguistically determined objects.

By his insistence that 'Grammar tells what kind of object anything is' (PI 373) Wittgenstein wanted to safeguard us from the philosophical perplexities which arise when it is assumed that every expression signifies an object in the way that proper names do. To avoid such perplexity, we must look at how a thing is spoken of before we can understand what kind of object it is. We must proceed through linguistics to ontology. In discussing the difference between sense impressions and physical objects (e.g. the physical tree) Wittgenstein said:

> . . . it confuses everything to say "the one is a *different kind* of object from the other", for those who say that a sense datum is a different kind of object from a physical object misunderstand the grammar of the word "kind", just as those who say that a number is a different kind of object from a numeral. They think they are making such a statement as "A railway train, a railway station, and a railway car are different kinds of objects", whereas their statement is analagous to "A railway train, a railway accident, and a railway law are different kinds of objects"' (BBB p. 64)

65

The possibility of confusion lies in the ambiguity of the expression 'a different kind of object'. On one interpretation it is all right to say that physical objects and sense data are different kinds of object, but not on another. On the interpretation which is not all right, a physical object and a sense impression are taken to be objects of fundamentally the same kind; that is, different members of the *same* class. It gets us nowhere to look for the differentiae between them on that basis. According to the interpretation which is all right, a physical object and a sense impression are not taken to be the same kind of object but different kinds, members of *different* classes. What it means to be an object differs radically in the two cases. This difference is revealed in the ways in which each is spoken of within its appropriate language-game. Observation and description of the rules of these language-games will tell us what kinds of objects physical objects and sense-impressions respectively are.

The parenthesis to the remark of Wittgenstein's which we have been discussing in this sub-section is particularly important for our purposes: 'Grammar tells what kind of object anything is (*Theology as grammar*)' (italics mine). Theology is the language-game (or set of games) within which we speak of God or god. The rules of that game reveal what kind of object God or god is. It is of vital importance in the philosophy of religion to be as clear as possible about this; and the only way to become clear is by observation and description of the way in which God or god is spoken about by religious believers. I am using 'God' and 'god' here as comprehensive terms for the object of religious belief; and I realise of course that there has been, and still is, the widest diversity in what religious believers take the object of their worship and service to be. But in so far as religious belief, for all its variety, forms a distinct kind of discourse, the object with which it is concerned will be of a distinctive kind. The divine beings in whom animists, polytheists and theists respectively believe are very different from one another, but all of them alike share certain differencies from other kinds of objects, such as material things sense impressions, moral values, or whatever. To discover what kind of object these divine beings are, whether as a whole or individually, we must look at how they are spoken of.

It seems to be the implication of what Wittgenstein said about the ultimacy of some language-games or forms of life (see above pp. 55–7) that we cannot question which of them are *true to fact*, or which of them are *rational*, if these questions presuppose criteria of truth and rationality over and above all language-games. It is not possible, on his view, to make sense of the notion of such criteria. Language-games, or some of them, are, according to Wittgenstein, 'proto-phenomena' (PI 654). What counts as the truth or falsity of a proposition, and what counts as a valid reason for saying something, depend on the language-game within which the proposition is stated or the reason offered. The belief that there is a truth which can be known or a rationality which can be apprehended *outside all language-games*, and by which their respective truth or rationality can be decided, is misconceived. But it does not follow that therefore any individual language-game (or set of games) can be isolated from the rest and regarded as a logically self-contained unit, so that no considerations except internal ones are relevant to its meaningfulness, truth or rationality. The mistake of supposing that to be the case is a matter to which we will return, with special reference to religion, in the last chapter.

3 The Mystical

In the *Tractatus*[1] Wittgenstein argued that there is something which cannot be put into words but which nevertheless *shows* itself. He speaks of it as 'transcendental'. That which is transcendental appears to have two forms or instantiations which I shall refer to as the 'logical' and the 'ethico-religious' respectively. '*Logic* is transcendental' says Wittgenstein at 6.13; and '*Ethics* is transcendental' at 6.421 (italics mine). In the latter of the two senses, i.e. the ethico-religious, he describes the transcendental as the 'mystical' (6.44, 6.45, 6.522), and it is with the mystical that I shall be concerned in the main body of this chapter. First, however, we must be clear about the difference between the logical and the ethico-religious instantiations and in particular about what is meant by saying that each shows itself.

In its 'logical' instantiation, the transcendental is 'logical form'. Wittgenstein was at great pains throughout the main part of the *Tractatus* to explain what he meant by logical form and by his doctrine that it cannot be put into words but simply shows itself in logical grammar or syntax. He was successful to the extent that, with the necessary application, one can understand what he meant and see how his arguments are related to those of other philosophers who have worked on the same problems. What Wittgenstein meant by the transcendental in its ethico-religious instantiation is also clear enough. At the end of the *Tractatus*, i.e. 6.4 to 7, he speaks of the mystical as having to do with moral goodness, i.e. ethics, aesthetic significance or artistic creation, i.e. aesthetics, and such matters as God, the meaning of life, immortality, i.e. religion. He goes on to say that these things also cannot be put into words. From other sources than the *Tractatus*, we learn that he believed they show themselves in art and action. Why he thought they do so is not as clear, to say the least, as why he thought that logical form shows itself

68

in logical grammar or syntax.

Wittgenstein did not differentiate as sharply between the two conceptions of the transcendental as I have done here and shall continue to do throughout this chapter. He evidently conceived of the argument of the *Tractatus* as a unity and saw his conclusions concerning the mystical in 6.4 to 7 as following from his discussion of the structure of language in the earlier part of the book. Whether or not there is any real connexion between the two conceptions will become clear, I hope, as we proceed.

I. THE LOGICAL INTERPRETATION

Wittgenstein defines the aim of the *Tractatus* in his preface thus: 'to set a limit to thought, or rather — not to thought, but to the expression of thoughts'. A 'thought', said Wittgenstein, is 'a logical picture of facts'(3). A fact is the existence of a state, or states, of affairs (cf.2). A proposition is the expression of a thought (cf.3.1). The aim of the *Tractatus* is therefore to set a limit to what can be put into those logical pictures of facts which propositions constitute.

One overall limitation on what can be expressed by a proposition is imposed by the laws of logic. The state of affairs of which any proposition is the logical picture must obviously be a logically possible state of affairs. 'It is as impossible to represent in language anything that "contradicts logic" as it is in geometry to represent by its co-ordinates a figure that contradicts the laws of space, or to give the co-ordinates of a point that does not exist,' said Wittgenstein (3.032). As an illustration of this kind of limitation on what can be expressed by a proposition, Wittgenstein referred approvingly to the interpretation of 'divine omnipotence' according to which that expression means, not that God can do anything at all, but only that he can do anything which is not contrary to the laws of logic (3.031). God cannot create anything contrary to the laws of logic because 'we could not *say* what an "illogical" world would look like' (3.031). The limitation which is here imposed on God's omnipotence does not consist in God's inability to do something such as to fashion recalcitrant material to his will; it consists in the impossibility of our saying that God has done X, where X constitutes a departure from the laws of logic. Nonsense does not cease to be nonsense simply because it is talked about God.

A more specific limitation on what can be expressed by a proposition hinges, according to Wittgenstein, on the distinction between a *logical picture* (i.e. a proposition) and its *logical form*. As we saw in chapter 2 a proposition needs pictorial or logical form in order to express a logical picture. I discussed above (pp. 28—32) some of the problems concerning what precisely is meant in the *Tractatus* by the expressions 'pictorial form' and 'logical form'. Leaving these aside, Wittgenstein's doctrine is that if some piece of language is a picture of some piece of the world, then there must be some logical correspondence between the two; that is, there must be some underlying structure which links *what pictures* and *what is pictured*. It is this, and only this, which makes the picturing logically possible. The whole notion of *re-*presentation — whatever use we may make of it — consists (logically) in the idea of the recurrence of the presence in that which re-presents of something which is also present in that which is re-presented. Unless this 'something' is deemed to be present in both, the notion of re-presentation — or picturing — is unintelligible. Picturing implies a *logically antecedent* community of form, or structure, in what pictures and what is pictured respectively. It is, therefore, logically impossible for this common form, or structure, to *be* what is pictured. To clarify the point, think how impossible it would be for an artist to paint us a picture of his way of painting. Every artist of significance has his own way of painting; that is, of representing the world around him. Whatever he decides to paint, his way of painting will be manifest in the finished product. His canvas will require no signature; an expert will be able to identify it as his work from the way in which it is painted. But what could we be asking for, if we said to one such artist, 'We don't want a picture of anything which you see in the world around you. What we want is simply a picture of your way of painting things. Not an example of that way, mark you! A picture of that way itself'!? Patently, this is a request which no artist could fulfil. No abstract painting, however abstract it might be, would meet our request; no self-portrait, however

70

revealing, could fulfil it. An artist's way of painting is manifest in his every picture, but it cannot (logically) be the subject matter of any of his pictures.

In the *Tractatus* Wittgenstein contrasts what can be *shown* with what can be *said*. I will quote one passage, where he does so, at length and then comment on certain parts of it. The impossibility of propositions being logical pictures of their logical form is explicitly stated in this passage; but, more than that, some indication is given of what logical form *is* and what it is for a proposition to *show* its logical form. In a moment I will try to make what is indicated on these latter points quite clear.

Propositions can represent the whole of reality, but they cannot represent what they must have in common with reality in order to be able to represent it — logical form.

In order to be able to represent logical form, we should have to be able to station ourselves with propositions somewhere outside logic, that is to say outside the world.

Propositions cannot represent logical form: it is mirrored in them.

What finds its reflection in language, language cannot represent.

What expresses *itself* in language, *we* cannot express by means of language.

Propositions *show* the logical form of reality.

They display it.

Thus one proposition '*fa*' shows that the object *a* occurs in its sense, two propositions '*fa*' and '*ga*' show that the same object is mentioned in both of them

If two propositions contradict one another, then their structure shows it; the same is true if one of them follows from the other. And so on.

What can be *shown*, cannot be *said*. (4.12–4.1212)

The opening sentence of this quotation simply reiterates the point which I have been making at some length: that a proposition cannot be a logical picture of its own logical form. Wittgenstein's next remark — that for any proposition to be such a picture, it would have to be 'outside logic' and so 'outside the world' — simply emphasises the necessary

71

correspondence between the logical form of language and that of reality, a point which is essential to the *Tractatus* philosophy of language. The contrast between what is *said* by a proposition and what is *shown*, which it is his main concern to draw, is highlighted in the above passage by the contrast between what '*we*' express *by means of* the proposition and what expresses '*itself*' *in* the proposition.

In order to understand the examples of logical form showing itself, which Wittgenstein proceeds to give, it is important to be clear about the distinction which he has drawn earlier between 'signs' and 'symbols'. 'A sign', he said, 'is what can be perceived of a symbol' (3.32). The *sign* may be a word or a proposition. If spoken, it will have a certain sound; if written, a shape and colour. But considered as a *symbol*, i.e. a meaningful piece of language, there is necessarily more to a word or proposition than such perceptible properties as sound or shape. If there were not more, then it would be impossible, as Wittgenstein points out (3.323), to distinguish between the meaning of the word 'is' when it is (a) a copula, (b) a sign of identity and (c) an expression for existence. The perceptible properties of 'is' are the same in all three cases, but the meaning is different. Wittgenstein comments that philosophy is full of confusions which have arisen from failure to remark such distinctions (3.324). What is needed is an ideal language which precludes these confusions. A symbol may be defined as a sign governed by 'logical grammar' or 'logical syntax', that is to say, by rules for its use which (ideally) make its meaning precise and unambiguous (3.325, 3.326, 3.327). These rules of logical syntax could be illustrated from the case of the *sign* 'is' of which I spoke a moment ago, by pointing out that, if 'is' in the sentence 'X is' is taken as an expression for existence, this sentence is a complete one; whereas, if it is taken as a copula, or sign of identity, the sentence is incomplete. We need to know such rules in order to understand the *symbol* 'is'. They constitute it.

Coming back, then, to the question 'What is the logical form which shows itself in a proposition?' we can see that, whatever it is, it will show itself *in the proposition, or parts of it, regarded as symbols*,[2] that is, in a proposition, or some component of a proposition, considered as an application of certain rules of logical syntax. This is the light in which Wittgenstein's two examples of logical form showing itself, towards the end of the passage just quoted above, must now be interpreted.

Consider, from the first of these examples, the remark:

one proposition '*fa*' shows that the object *a* occurs in its sense.

This is an example of logical form showing itself in a component of a proposition. The sense of a proposition is the possible state of affairs which it represents (cf.2.202, 2.221). The proposition '*fa*' does not *say* that the object *a* occurs in its sense; it simply says that the state of affairs of which *a* is a part exists. How then does '*fa*' *show* that the object *a* occurs in its sense? The first point to take is that '*fa*' is able to do so because the rules of logical syntax which constitute the *symbol '*a*'*, connect it with an *object, a*. The second point to appreciate is that this feature of the symbol '*a*' shows itself in the propositions within which '*a*' occurs (cf.3.263). As Wittgenstein remarks, 'only in the nexus of a proposition does a name have meaning' (3.3); and, again, 'an expression presupposes the forms of all the propositions in which it can occur' (3.311). (Name' and 'expression' in these two quotations respectively refer simply to the particular kind of symbol which '*a*' for instance is, as distinct from the kind of symbol which a whole proposition, such as '*fa*', is). So, '*fa*' shows that the *object a* occurs in its sense because *a* is the meaning of '*a*' in '*fa*' and what the object *a* is becomes apparent only when we see the rôle which the symbol '*a*' plays in the language to which it belongs.

This account of the matter is open to the immediate objection that the method by which it purports to explain the meaning of a symbol, such as '*a*' in '*fa*', presupposes the existence of the meaning which it is concerned to explain. How could anyone use a name in a proposition unless he already knew its meaning? If he could not, then it sounds like nonsense to say, as we have seen that Wittgenstein appears to say, that the meaning of the name presupposes its use in propositions. Fortunately, it is not our present purpose to defend Wittgenstein's doctrine of showing against this, or any other objection, but simply to get some idea of what he meant by it.

The second example of logical form showing itself which Wittgenstein offers in the above passage is as follows:

If two propositions contradict one another, then their structure shows it; the same is true if one of them follows from the other.

This is an example of logical form showing itself in a whole proposition. What does Wittgenstein mean when he says, as he does here, that the implication, or contradiction, of one proposition by another is something which their structure *shows*? Remember that propositions (just like the name '*a*' in the last example) are symbols constituted by rules of logical syntax. As such, they yield certain *tautologies* (4.461). For example, 'It is three o'clock' yields, 'It is not both three o'clock and not three o'clock' or again, 'If it is three o'clock, then either it is three o'clock or it is four o'clock.' These tautologies do not tell us anything new about the time: they do not give us new information in the way that, if we knew that it was three o'clock but had not heard that there was a train to London at three o'clock, it would give us new information to be told that the train to London was about to leave on time. These tautologies simply show us what, having uttered the symbol 'It is three o'clock', we must, or must not, go on to say. They explicate the logic of the symbol 'It is three o'clock'. The logic of a symbol is already implicit within the symbol. The structure of the symbol 'p' shows itself *in the fact that* e.g. 'Not both p and not-p' and 'If p then either p or q', are tautologies. As Wittgenstein puts it:

The fact that the propositions of logic are tautologies *shows* the formal — logical — properties of language and the world.

The fact that a tautology is yielded by *this particular way* of connecting its constituents characterizes the logic of its constituents.

If propositions are to yield a tautology when they are connected in a certain way, they must have certain structural properties. So their yielding a tautology when
74

combined in this way *shows* that they possess these structural properties. (6.12)

The logical form of a proposition shows itself in the tautologies which constitute its logic. When Wittgenstein insists that this logical form can do nothing but *show* itself, he is simply pointing out that the tautologies which constitute logical form *are tautologies*. That is, they do not *say* anything in the sense that they do not tell us anything which we did not know already. (Logically speaking, that is. To be taught logic will of course be, psychologically speaking, to learn something which one did not know before.) *What* one is being taught is merely the rules for the use of the language which one already uses. In that sense one learns nothing which one did not know before.

Wittgenstein developed his doctrine of showing in conscious opposition to what is known as the theory of types, which Russell propounded in his philosophy of mathematics. The issues between them are of a highly technical character and I shall not do more than touch on them here. What triggered off Wittgenstein's opposition was a so-called axiom of infinity which Russell had been compelled to postulate in order to make his theory of types work. This 'axiom' was to the effect that the number of objects in the universe is not finite. Russell's theory of types was propounded in the course of his attempt to prove that the whole of mathematics is derivable from logical axioms. In so far as it required the axiom of infinity to make it work, however, it rested, in the last analysis, not upon a logical truth but a contingent fact about the universe. Wittgenstein's way of designating this defect in Russell's theory was to say that the latter 'had to mention the meaning of signs when establishing the rules for them' (3.331). 'Meaning' here signifies the object or objects to which, as a matter of contingent fact, any sign refers, i.e. its actual referent(s). What Wittgenstein is calling attention to is the fact that Russell's derivation of mathematics, and in particular of arithmetic, from logic depended upon there actually being an infinite number of such referents in the universe. Frege, in the light of whose work both Russell and Wittgenstein did their philosophy of mathematics, had insisted on the need for *completeness* of definition. A definition of a concept, he said, 'must unambiguously determine, as regards any object, whether or not it falls under the concept (whether or not the predicate is truly assertible of it)'[3] The only way of achieving such completeness, it seemed to Wittgenstein, was to make logic entirely a matter of knowing the rules of logical syntax for any given symbol. 'Logic', he said, 'must look after itself' (5.473). It can do so, if, and only if, the propositions of logic are tautologies (cf.6.1); that is, if, and only if, they *show* the structure of language rather than *say* that anything is, or is not, the case. Russell's axiom of infinity manifestly falls under the condemnation that it is an attempt to look after logic by means of something other than logic alone.

Russell, for his part, at the end of his introduction to the *Tractatus*, suggests that, while the logical structure of any given language may well be inexpressible in *that language*, for the reasons which Wittgenstein gives, nevertheless we could conceive of its being expressible in some *other language* with a different structure. And so *ad infinitum*. To the obvious reply that Wittgenstein's argument would, in the last analysis, still apply to such a hierarchy of languages taken as a whole, Russell's answer is that this totality of languages is a fiction, a mere delusion. He seems to think that no one would wish to conceive of any such totality unless he had metaphysical ends in view.

Philosophy and logic, as Wittgenstein conceived of them are, to recall his words already quoted, concerned with drawing a limit to the expression of thoughts. That is to say, their concern is to show what can and what cannot be said. To *show* it, not to *say* it. The propositions of philosophy and logic are not themselves logical pictures of possible states of affairs. They show what the structure of language is, although this cannot be said. Russell, in his introduction to the *Tractatus*, points out the apparent paradox in Wittgenstein's position: 'Mr. Wittgenstein manages to say a good deal about what cannot be said.'[4] Wittgenstein himself was not unaware of this paradox. His way of dealing with it was to affirm that it is necessary to say the things which he had said in order to show that they cannot be said — a contention, which as Russell mildly remarks, leaves one with 'a certain sense of intellectual discomfort'.[5] Something of the same discomfort

76

was evidently felt by Wittgenstein himself for, at the close of the *Tractatus*, he suggests that philosophy should not really be taught as he has sought to teach it in his preceding pages, but as follows:

> The correct method in philosophy would really be the following: to say nothing except what can be said i.e. propositions of natural science — i.e. something that has nothing to do with philosophy — and then, whenever someone else wanted to say something metaphysical, to demonstrate to him that he had failed to give a meaning to certain signs in his proposition. Although it would not be satisfying to the other person — he would not have the feeling that we were teaching him philosophy — *this* method would be the only strictly correct one. (6.53)

A teacher of philosophy who employed this Socratic method would ask anyone who uttered a metaphysical proposition what he meant by the terms used in it, and then what he meant by the definitions offered in reply, and so on until a point was reached where the speaker could not say what he meant. In such a process no philosophical propositions would need to be employed. However, if philosophy must be taught by the more direct methods of the *Tractatus*, then the propositions used have to be seen, according to Wittgenstein, as ephermeral means to an end whose realisation will necessarily involve their elimination: i.e. as a ladder to be thrown away once one has climbed up by means of it (6.54).

What then, will someone who has been taught philosophy either by indirect or direct methods have learned? He will, says Wittgenstein, have climbed to a position from which he will see the world aright. And what is it to see the world aright? It is to see the need for silence.

> My propositions serve as elucidations in the following way: anyone who understands me eventually recognizes them as nonsensical, when he has used them — as steps — to climb up beyond them. (He must, so to speak, throw away the ladder after he has climbed up it.)

He must transcend these propositions; and then he will

77

see the world aright. What we cannot speak about we must pass over in silence. (6.54,7)

The logical doctrines of the *Tractatus* may be difficult to understand but they are not veiled in mystery. Whatever may be said for or against them, one can, with the required effort, form clear ideas of what they are. When Wittgenstein says that logic is transcendental we can discover what he meant. Given his conception of the relationship between language and reality, we can understand his notion of logical form and his reasons for thinking that it cannot be put into words but nevertheless makes itself manifest. It is not in the least unintelligible to say that logical form shows itself in rules of logical syntax. How could it do otherwise?

II. THE ETHICO-RELIGIOUS INTERPRETATION

The silence enjoined at the end of the *Tractatus* is not simply silence concerning logical form. That of which we cannot speak is also the whole subject matter of ethics, religion and aesthetics, for it is with these that Wittgenstein has concerned himself in the closing pages of his book. Now, therefore, we must consider what he meant by the transcendental in its ethico-religious instantiation i.e. 'the mystical', and why he thought that it cannot be put into words but nevertheless shows itself.

Feeling the World as a Limited Whole

In the closing paragraphs of the *Tractatus* (i.e. 6.4 to 7) 'the mystical' is spoken of as having to do with the following: 'the sense of the world', 'ethics', 'the will in so far as it is the subject of ethical attributes', 'death' and 'immortality', 'God', 'the problems of life' and 'the solution of the problems of life.' These matters were all conceived by Wittgenstein to be aspects of a certain 'view' of the world, or expressions of a certain 'feeling' about it. He wrote:

To view the world *sub specie aeterni* is to view it as a whole — a limited whole.
Feeling the world as a limited whole — it is this that is mystical. (6.45)

These words must be read with Wittgenstein's theory that
78

the limits of one's language are the limits of one's world (cf.5.6) in mind. What constitutes the limits of language? The only conceivable answer to this is that meaning rules do so. If anything purports to be language, then it lies within the scope of rules which determine what is meaningful and what is meaningless. According to the Wittgenstein of the *Tractatus*, as we have seen above, the meaning of language is that to which it refers. Language pictures, or mirrors, the world. The rules which prescribe the meaning of language indicate what parts of language refer to what parts of the world and how they so refer. So meaningful language is about the world, or reality, i.e. about what *is* the case.

There are two sorts of question about what is the case which, if they could be answered, would necessarily take us *beyond* what is the case. They are respectively questions concerning (a) the *sense*, and (b) the *value*, of what is the case. Of the former sort of question Wittgenstein said; 'The sense of the world must lie outside the world' (6.41); and, of the latter sort, 'If there is any value that does have value, it must lie outside the whole sphere of what happens and is the case' (ibid.). Answers to questions concerning the sense of the world must necessarily take us beyond the world (i.e. 'all that is the case' (1)). To say what the sense or meaning of any X is, must (logically) be to say something other, and more, than simply X. Again, answers to questions concerning the value of what is the case must necessarily take us beyond what is the case. To assess the value of what is the case, we must have, as our criterion, some conception of what *ought to be* the case. And what ought to be the case is, as a matter of logical necessity, distinct from what is the case. To reiterate Wittgenstein's view, if there is 'any value that does have value' — i.e. if there is any adequate criterion by which to judge the value of what is the case — then 'it must lie outside the whole sphere of what happens and is the case.' At 6.421 Wittgenstein says 'Ethics and aesthetics are one and the same.' Presumably, therefore, whatever is said about ethical value judgments in the *Tractatus* would apply with equal force to aesthetic judgements.

It follows from all this that, given Wittgenstein's picture theory of meaning, questions concerning the sense or value of what is the case cannot (logically) be answered. The kind of answer which they call for — i.e. one which goes beyond what is the case — cannot be given. It cannot be given in the sense that, if it is given, it will necessarily be meaningless. For, on the picture theory of meaning, as we have seen above, language has meaning in so far, and only in so far, as it pictures, mirrors, represents, what is the case. Since answers to questions about the sense or value of what is the case would need to go beyond what is the case, they would need to go beyond what could meaningfully be said.

To view or feel the world as a limited whole is to be aware of the limits which meaning-rules impose on what can be said. Just as Wittgenstein believed that it is impossible to put the structure of language into words, so he held that the *sense* or *value* of things cannot be expressed. However, he recognised that men frequently find themselves under a compulsion to try to express the inexpressible in religious or ethical terms.

In a published lecture, now called *'Ethics'*, he offered two examples of the kind of experience which people try to express in ethical or religious terms. This lecture was delivered in Cambridge ten years or so after the publication of the *Tractatus*. It first appeared in print in *The Philosophical Review*, 1965. One of the two examples was the experience of wondering at the existence of the world. Not, that is, at the existence of any particular thing *within* the world, but at 'how extraordinary (it is) that the world should exist'. Now, it makes sense, said Wittgenstein, to speak of wondering at the existence of something when you can imagine it *not* existing; one can, for instance, wonder at the fact that a certain house still stands because one can imagine that it might have fallen into ruins. 'But it is nonsense,' said Wittgenstein, 'to say that I wonder at the existence of the world, because I cannot imagine it not existing.' The second example which he gave is the experience of feeling absolutely safe whatever happens. Here again it makes sense to speak of feeling safe (e.g. from street accidents) when you can contrast your actual condition (e.g. sitting in your house) with some other conceivable condition (e.g. walking or driving along an 'accident black spot' part of a street). But 'it's nonsense to say that I am safe *whatever* happens,' said Wittgenstein, because there is nothing to contrast with

80

whatever happens.

In all cases such as 'wondering at the existence of the world' or 'feeling absolutely safe,' Wittgenstein maintained that we are misusing language. He gave the following reason. We are using expressions such as 'wondering' or 'feeling safe' to describe special experiences as if these expressions were similies or allegories. We are aware that our use of them in this context is different from their ordinary usage and we take it to be appropriate because allegorical. 'Wondering at the existence of the world'. we suppose, uses 'wondering' as an allegory with which to describe what we are really doing; 'feeling absolutely safe,' uses 'feeling safe' as a simile to which we can compare what we are really feeling. But, as Wittgenstein pointed out, if I say that X is a simile or allegory of Y, I must be able to say what Y is, otherwise I do not understand what I am saying. In the present case, however, this condition cannot be fulfilled because I cannot identify what it is that I am experiencing when I wonder at the existence of the world, or feeling when I feel absolutely safe, *apart from the simile or allegory which I am using*. It follows, said Wittgenstein, that 'what at first appeared to be a simile now seems to be mere nonsense.' He held that what he had to say about these two examples obtains for all religious language.

> Now all religious terms seem in this sense to be used as similes or allegorically. For when we speak of God and that he sees everything and when we kneel and pray to him all our terms and actions seem to be parts of a great and elaborate allegory which represents him as a human being of great power whose grace we try to win etc. etc. But this allegory also describes the experiences which I have just referred to. For the first of them is, I believe, exactly what people were referring to when they said that God had created the world; and the experience of absolute safety has been described by saying that we feel safe in the hands of God.[6]

Ethical terms are, Wittgenstein held in this lecture, subject to the same limitations as religious terms.Contrast 'He is a good man' with 'He is a good tennis player', for instance. If I were not a good tennis player and someone pointed this out to me, I might say 'Oh, that doesn't bother me, I don't want to be good' without this seeming to anyone a reprehensible thing for me to say. I might like playing tennis just for the fresh air and exercise. But suppose someone pointed out to me that I am not a good man and I said 'Oh, that doesn't bother me, I don't want to be good'. This would seem shocking to most people.

The imperative to be a good man is categorical, to use Kant's term, as distinct from merely hypothetical. *If* I want certain things which being good at tennis will bring, such as fame and money, *then* I ought to bother about being a good tennis player, but not otherwise. Being a good man, on the other hand, is something which I ought to care about *for its own sake* irrespective of any end to which it may be the means. Wittgenstein differentiated, in direct line with this distinction of Kant's, between *relative* value (e.g. a good tennis player) and *absolute* value (e.g. a morally good man). Ethics is about absolute value.

'Every judgment of relative value' he said 'is a mere statement of facts and can therefore be put in such a form that it loses all the appearance of a judgment of value.' He meant that 'He is a good tennis player,' for example, can be rewritten without loss or change of meaning, 'He has a strong service, his ground shots are accurate, he is quick at the net, his back-hand is powerful,' etc. In the case of absolute value on the other hand, so Wittgenstein wished to contend, 'no statement of fact can ever be, or imply, a judgment of absolute value.' You could rehearse all the facts there are and still have said nothing about that which has absolute value. In a comment on *Schlick's Ethic*, dated 17 December 1930 by Waismann (WWK p.115), Wittgenstein expressed in a rather curious way his conviction that the nature of the good has nothing to do with the facts. The view that God wills the good because it is good, as against the view that the good is good because God wills it, is generally regarded as the more profound. But Wittgenstein denies this: he takes the doctrine that good is what God commands to be the more penetrating. This view, he says, obviates any explanation as to why the good is good, whereas the other view pretends that the good might have some ground beyond itself. It has often been argued that the view which Wittgenstein favours is a glaring instance of the naturalistic fallacy. But here Wittgenstein says, by implication, that what God commands is not to be regarded as a fact at all. This is consistent with his general account of the mystical: to speak of something as God's command takes us beyond the limits of language and is, in effect, a refusal to say anything about it. In the ethical then, we come up against the limit of language which is the limit of the world. Since 'our words will only express facts' there is no language in which to describe categorical or absolute value. Absolute value, because it cannot be analysed into facts, cannot be put into words.

There are, I think, some fairly obvious objections to this account of religious and ethical language.

Take first Wittgenstein's account of religious language. It seems to me that he is mistaken in his view that religious belief necessarily takes God to be conceivable only allegorically. When a christian believer, for instance, says, that God loves us, I do not think he means to speak of God's attitude towards us as one of which love is an allegory; or when he says that God is almighty, I do not think he means that God has a characteristic of which almightiness is a simile. I think that in both cases he means literally what he says. If he did not, he would have no problem of evil on his hands. It is only because christians believe that God loves us in a perfectly normal sense of 'loves', and that God is almighty in the perfectly normal sense of being able to do whatever is logically possible, that they have to face the question 'Why then does God allow us to suffer pain and loss?' I know that some sophisticated apologists for Christianity have argued that the problem of evil can be solved by taking God's love to be 'infinite' love and so compatible with letting millions of his creatures suffer hunger or pain, but I have never met any believers who have been comforted by such considerations, just as I have never met any erstwhile unbelievers who have been converted to the faith by them.

Turning now to Wittgenstein's account of ethical language, for anyone to say, as he does, that judgments of relative or hypothetical value can be shown to be *mere* statements of facts is not correct. Many statements of fact could, for instance, be made about Bill Smith who is a good tennis player, e.g. that he plays only on Mondays, Wednesdays and Fridays, always has a shower after his game, uses Dunlop tennis balls and so on. None of these has anything to do with his being a good player. Why do certain of the facts, such as that he has a strong service, plays accurate ground shots, etc., make him a good player? Because these are the *criteria* of goodness in tennis players. Implicit within the statements of fact into which a judgment of relative value can be put are criteria or principles of evaluation which determine *what* facts constitute relative value as distinct from what facts do not. Again, to say of absolute value that 'no statement of fact can ever be, or imply, a judgment of absolute value' is not by itself to differentiate relative from absolute value. No statement of fact by itself can imply relative value either. 'He has a strong service' implies 'He is a good tennis player' if, and only if, the additional premise 'Whoever has a strong service is a good tennis player' is supplied. By the same token it makes perfectly good sense to ask why any man, or thing, which has absolute value, has it. The kind of reason which Wittgenstein himself gave is that a man is absolutely good, if he tells the truth. Absolute value implies the fulfilment of such criteria in exactly the same way as relative value does.

We see then what Wittgenstein meant by what he called viewing or feeling the world as a limited whole, i.e. by an awareness of the 'mystical'. He recognised that men experience this limitation as a restraint. They have a compulsion to ask questions about the mystical and they yearn for answers which can be put into words. But they cannot ask meaningful questions nor find meaningful answers. He saw men in this regard as being like prisoners who persistently dash themselves against the walls of their cage. Wittgenstein spoke about this kind of experience eloquently in the closing words of his lecture 'Ethics'.

> Now the answer to all this will seem perfectly clear to many of you. You will say: Well, if certain experiences constantly tempt us to attribute a quality to them which we call absolute or ethical value and importance, this simply shows that by these words we *don't* mean nonsense, that after all what we mean by saying that an experience has absolute value *is just a fact like other facts*

and that all it comes to is that we have not yet succeeded in finding the correct logical analysis of what we mean by our ethical and religious expressions. Now when this is urged against me I at once see clearly, as it were in a flash of light, not only that no description that I can think of would do to describe what I mean by absolute value, but that I would reject every significant description that anybody could possible suggest, *ab initio*, on the ground of its significance. That is to say: I see now that these nonsensical expressions were not nonsensical because I had not yet found the correct expressions, but that their nonsensicality was their very essence. For all I wanted to do with them was just *to go beyond* the world and that is to say beyond significant language. My whole tendency and I believe the tendency of all men who ever tried to write or talk Ethics or Religion was to run against the boundaries of language. This running against the walls of our cage is perfectly, absolutely hopeless. Ethics so far as it springs from the desire to say something about the ultimate meaning of life, the absolute good, the absolute valuable, can be no science. What it says does not add to our knowledge in any sense. But it is a document of a tendency in the human mind which I personally cannot help respecting deeply and I would not for my life ridicule it.[7]

So the mystical — i.e. ethics and religion — is, according to Wittgenstein, such that anything which is said about it must of necessity be nonsense. It is important now to recognise that, if this is the case, one could have either of two reasons for keeping silent about it.

One reason is simply that *one does not wish to talk nonsense and one will be doing so, if one talks about the mystical.* The other is the more complicated reason that *one does not wish to trivialise the mystical and one will be doing so if one talks nonsense about it.*

For a correct interpretation of Wittgenstein it is essential to know which of these was his reason for saying that one must be silent about the mystical.

There are grounds for thinking that Wittgenstein's reason was the latter, not the former, of the two. It is true that some parts of the *Tractatus* may admit of a contrary interpretation (e.g. 6.5, 6.521) but such a remark as 'There are, indeed, things that cannot be put into words. They *make themselves manifest*. They are what is mystical.' (6.522), seems to imply that Wittgenstein intended to do something more than to dismiss the mystical pejoratively as nonsense in the manner, say, of the logical positivists. I will discuss Wittgenstein's connexion with the logical positivists in the next chapter, but here I simply point out that there is justification, both in the *Tractatus* and in other sources, for attributing to Wittgenstein a respect for the mystical which is far removed from the hardline logical positivists' contempt for metaphysics.[8]

For instance, whatever Wittgenstein meant by his remark 'The solution of the problem of life is seen in the vanishing of the problem' (6.521), it is hardly possible to interpret it as amounting simply to an asseveration that metaphysics is contemptible as compared with science, if we place it alongside another remark in the *Tractatus*, viz. 'We feel that even when *all possible* scientific questions have been answered, the problems of life remain completely untouched' (6.52). Of course, this latter remark might conceivably be taken to imply that such problems not only do, but ought to, remain untouched because they are unworthy of the attention of intelligent men, but there is, as we shall see, some sound external evidence against this interpretation. We can find grounds for thinking that Wittgenstein not only sympathised with, but also shared, the concern about morality and religion which some of the best of men have felt. Indeed there is reason to believe that the *Tractatus* itself is an expression of such concern.

Consider, for instance, what Wittgenstein said when, after a number of unsuccessful attemps to get the *Tractatus* published, he approached Ludwig Ficker, editor of *Der Brenner*, for advice. In the course of correspondence with Ficker, he referred to the concluding paragraphs of the *Tractatus* (i.e. those concerning the mystical) as containing a most direct expression of the whole point of the book. That point, he went on to say, is an 'ethical' one. He told Ficker that he had once meant to include in the preface this sentence: 'My work consists of two parts: the one presented here plus all that I have *not* written' and that the book drew a limit to the ethical 'from the inside as it were' because this was the only '*rigorous*' way to draw it. 'I have managed',he said, 'in my book to put everything firmly into place by being silent about it.'[9]   I shall try to explain in due course what Wittgenstein meant by this. At the moment it suffices to point out that the part of the book which he called 'all that I have *not* written' (by which he must have meant what cannot be put into words) is described in the letter to Ficker as 'the important' part. This remark, whatever it may mean, is certainly incompatible with the conclusion that Wittgenstein thought of the mystical as nonsense and nothing more.

Other considerations also lead away from any such conclusion. Wittgenstein expressed fierce dissatisfation with all interpretations of the *Tractatus* which saw its main point in the arguments prior to 6.4 and little or no point in its concluding paragraphs from 6.4. That was why he disliked Russell's introduction to it so much and only consented to publishing it with that introduction when he found that no one would take it without. He seems to have been particularly anxious not to be taken for a logical positivist. Despite all their admiration of the *Tractatus*, he had difficulty in bringing himself even to discuss the book with the Vienna Circle and it is on record that, in early encounters with them, he perversely insisted on reading the poetry of Rabindranath Tagore aloud rather than talk about his book.[10] Eventually he did talk to some of them about philosophy, especially to Schlick and Waismann; but Carnap, who was present at some of these conversations, has put on record his early awareness of the gulf which separated them from Wittgenstein on the subject of religion.[11]

Paul Engelmann was one of Wittgenstein's most intimate friends at the time when the *Tractatus* first appeared and is presumably as reliable a source as we can find concerning Wittgenstein's own view about the point of the book. Engelmann says that Wittgenstein was mistaken for a logical positivist by a whole generation of disciples because he has this in common with the logical positivists — he differentiates what we can speak about from what we must be silent about.

87

But there the similarity ends. The positivists 'have nothing to be silent about'; they hold that 'what we can speak about is all that matters in life'. Wittgenstein, by contrast, 'passionately believes that all that really matters in human life is precisely what, in his view, we must be silent about'.[12]

It seems highly probable from evidence such as this that Wittgenstein's concern in the closing paragraphs of the *Tractatus* was not simply to deliver his readers from the inclination to talk nonsense. He had some point to make on the subject of ethics and religion which went beyond that. What, then was this point? The answer seems to be this: the mystical is trivialised when it is talked about and we must preserve it from such trivialisation by refusing to participate in all the 'gassing', the 'chatter', the 'twaddle' (to use Wittgenstein's expressions)[13] which brings ethics and religion into contempt.

Wittgenstein seems to have regarded as particularly obnoxious all attempts to give intellectual justification to either ethics or religion. He approvingly quoted Schopenhauer to Waismann on the subject of ethics: 'To teach morality is hard; to give it intellectual justification is impossible.' And speaking on the subject of religion with Norman Malcolm, after the latter had quoted to him a remark of Kirkegaard's to the effect 'How can it be that Christ does not exist, since I know that He has saved me?', Wittgenstein exclaimed, 'You see, it isn't a question of *proving* anything!'[14]

In this attempt to expound Wittgenstein's views about the mystical, I have been concentrating so far on the negative things which he had to say, that is, what cannot be said about the mystical. Moral goodness cannot be described as though it were a state of affairs in the world — 'propositions can express nothing that is higher' (6.42). Religious beliefs cannot be discussed as if anything which is the case would make them true or false — 'God does not reveal himself *in* the world' (6.432). And so on. But Wittgenstein had more positive things to say as well and to these I now turn.

The Derivation of the Doctrine of Showing
The *Tractatus* was not written in an intellectual vacuum. The thoughts which it expresses were, in part at least, the product of various influences operating within its author's intellectual

88

environment. Wittgenstein himself refers in his introduction to the stimulation which he had received from the works of Frege and Bertrand Russell.[15] For a long time interpreters of the *Tractatus* regarded these two philosophers as the main influence under which Wittgenstein had written. More recently, however, some interpreters have been turning their attention to the Viennese culture in which Wittgenstein spent his childhood and youth and by which, they have come to think, he was deeply and lastingly influenced. They have drawn out comparisons between some of the thoughts expressed in the *Tractatus* and some of the ideas which were current in *fin de siècle* Vienna.

Two notions, especially, may be instanced. These are to be found in the *Tractatus* and also, in one form or another, in the work of leading figures in Viennese culture at the turn of the century. One is the notion of two realms of experience which must be kept distinct; the other is the notion of something which, although we cannot express it, nevertheless shows itself.

To illustrate the currency of the former notion reference may be made to the work of Karl Kraus, the literary critic, and Adolf Loos, the architect. Kraus drew a sharp distinction between writing which is intended to report objective facts and writing which is meant to convey the author's emotions, opinions, fantasies or values. His purpose was not to denigrate either by contrast with the other, but simply to insist that both are corrupted if they are confused or compounded with each other. On this basis, he mounted a critical attack upon many of the writers of his day. One of his *bêtes noires* was the so-called *feuilleton*, or cultural essay, a prestigious form of journalism in his day wherein subjects were discussed in elegant language which purported to be both factually descriptive and emotionally evocative. Such writing Kraus believed to be doubly corrupt: it distorted the objective facts of a situation and it inhibited the creative imagination of the author. Loos drew the same kind of distinction as Kraus but with reference to the making of things, rather than the writing of literature. There are some things, artefacts, which exist for a practical purpose or use, such as tables or houses, and which should be made with, and only with, their function in mind; there are other things,

89

objets d'art, which exist to express the dreams or values of those who make them. Loos's *bête noire* was so-called 'applied art' which produced hybrid things, i.e. tables, houses, or whatever, embossed with useless external ornamentation. To make such things was in his view doubly offensive: it impaired utility and it debased art. Kraus summed up the distinction which he and Loos had been concerned to draw in this much-quoted and colourful way:

> Adolf Loos and I — he literally and I grammatically — have done nothing more than show that there is a distinction between an urn and a chamber pot and that it is this distinction above all that provides culture with elbow room. The others, those who fail to make this distinction, are divided into those who use the urn as a chamber pot and those who use the chamber pot as an urn.[16]

There is evidence that Wittgenstein must have been familiar with the work of both Kraus and Loos. For example, when he went to Norway, he continued his subscription to Kraus's journal *Die Fackel* and had it sent out to him,[17] from which we may safely infer that he read it regularly. And it is recorded that Loos once made to Wittgenstein the curious remark, 'You are me!'[18] from which we may infer that Wittgenstein's views about architecture were influenced by Loos.

The distinction between the realm of *fact* and the realm of *value*, which is central to the thought of the *Tractatus*, especially in those passages concerned with the mystical, may well have been drawn in the light of the distinction which Kraus and Loos had brought out between two realms of experience, those of fact and fantasy, of artefacts and *objets d'art*, of urns and chamber pots, respectively.

The other notion to which I referred above is that of something which, though we cannot express it, may nevertheless show itself. For an example of this idea in a writer who doubtless influenced Wittgenstein, we may turn to Heinrich Hertz. In his important work on mechanics, he gave an account which represents the latter as a quest for mathematical models of objects, which will be 'logically permissible' (they are this if they do not contradict the laws

90

of thought), 'correct' (they are this in so far as their essential relations correspond to the relations of the external objects which they purport to explain), 'appropriate' (they are more appropriate as they include more of the essential relations of the object), 'simple' (they become simpler as they include fewer superfluous or empty relations).[19] Hertz maintained that his account of mechanics showed the limitations of the subject from within because its method of explanation was 'too simple and narrow to account for even the lowest processes of life'.[20] Wittgenstein had been trained as an engineer in his early days and presumably that is how he first became acquainted with Hertz's theories. In the *Tractatus* he refers explicitly to Hertz twice (see 4.04 and 6.361). Reference was made in the last chapter to the debt which Wittgenstein's picture theory of language owed to Hertz's model theory of the language of mechanics. In particular, this applies to the doctrine of showing. Just as Hertz's account of the limits of mechanics from within showed something about life, namely that it lies beyond purely mechanistic description or explanation, so Wittgenstein's attempt in the *Tractatus* to draw a limit to the expression of thoughts showed something about the mystical, namely that it lies beyond expression in words.

My intention in the last two paragraphs has not, of course, been to make out a case to the effect that the *Tractatus* is simply a product of the influence of Kraus, Loos or Hertz; it has been merely to catch a glimpse or so of the intellectual climate with which Wittgenstein was familiar before ever he became acquainted with the work of Frege or arrived in the Cambridge of Russell and Moore. A detailed description of the Vienna in which Wittgenstein grew up and of the thinkers whose work constituted its cultural environment is offered by A. Janik and S. Toulmin in their *Wittgenstein's Vienna* (London, 1973). Whatever may be the defects of that book, there is more than a little likelihood that its authors are correct in their general view that when Wittgenstein came to England he was already preoccupied with a philosophical problem, which the *Tractatus* is an attempt to solve. This was the problem of drawing a clear distinction between what can, and what cannot, be said and thereby delivering what cannot be said from the corruption which sets in when any attempt is made to say it. Art, ethics, religion, as we have seen, belong according to Wittgenstein within the realm of what cannot be said. In his view, it was undoubtedly of the first importance to draw the distinction which differentiates them from science or common sense; but I think we have found reason to believe that it was for him equally important to recognise that, though we cannot express the mystical, it can, and does, show itself. When we set the *Tractatus* against the background of Wittgenstein's Vienna, it certainly becomes easier to understand, and accept, his expressed opinion that its aim was to put *everything of importance* into place by being silent about it (cf. above p. 87).

The Difference Morality or Religion Makes

Morality is for Wittgenstein, as for Schopenhauer, a sphere for the exercise of will rather than reason. It makes all the difference how a man exercises his will morally, but this is not a difference which can be put into words. *What* he wills cannot be expressed in propositions whose truth or falsity is determined by how things are in the world. This does not render the exercise of the will futile, or reduce it to empty, idle fantasy. On the contrary, it is the will alone which can break out from the limits imposed by language. In the nature of the case, however, the will cannot effect this escape in language for then there would have been no escape.

In the *Tractatus* Wittgenstein said cryptically:

If the good or bad exercise of the will does alter the world, it can alter only the limits of the world, not the facts — not what can be expressed by means of language.

In short the effect must be that it becomes an altogether different world. It must, so to speak, wax and wane as a whole.

The world of the happy man is a different one from that of the unhappy man. (6.43)

Whatever Wittgenstein was saying in this difficult passage, it cannot have been that the limits of language or the world can be eliminated or changed in a *literal* sense simply because someone wills them to be. 'The world is independent of my will.' (6.373). By an exercise of will we could not change the world

92

which gives language its sense, or the sense of language so given. Wittgenstein must, therefore, have meant that an exercise of will can make the world of the happy man different from that of the unhappy in some *metaphorical* sense. The difference, he says, which the good or bad exercise of will makes cannot be a difference in 'the facts.' What other sort of difference could it be? Wittgenstein's answer appears to be as follows.

A man who exercises his will in doing something morally right or good cannot look for something *other than this act itself* which makes his world different from that of the man who wills otherwise. Ethics can have nothing to do with what is the case, conceived as reward or punishment. The difference is *in the act itself.* As Wittgenstein has it:

> It is clear . . . that ethics has nothing to do with punishment and reward in the usual sense of the terms. So our question about the *consequences* of an action must be unimportant. — At least those consequences should not be events . . . There must indeed be some kind of ethical reward and ethical punishment, but they must reside in the action itself. (6.422)

In the section of the *Tractatus* which immediately follows (i.e. 6.431–6.4312) Wittgenstein says something similar about religion. The religious believer must not expect any fulfilment or authentication of his beliefs in the form of spatio-temporal events. Any such event will be part of *the world* and so necessarily cannot be part of *the sense of the world.* Belief in 'life after death' is a case in point. Death, said Wittgenstein, 'is not an event in life: we do not live to experience death' (6.4311). We see his point if we ask what sense it would make to say, for instance, 'First I died, then I saw X', as though death were one event in a sequence of events which happened to us and went on after death, like, for example, 'First I wrote a letter, then I saw X.' Wittgenstein's concern here was not to undermine belief in immortality but to bring out what such belief is, or rather what it is *not.* It is *not* a matter of believing that events will go on happening to one after death. So to regard it takes the point out of belief in it as part of the meaning of life or the sense of the world. If surviving death is one event in life, or

93

one fact in the world, then it is part of what needs to be given a meaning or sense, not part of that meaning or sense. Said Wittgenstein:

> Not only is there no guarantee of the temporal immortality of the human soul, that is to say of its eternal survival after death; but, in any case, this assumption completely fails to accomplish the purpose for which it has always been intended. Or is some riddle solved by my surviving for ever? Is not this eternal life itself as much of a riddle as our present life? The solution of the riddle of life in space and time lies *outside* space and time. (6.4312)

Immortality, he said, should be taken to mean 'not infinite temporal duration, but timelessness' and 'then eternal life belongs to those who live in the present' (6.4311).

As Wittgenstein saw it, then, morality and religion are activities the justification of which lies, so to say, within themselves. The difference they make is not heteronomous. The difference simply *is* the ethical act itself not anything consequential upon it; it *is* the religious belief as such, not anything determined by it. To act ethically, or believe religiously, *is* to be in 'an altogether different world' which 'must, so to speak, wax and wane as a whole' (6.43).

How the Mystical Shows Itself
Wittgenstein evidently believed that we can discover, and even create, situations in which the mystical shows itself. This becomes apparent from his correspondence with Engelmann and from what he himself did after the publication of the *Tractatus*. The two spheres in which he apparently thought that the mystical can show itself are *art* and *action*.

(i) *Art*. Consider art first. To take an example, Wittgenstein wrote the following in a letter to Engelmann (dated 9 April 1917) about a poem which the latter had sent him: '...The poem by Uhland is really magnificent. And this is how it is: if only you do not try to utter what is unutterable then *nothing* gets lost. But the unutterable will be — unutterably — *contained* in what has been uttered!'[21] Engelmann tells us that this letter was written 'when Wittgenstein was working on the completion of the *Tractatus*

— possibly before he had given final shape to the statement of his mystical insights.'[22] The poem sent to Wittgenstein was Uhland's *Graf Eberhard's Weissdorn*. Engelmann takes Wittgenstein's comments upon it to indicate that the latter considered this poem to be an instance of what is meant in the *Tractatus* (6.522) by the mystical making itself manifest. The poem in A. Platt's English translation of 1848 is as follows:

COUNT EBERHARD'S HAWTHORN[23]

Count Eberhard Rustle-Beard
From Wurttemberg's fair land
On holy errand steer'd
To Palestrina's strand.

The while he slowly rode
Along a woodland way;
He cut from the hawthorn bush
A little fresh green spray.

Then in his iron helm
The little sprig he plac'd;
And bore it in the wars,
And over the ocean waste.

And when he reach'd his home,
He plac'd it in the earth;
Where little leaves and buds
The gentle Spring call'd forth.

He went each year to it,
The Count so brave and true;
And overjoy'd was he
To witness how it grew.

The Count was worn with age
The sprig became a tree;
'Neath which the old man oft
Would sit in reverie.

95

The branching arch so high,
Whose whisper is so bland,
Reminds him of the past
And Palestrina's strand.

Engelmann says that he himself had considered this poem an instance of how poetry can produce a profound artistic effect *beyond* (but never without) the immediate effect of its language. He had learned from Karl Kraus that this was a possibility in general; in Uhland's poem he had found a particular example of its realisation. He was delighted to discover that Wittgenstein thought the same about the poem. Of Wittgenstein's letter Engelmann says: 'It seems to me indeed that his discovery of what a proposition cannot make explicit because it is manifest in it — in my view the essential core of the *Tractatus* although only adumbrated in the book — has found a lasting expression in this letter.'[24] He evidently takes 'what is manifest in' a proposition here to mean what the propositions of the poem convey concerning ethical or religious reality. There is no indication in Engelmann's remarks that he thought there to be any distinction between what I have called the 'logical' and the 'ethico-religious' interpretations of the transcendental. Engelmann would presumably have claimed that it is the same phenomenon for language to 'show' its logical structure and for poetry to 'show' absolute aesthetic value; or, at least, that these are simply two manifestations of the same phenomenon. He would evidently have taken this to be Wittgenstein's view of the matter also, had he considered that question. To this we shall return (pp. 111–12).

Wittgenstein had a high regard for certain forms of literature or art besides poetry. He valued in particular Tolstoy's stories; but he also praised detective stories and Wild West films. Janik and Toulmin in their *Wittgenstein's Vienna* offer the explanatory comment that 'these fables reach out to a man in his *Innerlichheit*, and so are the means of touching the fantasy, which is the fountainhead of value.'[25] If, as seems likely, Wittgenstein regarded such stories and films as vehicles through which the mystical can show itself, then it was presumably the direct or honest quality of these art forms, the genuineness of the emotions or situations

96

described in them, which he appreciated.

Whatever the explanation of Wittgenstein's particular predilections, it is quite clear that he saw art as a means whereby the highest which cannot be spoken might nevertheless show itself. Literature as diverse as the poetry of Goethe and American detective magazines, the drama of films, architecture — in all these art forms the mystical which cannot be put into words can, in his view, make itself manifest.

(ii) *Action.* Wittgenstein taught from 1920—26 in elementary schools in Lower Austria, at the villages of Trattenbach (1920—22), Puchberg (1922—24) and Otterthal (1924—26). It has sometimes been assumed that the only significance of his so doing lies in the fact that, having to his own satisfaction at least solved all philosophical problems in the *Tractatus*, he had to find something else to do and, with characteristic eccentricity, chose elementary school teaching. But that is almost certainly too simple an account of the matter. In a recent study[26] Professor W. W. Bartley contends that Wittgenstein's decision should be seen as an application of the doctrine of showing. Wittgenstein, he thinks, deliberately intended to let the mystical show itself in his schoolmastering. From August 1965 to September 1971,[27] Bartley conducted research into Wittgenstein's activities as a school teacher. The populations of the lower Austrian villages concerned are not very mobile; Bartley found many of Wittgenstein's old pupils still living there and recorded their memories of him as a teacher and friend. In what immediately follows I shall draw freely on Bartley's investigations.

Wittgenstein may have taken up school teaching with the practical intention of helping to promote what is commonly referred to as the Austrian school-reform programme. After the 1914—18 war some educationalists in Austria, most notably Otto Glöckel and Karl Bühler, launched an attack on the authoritarian, repressive, and mechanical methods of teaching which had hitherto prevailed in their elementary schools. Pupils were required to accept uncritically all that their teachers told them and to learn primarily by commiting information to memory. Elementary schools were appropriately called 'drilling schools' (*Drillschule*). The reformers wished to make them into 'working schools' (*Arbeitsschule*);

97

that is, they wished to replace learning by rote with learning through active participation in projects or experiments. They wanted young children to be encouraged to ask questions and to think things out for themselves, rather than to be repressed and compelled to accept all that they were told without ever asking why. Wittgenstein preserved a characteristic independence in his attitude to the school-reform programme. He is known to have called Bühler a charlatan; and some of his friends, such as Rudolf Koder and Miss Anscombe, seem to object to any linking of his name with the programme.[28] But his method of teaching seems to have been influenced by it. Its two central principles were: *self-activity*, i.e. finding out things for oneself, and *integrated instruction*, i.e. relating what is taught to the pupil's local environment and relating the subjects which are taught to each other. Wittgenstein's teaching clearly evinced both.

In accordance with 'self-activity' he got the children to help him compile a *Wordbook* which was subsequently published. Such *Wordbooks* were commonly used in Austrian schools, but their examples were usually drawn from literary sources beyond the experience and understanding of many children. Wittgenstein's was put together in a new way. He asked the children to write essays on subjects which interested them, without worrying too much about the spelling or grammar; and then he took up the language which they had actually used and extracted the principles of grammar from within it. For instance, his *Wordbook* teaches the difference between *ihm* (the dative 'to him') and *ihn* (the accusative 'him') on the basis of the difference between the local dialect forms, *eam* (for *ihm*) and *n* or *m* (for *ihn*). This is said to be the first *Wordbook* to use local dialect as a medium of instruction. In the same spirit of self-activity, Wittgenstein got his children to help him make models of steam engines, pulleys and other mechanical devices which they saw in the wool mill at Trattenbach. They also helped him to put together skeletons of local small animals. The skeleton of a cat which he had made was still used in the school at Puchberg when Bartley went there.

All this was not only 'self-activity' but also 'integrated instruction', whereby what children were taught was related as closely as possible to their local environment and customs.

98

What was meant by the locality could of course be widened and Wittgenstein tried to extend his children's environment by taking them on trips to Vienna at his own expense. Some of the Trattenbach pupils recalled for Bartley, how, from the moment they set out on the twelve mile walk through the woods to the railway station at Cloggnitz until they got on the train in Vienna to return home, Wittgenstein would be constantly directing their attention to the things around them — local plants and stones in the woods on the way to the station, buildings in Vienna with differing styles of architecture, machines on the streets, exhibits in museums, etc. He kept up throughout these trips a barrage of questions. In class he had told them about the kind of things which they would see and his questions were designed to test whether or not they could identify and explain for themselves what he had told them about in the village schoolroom.

Wittgenstein's life style during these years of teaching was austerely and self-consciously simple. He made no secret of the fact that he came from a wealthy family and seems indeed to have gone out of his way sometimes to ensure that the villagers knew that he had once lived in a great house and had servants to wait on him. When told by a colleague at school that the local peasants thought him 'a rich baron', Wittgenstein seemed pleased. He also told the villagers that he had written a book, the *Tractatus*, of which they would not be able to understand a word; and he spoke freely of his friendship with famous men. It seems as if he wanted to call attention to the simplicity of the life he now lived by contrasting it with that which he might have been living. At Trattenbach he stayed first in an inn but then moved into the school kitchen and subsequently into a small attic over the grocery store. His accommodation when he moved to Puchberg and Otterhal was equally poor. He ate peasant food of the most frugal kind; for instance, while in Trattenbach, he lunched with one of the poorest families and dined every evening on cocoa and outmeal. In dress, he dispensed with hat, collar and tie, and the three-piece suit which a schoolmaster was expected to wear, in favour of an open-necked shirt, flannel trousers and, when necessary, a leather windcheater. He was seen every day striding along hatless with a bamboo walking stick or books in his hand.

99

Most of his pupils seem to have liked him; that, at any rate, is the strong impresson which some of them gave to Bartley forty years later. This makes it the more astonishing that he was actually brought to trial in 1926 at Gloggnitz on a charge of ill-treating his pupils. There can be no doubt that Wittgenstein's discipline was strict and that, unlike some teachers who supported the school-reform movement, he did not hesitate to use corporal punishment when he thought it well deserved. But Bartley plausibly argues that this tendency to be strict was simply made use of by Wittgenstein's enemies to bring him down, their hostility being based in reality on other grounds. Matters came to a head in Otterthal, but during his previous appointments in Trattenbach and Puchberg Wittgenstein had alienated parents and colleagues. Talented children liked to stay behind after school, sometimes till as late as eight o'clock, learning new subjects or going out to collect plants and stones with Wittgenstein. The parents of Wittgenstein's pupils were, for the most part, poor and they needed their children in the evening to earn money or help on their little farms. These after-hours classes interfered with evening labour and that was perhaps the chief reason why many villagers disliked Wittgenstein. Moreover, they resented the admiration and affection which some of their children evidently had for a man who, in his dealings with older people, was usually arrogant or reserved. Tensions inevitably arose. To take one example, Wittgenstein's most gifted pupil, a poor boy named Karl Gruber, had gained a good knowledge of Latin, Greek and mathematics through these evening sessions, and Wittgenstein wanted to adopt this boy so that he could ensure his further education in Vienna. Though the boy and his mother were in favour of the arrangement, the boy's father vetoed it in a painful interview with Wittgenstein. Afterwards he said that his son must get away from 'that crazy fellow' and go out to work.

Wittgenstein was able occasionally to help the villagers. For instance, there is an oft-told tale that, when the steam engine in the wool factory at Trattenbach broke down, engineers called in from Vienna could not discover what was wrong, and recommended that it be taken to pieces and sent to Vienna for further inspection; but to avoid the loss of employment which this would entail, Wittgenstein asked permission to examine it and then told four workmen to tap the machine with hammers in rhythm whereupon it began to work. Refusing payment for himself, Wittgenstein accepted a gift of woollen cloth from the mill, which he asked Father Neururer, the parish priest, to distribute to needy people in the village. But despite this dramatic incident and other less spectacular help, e.g. in prescribing cures for illness, which Wittgenstein was able occasionally to give the villagers, they did not warm to him.

Some of his disaffected pupils who had been severely dealt with for various offences, cunningly capitalised on the gossip about Wittgenstein's cruelty when it began to spread. Karl Gruber's brother, Konrad, confessed to Bartley that, having been slapped by Wittgenstein for poor work in one lesson, he put a pencil into his nose to make it bleed and, when permitted to go outside to stop the bleeding, made it last forty-five minutes till the end of the lesson. Other crafty children pretended to faint when made to stand in a corner. At last, in Otterthal, a man called Piribauer, who hated Wittgenstein, seized the opportunity to stir up real trouble when a boy who lived in his house was carried from the classroom fainting after being slapped on the cheeks by Wittgenstein. The boy's fellow-pupils told Bartley long afterwards that they believed that the boy faked the fainting. However, through Piribauer's agitation Wittgenstein was brought to court. After being examined by a psychiatrist, he was acquitted; but it finally decided him to leave the district in despair and to give up school-teaching for ever.

Wittgenstein did not really inflict stricter corporal punishment than other teachers and he did not beat pupils spasmodically or unpredictably, but only for known offences such as dishonesty, bad work and unruliness — or such was the consensus of opinion among his old pupils. If this was so, it is sad that his school teaching career ended as it did. Wittgenstein had gone to Lower Austria to — as he himself put it — 'get the peasantry out of the muck'. He firmly believed that education would be their salvation and that the instruction which he could give them would make a great difference for good to life in the villages. For instance, he told the father of Emmerich Koderhold, another talented pupil whom he wanted to send for further education to

Vienna, that when the boy returned to the family farm he would 'even carry the manure better if he studies'. Unhappily, all Wittgenstein's confidence in his ability to improve the life and lot of the peasants in Lower Austria was destroyed by the end of the six years and he was thoroughly disillusioned and dispirited. This process had begun very early on; he had written to Russell after his first year in Trattenbach, 'I know that human beings on the average are not worth much anywhere, but here they are much more good-for-nothing and irresponsible than elsewhere.'[29] The 'odiousness and baseness' of which he then suspected them became intolerable in his eyes as the years passed.

Wittgenstein had many sombre elements in his personality. Russell has said that he had 'the pride of Lucifer'[30] and many of the stories told about his relationship with people in Cambridge and elsewhere bear that out. We know from the letters which Wittgenstein wrote to Engelmann that he suffered agonies of guilt and despair which sometimes drove him to contemplate suicide. There has been controversy about the reasons for this self-reproach. Bartley's book openly states that Wittgenstein's perpetual bad conscience arose, in part at least, from the fact that he regularly consorted with the most repellent kind of male prostitute in London and Vienna. His evidence for regarding Wittgenstein as a homosexual of a highly compulsive kind has, however, been called in question. Professor Anscombe has suggested that before any weight is placed upon it, far more information ought to be given by Bartley about his sources. M. O'C. Drury, a psychiatrist who was also a close friend of Wittgenstein's, has said that in confessions of 'matters in his past life of which he was most ashamed' Wittgenstein made no reference to homosexuality, and has asserted that 'sensuality in any form was entirely foreign to his (Wittgenstein's) ascetic personality.' Against this, it has been stated by Irina Strickland that Bertrand Russell said to her in May 1952, that Wittgenstein was a homosexual; and Bartley's revelations certainly did not come as any great surprise to many people in the philosophical world. (See letters in *Times Literary Supplement* 16 November 1973 and 22 February 1974, with Bartley's replies 11 January 1974 and 8 February 1974.) Leaving this matter aside, a combination of intellectual

102

arrogance, natural shyness, passionate temper and self-conscious guilt, whatever its source, such as characterised Wittgenstein, is hardly calculated to endear a man to anybody, least of all to his social and intellectual inferiors. The reason for Wittgenstein's failure to 'get the peasantry out of the muck' was not simply their own stupidity or malice. He himself was part of that reason. He was a curious mixtures of opposites, much too curious a mixture for simple people to be expected to like or trust.

Our prime interest, however, is in the intention with which Wittgenstein went into school teaching. Bartley suggests that he was 'consciously or unconsciously, for better or worse, engaging in an imitation of Christ,[31] when he set off to 'get the peasantry out of the muck'. We know that he was greatly influenced by the *Gospels* (see p. 9). Amongst the actions which he performed in pursuit of his aim were some which in one sense put ethics and religion into words. It is important, however, to distinguish such actions from talk about ethics or religion. A verbal act, like any other act, may presumably be the vehicle whereby the mystical shows itself but such a verbal act will be distinct from saying things like 'Duty is such and such' or 'God is so and so'. Take two examples, one concerned with honesty and one with God. As Wittgenstein's pupils recalled for Bartley, he sometimes inculcated honesty. If they put up their hands in response to a question and it then turned out that they were only pretending to know the answer, he became very angry; but on one occasion Konrad Gruber confessed that he had done so because he was ashamed not to know and Wittgenstein responded to this honesty by refraining from any punishment. Sometimes Wittgenstein advocated trust in God. Bartley was told by Wittgenstein's old pupils how, after a trip to Vienna, on the walk back home from Cloggnitz through the woods in the dark, many of them became frightened. Wittgenstein went from one to the other asking 'Are you afraid? Well, then, you must think only about God.'[32] ,

Was it then Wittgenstein's conscious intention to give profound expression to ethical or religious reality by the example which he set? It is a pity that the controversy about Wittgenstein's homosexuality which Bartley's book aroused in the press may have somewhat obscured what I take to be one of its main intentions; this was certainly not to denigrate Wittgenstein but rather to represent him as a human being who was desperately and sacrificially trying to put ethical, and perhaps also religious, reality into action. Bartley's reports of conversations with his former scholars often give this impression of him, and it was one which his close friend Engelmann undoubtedly gained.[33] Engelmann says explicitly that Wittgenstein made a conscious effort to live out the implications of the *Tractatus*, that is to *do* what could not be said but could be shown. 'Wordless faith' is how Engelmann defines this attempt. For his part, he sees such 'wordless faith' as a way of reconciling the conflicting ideologies of the modern world. It will provide, he anticipates, a 'temporary home for human society' until a 'new language' can be found for this 'new way' of life. The Wittgenstein of the *Tractatus*, Engelmann recognises, would not have gone along with this idea that there ever could be such a language, but that is not, in his opinion, the main issue. The important point is that Wittgenstein found a way of dealing with the fact that 'any doctrine uttered in words is the source of its own miscon- struction by worshippers, disciples, and supporters.'[34] The thing to do is to *say* nothing about ethics or religion but simply to act.

In What Sense is the Mystical Inexpressible?

Two questions seem to me to call for some discussion in the light of these attempts which I have been making to say how the mystical shows itself in art and in action according to Wittgenstein. One is: in what precise sense is the mystical, as Wittgenstein conceived of it, inexpressible? Another is: is it logically possible to identify the mystical, as he conceived of it? I shall deal with the former in this sub-section and the latter in the next.

On a logical interpretation, as we saw in section I, the transcendental is the structure of language, and the reason why it cannot be put into words is the logical impossibility of putting into language that which must be in it already for it to be language. A painter must have a method of painting but he cannot paint it; nor can that which is the necessary condition of anything being said itself be something which is said. The point is a logical one. It rests in the last analysis on

104

the law of non-contradiction. It would apply, whatever theory of meaning were adopted.

Matters become more complicated, however, when we turn to the ethico-religious interpretation of the transcendental. Wittgenstein appears to have had two kinds of objection to putting this, the mystical, into words, which I will differentiate as the *logical* and the *moral* respectively.

To begin with the former, we saw above (p. 79) that Wittgenstein regarded as instances of the mystical 'the sense of the world' and 'any value that does have value'. He argued that nothing can be said about such matters. His argument to this effect, as we saw, ran as follows. Language has meaning if and only if it pictures what is the case. It is logically impossible for the sense of the world to be itself a part of the world, since the meaning of anything cannot be part of that of which it is the meaning. Again, it is logically impossible for evaluative judgments to be analysed into statements of what is the case and nothing more because such judgments always necessarily invoke some criterion of what ought to be the case and what ought to be the case is not logically reducible to what is the case. The sense of the world and any value that does have value, therefore, 'lie outside' (6.41) what is the case. Given the picture theory of meaning, this makes them inexpressible. The argument is perfectly valid. The major premise is the picture theory of meaning. The minor premise is the definition of the mystical as the sense of the world or any value that does have value. The conclusion is that the mystical is inexpressible. There is, of course, the problem of how expressions such as 'the sense of the world' or 'any value that does have value' can, on Wittgenstein's theory, themselves have any meaning; but, presumably, it was part of what he meant by throwing away the ladder after one has climbed up it (6.54) to recognise that such expressions have no meaning.

Alongside this logical objection to putting the mystical into words Wittgenstein seems also to have had what I can only call a moral objection. I quoted above (p. 104) Englemann's remark that Wittgenstein had found a way of dealing with the fact that 'any doctrine uttered in words is the source of its own misconstruction by worshippers, disciples and supporters.' This remark implies that there is a power of corruption in words. The moment the mystical is expressed, this corruption begins to work. The mystical must be protected by silence. Recall Wittgenstein's remark to Ficker that he had 'put everything firmly into place by being silent about it';[35] or again, his use of pejorative expressions such as 'gassing', 'chatter', 'twaddle', (cf. p. 88 above) to describe talk about ethics and religion. Behind such remarks, it seems to me, lies the objection that talk about the mystical trivialises or destroys the very things which such talk is supposed to be explaining, defending or expressing.

There is, of course, some force in this moral objection. Talking *about* ethics or religion is undoubtedly a dangerous business. Where ethical issues are at stake there is always a fatal temptation to make talk a substitute for action. Perception as well as humour lay behind Carlyle's reported suggestion to Emerson, after the latter had said that he had lost all belief in the Devil, that they should visit the debating chamber of the House of Commons where it would quickly be restored! Moreover, there is a sense in which the content of morality can be adequately expressed only in actions, not words. The highest cannot be spoken; it can only be done. All this is, of course, the staple of schoolmasters, parents, and other exhorters of the young, but it is none the less sound for that. If our aim is moral education, rather than education in moral philosophy, then it is far better to define courage, or any other virtue, ostensively through tales, true or legendary, of the deeds of saints or heroes, than verbally through disquisitions upon the meaning of the word 'courage', or whatever. What I have just been saying about ethics applies *a fortiori* to religion. Deeds not words are what matter. The believer needs to know that he is not heard for his much speaking;[36] and that it is better to be the son who says 'I will not' but goes, than the one who says 'I go sir' but goes not.[37] Once more, all this is commonplace, the diet served for countless generations by priests and preachers to their flocks.

Wittgenstein, however, is spoken of by his friend and admirer, Engelmann, in places as though he were the first to have thought of this moral objection to talk about ethics or religion. He is represented as a kind of saviour of mankind, the exemplar of 'wordless faith', a new way of life which will reconcile conflicting ideologies and unite humanity. Engel-

106

mann concedes that 'some great men of the past' lived like Wittgenstein; but, he says, 'only in our epoch has this example come to point the way to a universal new way of life'![38] Whether or not Wittgenstein saw himself in the same light is uncertain. Perhaps he should be given the benefit of the doubt; but, on the other hand, a man who feels that he has provided 'the final solution' of all essential problems of philosophy may not have found it all that hard to believe that he was also the saviour of mankind.

Putting such unsavoury speculations aside, it must nonetheless be remarked that if he has been rightly interpreted above, then Wittgenstein grossly over-estimated the moral objection to putting ethics or religion into words. It is simply not true as he evidently thought that all those who have attempted to justify ethics or religion intellectually were morally corrupted in the process. Nor is it true, as Engelmann no doubt rightly supposed he thought, that any doctrine uttered in words is bound to be misconstrued by those who embrace it. The moral effects of talking about ethics or religion are not always deleterious. Verbal discussion of what it is morally right to do may result, and often has resulted, in more intelligent, sensitive and beneficial human behaviour. Similarly, it is doctrinaire in the extreme to hold that all talk about religion has had a morally harmful effect on those who engaged in it. The view that religion has been bad for men is, of course, arguable, but it is not that view which is in question. Wittgenstein thought simply that all talk concerning the nature or attributes of God is corrosive of true religion, and that view is, to say the least, an exaggerated one.

Can the Mystical be Identified?

I turn now to the second of the two questions which are raised by the doctrine that the mystical shows itself in art and action: is it logically possible to identify the mystical?

Poetry such as the poem by Uhland quoted above (pp. 95–6) shows it. Action, such as Wittgenstein's in exchanging a mansion in Vienna or a college in Cambridge for attic accommodation in Trattenbach in order to 'get the peasantry out of the muck' shows it. But precisely *what* is it that such things show? How do we identify the mystical in such art or action?

107

Two opinions were clearly held by Wittgenstein: one that the mystical *cannot* be identified *in* words; the other that it *can* be identified *without* words. We must proceed in the light of them as far as we can.

First of all, if the mystical cannot be identified in words, then it cannot be equated with any property which is verbally definable. A poem's literary characteristics, for instance, such as metre, rhyme, cadence, etc. can all be defined verbally, so whatever it is which gives a poem like Uhland's the property, mystical, it cannot be any such feature. Similarly, it is no use saying that it is the self-sacrifice evident in Wittgenstein's going to teach in Lower Austria which identifies the mystical for us, because self-sacrifice can be verbally defined. The 'mystical' necessarily refers to some inexpressible property which works of art or courses of action have. How then is such a property to be identified?

If the mystical can be identified without words, then presumably it admits of ostensive definition. It must be possible to point to some observable property which is distinct from every property which can be put into other words and in effect say 'That's what "mystical" means' — in the way in which redness, for example, could be defined ostensively. Now, when an individual has seen red in one instance, he can identify it in another as the same again. He sees, say, the redness of a telephone kiosk and then the redness of a traffic light and recognises the same again. Moreover, he can, within limits, check his identification of redness, i.e. what he calls 'red', against other people's identification of it by discovering whether they see 'the same again' where he does, in order to confirm that what he means by red is the same as what they mean. Well, no doubt one could do something of the same kind, if one perceived a verbally indefinable property, the mystical, in works of art or courses of action. One could identify it as the same again, when it recurred in one's experience; and one could check what one meant by 'mystical' against what others evidently meant by it.

But suppose it is the case that the ability to 'see' the mystical is restricted to certain individuals. Suppose some

108

men, as a matter of empirical fact, cannot see it. However many *objets d'art* or life stories are set before them, the mystical does not make itself manifest; they are like colour-blind men who cannot see red, however many red objects are shown to them. If the mystical is definable only ostensively, then of course it could never be identified for such men. This state of affairs need not distress anyone, least of all those who can see the mystical. An élite does not have to feel sorry that it is an élite. Activities such as artistic criticism, moral exhortation, religious worship, all frequently proceed happily on the assumption that relatively few will understand what is being said. But the fact must be recognised that if the mystical is perceived only by some people, then these individuals cannot spread any kind of gospel concerning it to *all* mankind. And that is what they may well wish to do. Engelmann evidently thought it highly desirable and perfectly possible that Wittgenstein's life and work should 'point the way to a *universal* new way of life' (italics mine).[39] He evidently thought that the ideals which Wittgenstein's life and work evince do not need to be communicated by talk because they have been 'lived and thus made manifest'.[40] Well, true enough, Wittgenstein has lived and anyone who wishes can confirm that he has; but the relevant question is, why should any given individual take Wittgenstein as an example? If Wittgenstein's actions are to be more than mere facts which can be known as such, if they are also to be ideals for *all* men, then there has to be *a reason why* they should be pursued which is a reason for any and every man. Engelmann's reason for thinking that Wittgenstein should be taken as an example is quite explicitly his certainty that in the latter's life and work the mystical shows itself. But that could be offered as a reason to all men to follow a similar way of life, if and only if all men were capable of identifying the mystical. On our present hypothesis, they are not: only an élite can do so. This élite cannot, therefore, set Wittgenstein before others as an ideal or an example which they expect these others to see the point of following. As a putative saviour, Wittgenstein will necessarily be unintelligible to those who are not already among the elect. I have *not* been saying in these last remarks that I think some men can identify the mystical; I have simply been drawing out the implications of the supposition that the mystical is an ostensively definable property evident to some men but not to others. I *have been* saying that it would make sense to present Wittgenstein's life as a universal ideal, if, and only if, all men could perceive the mystical in it.

But even if all men could do so, there would be a further problem. The mystical, on the view of it which I have been considering here, is comparable to what some moral philosophers have called 'non-natural' properties. Rightness, for instance, may be represented as a non-natural property which men intuit in certain actions. The rightness of the action, on this view, is the ground of the obligation to perform it. But the objection has been raised: how is one to differentiate between the descriptions 'M is a man who thinks he ought to do X' and 'M is a man who thinks he ought to do X because he thinks X is right'? Is not the latter tautologous? What is thinking X right, if it is not thinking that X ought to be done? Reflections of this sort have led many moral philosophers to use Occam's Razor against 'non-natural' properties. By the same token, I ask what more there is to the description 'M sees Wittgenstein's life as an instance of the mystical and so adopts it as an ideal to aim at' than there is to 'M adopts Wittgenstein's life as an ideal to aim at' *simpliciter*? What does it mean to speak of cherishing works of art or following courses of action *because they are mystical*, if the mystical is a property about which nothing whatever can be said other than that it is the 'mystical'? What sort of an explanation of, or ground for, the cherishing of *objets d'art* or the following of courses of action could 'because they are mystical' be conceived to provide? There is supposed to be a mysterious something, the mystical, which makes works of art, or courses of action, worth valuing, but the only evidence I would ever have that a man perceived it in any X is that he valued X. What *more*, then, have I been told, when I have been told, not simply that he values it, but that he does so because he perceives the mystical in it? Perception of the mystical seems to be as superfluous, when taken for a ground of pursuing any ideal, as perceiving 'non-natural' properties is when considered as the ground of

110

obligation.

Is There a Connexion between the Two Interpretations of the Doctrine of Showing?

Early in this chapter, I expressed the hope that it would become clear as we proceeded whether or not there is a connexion between what I call the logical and the ethico-religious doctrines of showing. It has been difficult to find any connexion. What Wittgenstein meant by the trans-cendental seems to have been quite different in each of its two instantiations; and what he meant by its showing itself equally dissimilar.

The transcendental, in what I called its logical instan-tiation, is logical form. In what I called its ethico-religious instantiation, it is the sense of the world and the value of certain things. These two instantiations are not at all the same kind of thing, as may be seen from the following consideration. The mystical, as conceived by Wittgenstein, is something which cannot be put into words, given the picture theory of meaning. If, and only if, it is a necessary condition of significant language that it should picture what is the case, may we say that the meaning or value of what is the case cannot be put into words (see above p. 79). But whatever general theory of meaning we were to adopt, we could say that anything which is a necessary condition of language being language cannot itself be put into language. Wittgen-stein takes logical form to be such a necessary condition. It is not because his account of logical form is what it is (viz. a by-product of his picture theory), but because he takes it to be the necessary condition of language that he says it cannot be put into words.

In both instantiations, the transcendental is indeed said to show itself. But this common feature is a purely verbal coincidence. It is difficult to see any similarity between the *way* in which the transcendental is conceived to show itself in the logical and the ethico-religious instantiations respectively. As to the former,Wittgenstein said that the structure of language, i.e. its logical form, shows itself in propositions, or their components, regarded as symbols. Propositions yield tautologies and these tautologies explicate the logical form of the propositions. The fact that they are tautologies con-

111

stitutes the point that the transcendental cannot be said but only shown (see above p. 75). There may be many things wrong with this view but the way in which the transcendental shows itself on this interpretation is intelligible. Logical form is something which could be shown through logical implication. In its ethico-religious instantiation the transcendental shows itself in art and action. We have seen that it is a problem to know just what Wittgenstein had in mind here. If he meant something trivial, such as that art can make one think of God or goodness, or have aesthetic value, then of course that is true. If again, he meant that actions can be ethically good or express religious devotion, that is equally indisputable. But whatever it could mean to say that the highest cannot be spoken but only shown — in art or action — this sense of 'showing' does not seem to be conceivable in anything like the sense in which logical form may be said to show itself in logical implications.

It is hard to avoid the conclusion that there is simply *no* similarity between either what is *meant* by the transcendental, or what is *meant* by its showing itself, on the respective interpretations of it which are to be found in the *Tractatus*. Wittgenstein evidently thought that there was some essential connexion on both counts; but we have found it impossible to form any clear idea of what this could be.

4 Verificationism

The best known exponents of verificationism are the logical positivists. They were deeply influenced by the *Tractatus*. There are good reasons to think that what they took it to be saying about metaphysics was quite different from what Wittgenstein intended it to show about the mystical, as we saw in the last chapter;[1] nevertheless, there is no denying that in the development of their verificationism, the *Tractatus* played an important part. Some of Wittgenstein's later writings seem to indicate that, in the late twenties and early thirties at any rate, he himself subscribed to a verificationism similar to theirs. The logical positivists had firm things to say about religious belief in the light of their verification principle and some of Wittgenstein's remarks, in the years referred to, seem to echo these. Any consideration of the bearing of his philosophy upon religious belief must, therefore, give some account of the attack which verificationists — or falsificationists — have launched upon it, and assess how damaging that attack may have been.

In this chapter I intend to discuss the following matters. First, I shall indicate the debt which the Vienna Circle evidently owed to the *Tractatus*. Then I will give some account of the verificationism to which Wittgenstein himself, at the time mentioned above, seems to have subscribed. Certain philosophical problems arise concerning the central principle of verificationism, and I will next discuss these. Finally, I will consider how religious belief really fares in all this and whether or not it can be discredited by the kind of attack which verificationism has inspired.

I. LOGICAL POSITIVISM'S DEBT TO THE *TRACTATUS*
The Vienna Circle consisted of a group of philosophers, scientists and mathematicians which gathered around Moritz Schlick in the early 1920s when he became professor of

113

philosophy at the University of Vienna. Among its leading members were Rudolf Carnap, Friedrich Waismann, Herbert Feigl and Kurt Gödel. Its views were made known in Britain largely through A.J. Ayer's *Language, Truth and Logic*, which was published in 1936 after Ayer had spent some time in Vienna. In 1930 the Circle had taken over the journal *Annalen der Philosophie* and renamed it *Erkenntnis*. This became the principal organ of logical positivist thought for some years. The first article in its first number was written by Schlick and entitled 'The Turning Point in Philosophy'.[2] It reveals very clearly the profound influence which the *Tractatus* must have had upon the Vienna Circle. Indeed, it reads like a commentary on Wittgenstein's claim, in the introduction to the *Tractatus*, that he had found 'on all essential points the final solution of the problems' of philosophy.

Schlick expresses the conviction that a decisive turning point in philosophy has been reached. An end is now in sight to what he calls the fruitless conflict of systems. Leibniz foresaw it dimly; Russell and Frege, more clearly. But says Schlick, '. . .Ludwig Wittgenstein (in his *Tractatus Logico-Philosophicus*, 1922) is the first to have pushed forward to the decisive turning point.'[3] Throughout the article what Schlick has to say can be paralleled from the *Tractatus*. The turning point, it appears, is the recognition that philosophy, in Schlick's words, is 'not a system of cognitions, but a system of *acts*'[4], or as Wittgenstein had expressed it, 'not a body of doctrine but an activity' (4.112). This activity Wittgenstein had called 'the logical clarification of thoughts' (ibid.); Schlick describes it as 'that activity through which the meaning of statements is revealed or determined'.[5] Schlick believed that philosophy can at last make the meaning of statements crystal clear because of the decisive insight into the logical relationship between language and reality which Wittgenstein has given us.

Schlick's account of this logical relationship follows meticulously Wittgenstein's in the *Tractatus*. True statements, or cognitions, express or represent facts (cf. e.g. 4.1). They are able to do so because they severally have logical form in common with the facts which they represent (cf. e.g. 2.18). This logical form cannot itself be represented but

114

shows itself (cf. e.g. 4.12 and 4.121). Philosophy's task of making clear the meaning which any statement has cannot be effected in the last analysis by other statements because the meaning of these latter would, in their turn, have to be clarified and so on *ad infinitum*. The analysis must therefore come to an end, says Schlick 'in actual pointings'[6] i.e. in ostensive, not further verbal, definition. This parallels Wittgenstein to the effect that analysis is only complete when a proposition has been dissected into names (or combinations thereof), where 'name' means a simple or primitive sign which 'cannot be dissected any further by means of a definition'. (3.26).

On a view of philosophy such as that which Schlick took from Wittgenstein its task is always to make itself dispensable: to clear up confusions about the meaning of what is being said so that, once clarity is achieved, there will be no further need for philosophy. To illustrate this view Schlick points out that the physical sciences are now independent of philosophy because a clear meaning has been given to their fundamental concepts and successful work can therefore proceed within them. By contrast, ethics, aesthetics and frequently psychology continue to be branches of philosophy because those who work in these fields are still trying to clarify their basic conceptions. Schlick recognises, of course, that the physical sciences may still need philosophy from time to time. Einstein's work which gave new meanings to space and time was philosophical, and further conceptual revolutions of that kind may be necessary. Schlick shares Wittgenstein's view that philosophy is a ladder which must be thrown away once we have climbed up it (6.54). But all this does not imply that the claims which Wittgenstein and Schlick made for philosophy were modest. Quite the contrary. Schlick said that philosophy must supply 'the ultimate support' of knowledge. The decisive turning point has made it impossible to attribute any uncertainty or mere probability to 'the acts of giving meaning which constitute philosophy'.[7] He goes on: 'It is a matter of positing the meaning of statements as something simply final. Either we *have* the meaning and then we know what is meant by the statement, or we do not possess it, in which case mere empty words confront us and as yet no statement at all. There is nothing in between and there can be no talk of the probability that the meaning is the right one. Thus after the great turning point philosophy shows its decisive character even more clearly than before.[8] This is in the same spirit as Wittgenstein's claim in the introduction to the *Tractatus* that 'what can be said at all can be said clearly', and as remarks in the text of his book such as 'What a proposition expresses it expresses in a determinate manner, which can be set out clearly . . .' (3.251).

At the end of the *Tractatus* Wittgenstein held that 'if a question can be framed at all, it is also *possible* to answer it.' (6.5). In the same vein, Schlick holds that because everything is knowable which can be expressed, and this is the total subject matter about which meaningful questions can be raised, 'there are consequently no questions which are in principle unanswerable'.[9] No meaningful ones, that is. There are, of course, some questions which conform to the customary rules of grammar and so appear to be meaningful 'but in truth they consist of empty sounds, because they transgress the profound inner rules of logical syntax discovered by the new analysis'.[10] These meaningless questions are ones which we have no idea how to answer even in principle. Said Schlick: 'Whenever there is a meaningful problem one can in theory always give the path that leads to its solution. For it becomes evident that giving this path coincides with the indication of its meaning'.[11]

Wittgenstein may not have wished to be mistaken for the logical positivists' mentor but in their early days at any rate they adopted him as such. There are two basic doctrines of Logical Positivism, which are beyond doubt attributable to his influence. One is to the effect that all significant logical statements are either tautologies or contradictions, the former if true and the latter if false. The other is the view that all statements of other-than-logical fact can, in principle, be analysed into elementary statements of absolutely simple fact; they are significant only in so far as they give a picture of the atomic facts of the situation which they represent. To these doctrines I shall return below (see pp. 124—6).

II. WITTGENSTEIN AND VERIFICATIONISM

The logical positivists held that every meaningful statement of other-than-logical fact can, in the last analysis, be verified by direct sense experience. No such doctrine is found in the *Tractatus*; but during the late 1920s and early 1930s, Wittgenstein seems to have gone along with it. After his return to Cambridge in 1929 he had conversations with Schlick and one or two members of his Circle on visits to Europe and Waismann has left some account of these in his *Ludwig Wittgenstein und der Wiener Kreis* (Oxford, 1967). Waismann also included in his book certain *Thesen* which may be taken to represent opinions held by Wittgenstein at the time. G.E. Moore's notes on Wittgenstein's Cambridge lectures 1930—33 were published in *Mind* 1954—55 and are also to be found in Moore's *Philosophical Papers*(London, 1962). Wittgenstein's own book *Philosophical Remarks* was written in the early thirties, though not published until 1964. From each of these works I shall quote evidence of Wittgenstein's inclination towards empiricist verificationism during this period of his life.

It may be useful to say first of all, however, that there is a remark in the *Tractatus* which must be carefully differentiated from the logical positivists' verification principle. Wittgenstein said: 'To understand a proposition means to know what is the case if it is true' (4.024). This is quite different from the Vienna Circle's famous verification principle: 'The meaning of a proposition is the method of its verification'. The *Tractatus* quotation says, in effect, that the meaning of a proposition is its truth-condition; the verification principle, that its meaning is its verification-condition (or perhaps more accurately, the verification-procedure appropriate to its verification-condition). The nature of the difference between truth-conditions and verification-conditions (or -procedures, see below p. 119) will become clear, if we recall a distinction which Wittgenstein drew in some of his later writings between what he called 'criteria' and 'symptoms'. 'Criteria', in this sense, are *truth*- (or *falsity*-) *conditions*, i.e. the conditions under which a statement of fact would be true (or false). 'Symptoms', by contrast, are *verification*- (or *falsification*-) conditions, i.e. the conditions under which we would know, or have good reason to think, that a statement of fact was true (or false). Wittgenstein explains these terms in *The Blue Book* thus:

> Let us introduce two antithetical terms in order to avoid certain elementary confusions: To the question "How do you know that so-and-so is the case?", we sometimes answer by giving '*criteria*' and sometimes by giving '*symptoms*'. If medical science calls angina an inflammation caused by a particular bacillus, and we ask in a particular case "why do you say this man has got angina?" then the answer "I have found the bacillus so-and-so in his blood" gives us the criterion, or what we may call the defining criterion of angina. If on the other hand the answer was "His throat is inflamed", this might give us a symptom of angina. I call "symptom" a phenomenon of which experience has taught us that it coincided, in some way or other, with the phenomenon which is our defining criterion. Then to say "A man has angina if this bacillus is found in him" is a tautology or it is a loose way of stating the definition of "angina". But to say, "A man has angina whenever he has an inflamed throat" is to make a hypothesis. (BBB pp.24–5)[12]

The conditions defining the meaning of a cognitive sentence are here identified with the conditions under which the statement made by this cognitive sentence would be true. 'He has angina' (angina here is quinsy) *means* 'He has bacillus so-and-so in his blood' in the sense that the former is true if and only if the latter is. The latter gives us the '*criterion*' of the former. But 'His throat is inflamed' only states what is taken to be a '*symptom*', or a piece of evidence, on the basis of which it may be said that a person has angina.

To confuse 'criteria' with 'symptoms' is to confuse meaningfulness with verifiability. It was just this confusion of which the logical positivists were guilty when, in their verification principle, they identified the *verification-conditions* (or procedures) whereby we determine whether a statement is true or false with that statement's *truth-conditions*. I do not understand the meaning of a cognitive sentence unless I know the truth-conditions of the statement which it makes. But this is quite different from saying, as the

118

Vienna Circle did, that the meaning of a sentence is identical with the verification-conditions (or procedures) of the statement which it makes. I do not know, for example, what 'He has angina' means unless I know that 'He has bacillus so-and-so in his blood' states its truth-condition; but I may know what it means before I know that 'His throat is inflamed' states its verification-condition.

However, in the works which represent Wittgenstein's thought in the late 1920s and early 30s this distinction between 'criterion' and 'symptoms' does not appear.[13] He seems to subscribe uncritically to empiricist verificationism. In *Thesen* we read: 'To get to the meaning of a sentence one must clarify the procedure which leads to the determination of its truth. If one does not know this procedure, then one cannot understand the sentence either. A sentence cannot say more than what is determined by the method of verification... The meaning of a sentence is the mode of its verification.' (WWK p.244)[14]

Here, meaning is identified with verification-procedures. Verification-conditions, i.e. evidence or 'symptoms', are discovered by verification-procedures. The two, conditions and procedures, are not identical. However, they are related. The procedures suggest the conditions, and *vice versa*. If when testing for acid, one knows that the verification-procedure is to dip litmus paper into it, one may infer that some effect on the paper is the verification-condition; and if one knows that the latter is the condition one may infer that the former is the procedure. So nothing very much turns on whether meaning is identified with verification-procedures or verification-conditions.[15] Verificationists usually identify it with the former as Wittgenstein, echoing Schlick's verification principle, does in the above passage.

Wittgenstein seems in some places to have subscribed, during this period, to the phenomenalism which many early logical positivists professed. In *Thesen*, for instance, we read: 'If I say "My friend is angry" and if I find this out because of his showing a particular perceptible behaviour, then by this sentence I also only *mean* that he is showing this behaviour. And if I mean more, then I cannot state what this more consists in' (WWK p.244). Wittgenstein appears to be saying quite clearly that behaviourist and mentalist accounts of

119

human action mean the same thing. The impression that he held such a view may be reinforced when we read in *Philosophical Remarks*: 'According to my principle, two assumptions must be identical in sense, if every possible experience that confirms the one confirms the other too. Thus if no empirical way of deciding between them is conceivable (op.cit.p.282). But earlier in the *Remarks* Wittgenstein had said, during a discussion of behaviourism: 'If I say I believe that someone is sad, it's as though I am seeing his behaviour through the medium of sadness, from the viewpoint of sadness . . .' (pp. 89–90). Kenny suggests that this may express the view that from the fact that no experience could settle the matter between the behaviourist and the mentalist positions, it follows, not that the two positions mean the same thing, but that the difference between them is 'somehow given prior to experience'.[16]

Empiricist Verificationism is implicitly defended by Wittgenstein against certain conceivable objections. The objection, that the meaning of a sentence logically precedes its verifiability because we cannot know whether or not it is verifiable unless we already know its meaning (cf. p. 133 below), is rejected by Wittgenstein: 'The method of verification is, of course, not something which is subsequently added to the meaning. The sense already *contains* the method of verification. A method of verification is not something we can *look for*'. (WWK p.244). I cannot speak of verifying a sentence in this way or that, as I might speak of going to A either on foot or on horseback. The method of verification is determined in the meaning of the sentence. Again, the objection that meaningfulness is a matter, not of verifiability, but of the grammatical structure of the sentence is firmly put aside. 'A statement does not have meaning because it is constructed properly but because it is capable of verification'. (WWK p. 245). Every verifiable sentence is *as such* constructed correctly. If I state the method of verification, I thereby determine the form of the sentence, the meanings of its words, rules of syntax, and so forth. In order to find out what a sign means one must ask how the sentence in which it occurs is verified. The same word can have different meanings in sentences which are verified in different ways; e.g. 'yellow' is a sign common to physics and daily life, but the symbol

120

'yellow' means something different in the one from what it means in the other and the essence of this difference lies in the fact that in the one case sentences about it are verified by looking at a coloured surface but in the other by measuring wave-lengths.

The verification principle may be cast in either a strong or a weak form. In the strong form, it requires an empirical proposition to be *conclusively* verifiable; in the weak, to be rendered *probable*. Wittgenstein seems to have moved from the one to the other. In a conversation with Schlick in December 1929, he voiced an emphatically strong version of the principle: 'If I can never conclusively (*vollstandig*) verify the meaning of the sentence, then I cannot have meant anything by the sentence. The sentence in fact does not say anything'. (WWK p.47). But in the *Philosophical Remarks* we find him saying: 'All that's required for our propositions (about reality) to have a sense, is that our experience in *some sense or other* either tends to agree with them or tends not to agree with them. That is, immediate experience need confirm only something about them, *some* facet of them'. (PR p.282). What explains this change? In the *Remarks*, Wittgenstein uses the words 'hypothesis' and 'proposition' sometimes as though these words were synonymous (see PR p.282), and sometimes as though they were quite distinct in meaning (see PR pp. 282–6). This is rather confusing; but it seems evident that he intended to draw an important distinction by means of these terms. In the early stages of his argument, at any rate, he appears to have meant by a 'hypothesis' a proposition of ordinary language: he speaks, for instance, of 'the hypothesis "There is a book lying here"', (PR p.284). This is in line with the logical positivists' view that common sense factual statements are hypotheses concerning future experience (cf. below p. 125). By 'proposition' he seems to have meant a record of immediate experience which confirms, or disconfirms, such a 'hypothesis'. Now, Wittgenstein says that when he points out that a 'hypothesis' cannot be conclusively or definitely verified, he does not mean 'that there is a verification of it which we may approach ever more nearly, without ever reaching it,' but that 'an hypothesis simply has a different formal relation to reality from that of verification'. And he adds the parenthesis: '(Hence, of course, the words "true" and "false" are also inapplicable here, or else have a different meaning.)' (PR p.285). He calls the formal relation a 'looser' one (PR p.284). 'What is essential to a hypothesis is, I believe, that it arouses an expectation by admitting of future confirmation. That is, it is of the essence of a hypothesis that its confirmation is never completed' (PR p.285). How is a hypothesis related to 'propositions'? Said Wittgenstein: 'An hypothesis is a law for forming propositions .,. .a law for forming expectations . . .A proposition is, so to speak, a particular cross-section of a hypothesis' (PR pp. 285–6). 'Propositions' express observations which when they verify their 'hypothesis' stand to it as the points of a graph do to the line of the graph: ' . . . the verifications of particular cases correspond to cuts [sc. in the graph] that have actually been made' (PR p. 284). Our immediate experiences, then, are expressed in these 'propositions'. This is done correctly or incorrectly, truly or falsely. New experiences are always occurring and the 'propositions' which record them may, or may not, tally with their relevant 'hypothesis'; but if they do not tally, it becomes necessary to modify the hypothesis. This takes cognisance of what Waismann once called the 'open texture' of empirical concepts. There are perhaps also affinities between the above views of Wittgenstein and what, as we shall see, Ayer had to say about 'primary' and 'secondary' systems (below p. 135). But it would be beyond our present purpose to pursue such comparisons.

Turning now to G.E. Moore's notes on Wittgenstein's Cambridge lectures in the early 1930s, we find Moore reporting as follows: 'Near the beginning . . . . . he made the famous statement "The sense of a statement is the way in which it is verified;" but (later) he said this only meant "You can determine the meaning of a proposition by asking how it is verified" and went on to say "This is necessarily a mere rule of thumb, because 'verification' means different things, and because in some cases the question 'How is it verified?' makes no sense." ' [7]

Here Moore appears to be attributing three modifications of the verification principle to Wittgenstein. The first is to the effect that, whilst the meaning of a proposition is not equivalent to the way in which it is verified, nevertheless we

122

can best determine its meaning through getting to know how it is verified. This does nothing to redeem verificationism from the objections to it which we have already noted. If you ask how to verify a given statement the answer is neither a necessary nor a sufficient condition of knowing what the statement means. I may discover that the way, or one of the ways, to test the statement 'He has angina' is to look at his throat in order to see whether it is inflamed, but this is not sufficient to tell me what the statement means. Similarly, I may know what 'He has angina' means but not know that the way to verify it is to see whether or not he has an inflamed throat.

The second modification — 'verification' means different things — is no doubt true in one sense. Verifying 'He has angina' may mean seeing that he has an inflamed throat or seeing that he has a swollen neck, or both. But in another sense what it means to verify the original statement is the same in both cases, viz. to observe 'a phenomenon of which experience has taught us that it coincided, in some way or other, with the phenomenon which is our defining criterion' (cf. Wittgenstein's definition of a 'symptom' quoted on p. 118).

The third modification — that in some cases the question 'How is it verified?' makes no sense — is the most interesting of all. It suggests an awareness of two things. First, that there are other kinds of meaning besides cognitive. Secondly, that there may be cognitive meaning in the absence of verifiability. To both we shall have occasion to return in our discussion of verificationism and religious belief.

III. THE VERIFIABILITY CRITERION

What is to be said for verificationism? Though Sir Alfred Ayer differs, even in his earliest publications, from some of the Vienna Circle in important ways, he has been the foremost British exponent of Logical Positivism, so I shall attempt an assessment of its central principle on the basis of his writings. In the first edition of his *Language, Truth and Logic* (London 1936), Ayer defined the verifiability criterion thus: 'a sentence is factually significant to any given person if, and only if, he knows how to verify the proposition which it purports to express — that is, if he knows what observations would lead him, under certain conditions, to accept the proposition as being true, or reject it as being false'.[18] When he published the second edition of his book, ten years later, Ayer was dissatisfied with the wording of this formulation. He recognised that unless a sentence is factually significant, it is logically impossible for it to express a proposition, and so it is otiose to speak of further necessary conditions of factual significance in the case of sentences expressing propositions, as the above formulation does. Accordingly, Ayer reformulated the criterion thus: 'a statement is held to be literally meaningful if and only if it is either analytic or empirically verifiable.'[19] Ayer now defined a 'sentence' as 'any form of words which is grammatically significant;' and defined a 'statement' as an 'indicative sentence whether it is literally meaningful or not.' He differentiated a statement from a proposition, defining the latter as 'what is expressed by sentences which are literally meaningful.' By 'literally meaningful' he meant capable of being either true or false. He now restricted the expression 'factually significant' or 'factually meaningful' to empirically verifiable propositions.[20] Indicative sentences which are mutually translatable he took to express the same statement; and, if literally meaningful, the same proposition.

The two key expressions in Ayer's second formulation of his criterion are 'analytic' and 'empirically verifiable'. These indicate *how* a statement can be tested for literal meaningfulness. They take up the two basic ideas which, as we noted at the end of section I, the logical positivists inherited from Wittgenstein (see above p. 116).

An *analytic* proposition is one which can be verified simply by appeal to the definitions of the signs used within it, e.g. '2 + 2 = 4', 'A bachelor is unmarried', 'Every effect has a cause', etc. These examples are all true propositions and they are true because they are tautologous. False analytic propositions — e.g. '2 + 2 = 5', 'In New Guinea there are married bachelors', 'This is an effect without any cause' — are false because self-contradictory. Mathematical as well as logical propositions can, according to Ayer, be verified analytically. All other meaningful propositions, he maintains, are *empirically* verifiable, i.e. they can be tested for truth or falsity by appeal to sense-experience. In fact, they are all hypotheses concerning further experience.[21] The propositions of common sense, science, history, etc., express what anyone will experience if they are true. Roughly speaking that is to say, historical propositions, such as 'Caesar crossed the Rubicon,' are predictions of what anyone will observe who delves into the relevant documents; scientific propositions, such as 'Water boils at 100°C', predict what anyone will see who conducts certain experiments; common sense remarks, such 'There is a policeman in the garden', tell us what we shall experience if we attend at the appropriate time and place to the relevant evidence.

The logical positivists did not, of course, maintain that a statement must be verifiable in practice in order to have literal meaning, but only in principle. It may be a practical impossibility to complete the necessary investigation but that is not to the point. There are problems in mathematics and logic which are as yet unsolved; but those trained in these disciplines know what kind of thing would count as a solution. In science there are theories which cannot be tested because equipment or opportunity to test them does not exist, but the scientists concerned know what sort of observation would verify, or at least falsify, their theories.

I add 'falsify' here because, in fact, scientific hypotheses cannot be empirically verified, but only falsified. Such hypotheses are of the form 'It is always the case that if A then B' and are expressed in universal propositions. Now whatever A may stand for, we can never be sure that we have observed all instances of the occurrence of A in the universe, and so can never verify this proposition. However, one instance of A occurring and B not occurring would suffice to falsify it. When the scientific hypothesis is to the effect that if A occurs, there is such-and-such a degree of probability that B will occur, this does not affect the universal character of the proposition which expresses it: it affirms that, whenever A occurs, there is that degree of probability that B will occur, and one instance where this is shown not to be so will be enough to falsify it. It seems more satisfactory, then, to hold that propositions expressing scientific hypotheses are factually significant if and only if they can be empirically falsified. But this modification, as we shall see in a moment, is far from repairing all that is unsatisfactory about Logical

125

Positivism's criterion of meaning.

The Rejection of Metaphysics

The main concern of the logical positivists was to discredit metaphysics and exalt science. Ayer defined a metaphysical statement as one which purports to express a genuine proposition but does in fact express neither a tautology nor an empirically testable hypothesis and so is 'nonsensical'.[22] All statements to the effect that a transcendent God exists or has certain attributes are classified by him as metaphysical and therefore nonsensical.[23] This is because, on the one hand such statements are not normally taken to be analytic. It is true that Anselm and other proponents of the ontological argument for God's existence have thought that the latter can be shown to be a logical necessity, but they have all regarded the proposition 'God exists' as a synthetic one. We need not concern ourselves here with objections to that way of thinking; it suffices to point out that, if all logically necessary propositions are analytic, as the logical positivists thought, then, given that 'God exists' is logically necessary, this proposition will be about nothing except the meaning of the word 'God'. But the belief that God exists is normally taken to be about more than that, and so its significance cannot be saved by regarding it as analytic. On the other hand, this belief is not empirically verifiable. Statements about an anthropomorphic God could conceivably be empirically verified, but if God is said to be transcendent, and 'transcendent' is taken to mean something like 'beyond all human comprehension', then 'God exists' cannot (logically) be empirically verified. To this subject I return below (see pp.140–2).

Logical Positivism's condemnation of religious belief must not be confused with agnosticism or atheism. An agnostic is someone who suspends judgment as to whether the statement 'God exists' is true or false; an atheist, someone who thinks that it is false. Both points of view imply that the statement 'God exists' has factual significance. A logical positivist, by contrast, holds that it does not make sense to say that God either does, or does not, exist, nor even that he may.

The logical positivists' criterion of meaning, on which their condemnation of religion was based, has proved a hornets'

126

nest of philosophical problems. I will touch on three of these: (i) What is the logical status of the criterion?; (ii) Can the criterion be satisfactorily formulated?; (iii) Does it misrepresent the meaning of factual statements?

The Logical Status of the Criterion

There has been some difficulty in determining precisely what the verifiability criterion itself is.[24] Is it *simply* an empirical proposition about how the word 'meaning' is normally used? If so, it is plainly false. Ordinary language users would not find it at all odd to be told that metaphysical, moral or religious statements have meanings. Some of them may regard such statements as false, but none of them would regard them as meaningless. This is so obvious that the verifiability criterion can hardly have been intended as a reportive or lexical definition pure and simple.

Nevertheless, Ayer says that it is a definition and describes it as not entirely arbitrary.[25] He evidently thinks of it as both reportive and stipulative. It reports what is ordinarily understood by statements of logical or scientific fact respectively. Unless a statement were rendered true or false solely by the definitions of the terms used in it, it would not normally be taken for a logical proposition; and unless it were verifiable, or falsifiable, by appeal to sense-experience it would not be taken to inform us about a matter of empirical fact, at any rate in science or common sense talk. The verifiability criterion becomes stipulative in so far as it proposes that only statements which can be analytically or empirically tested should be regarded as meaningful. It will appear as we proceed why Ayer did not consider this proposal to be entirely arbitrary (see especially pp. 133–6).

Attempts to Formulate the Criterion Satisfactorily

Logical positivists have not been able to formulate their verifiability criterion in a way which they find entirely satisfactory.

In so far as the meaningfulness of statements is made to depend on what is empirically observable, there are some immediate and fairly obvious objections to making either verifiability or falsifiability the test. We have already seen (p. 125) that universal propositions of the form 'It is always the case that if A then B' cannot be empirically verified because we can never be sure that we have observed all the occurrences of A in the universe. This excludes all scientific hypotheses (laws, theories) since they are all universal propositions of this form. But if we make empirical falsifiability the test, what of those propositions of common sense which have the form 'Some A's are B'? These cannot be falsified because, however many A's we found which were not B, it would always be possible that there were some somewhere which were B. Such conclusions were abhorrent to logical positivists. To exclude science and common sense as meaningless was the very reverse of what they set out to do.

There are more complicated difficulties about the verifiability criterion. Even in the first edition of *Language, Truth and Logic* Ayer recognised that no proposition can be *conclusively* verified or falsified except an analytic one.[26] We can know for certain that the statement 'Bachelors are unmarried' is true because it is tautologous; and that 'Bachelors are married' is false because it is self-contradictory. But we cannot know for certain that any other-than-logical proposition is true or false. Such propositions being empirical hypotheses, we can only hope to discover with a certain degree of probability that they are either true or false. It is always logically possible (a) that we have not observed all the relevant evidence and (b) that we have mistaken some evidence which we have observed. It is clear, that scientific laws, since they are intended to cover an infinite number of cases, could not even in principle be conclusively verified. But neither could they be conclusively falsified because when we take certain observations as proof that a given hypothesis is false, certain conditions are always presupposed and it is always logically possible that we are deceived in supposing these conditions to be fulfilled. We can never be sure, for instance, that our physical senses are not deceiving us. We may disallow any saving hypothesis unless it makes the hypothesis which it is introduced to save more, not less, vulnerable to empirical evidence; but that does not affect the point that if we make empirical falsifiability a general criterion of meaning we can (logically) never know for certain that some empirical hypothesis (i.e. some pro-

128

position in common sense, or history, as well as science) has really been falsified.

The verifiability criterion must accordingly be interpreted in a sense which does not require the conclusive testing of empirical propositions. We must be content to consider how experience may render a statement *probable*. It can do so, says Ayer, if some possible sense-experience would be 'relevant'[27] to the determination of its truth or falsehood. But what is being 'relevant'? To make this clear, Ayer puts forward his 'weaker' criterion. Taking 'experiential proposition' to mean a proposition which records an actual or possible sense-experience, this criterion runs; '... it is the mark of a genuine factual proposition ... not that it should be equivalent to an experiential proposition, or any finite number of experiential propositions, but simply that some experiential proposition can be deduced from it in conjunction with certain other premises without being deducible from these other premises alone.'[28] In passing we note the explicit exclusion of phenomenalism here; but our main concern is with other matters. Ayer commends this weaker criterion as 'liberal enough' to allow factual significance to universal propositions and statements about the past.

In the introduction to the second edition of *Language, Truth and Logic,* however, he recognises that this weaker criterion also has defects. For one thing, it overlooks the vagueness of at least some empirical propositions. There is never any single experiential proposition (or as Ayer here prefers to call it 'observation statement'), or single set of such, of which it can be said that precisely this one is entailed by any given empirical statement. The occurrence of one or other of a fairly indefinite range of sense-experiences would normally be taken to verify any given empirical statement. The 'open texture'[29] of empirical concepts makes it possible to extend this range infinitely. However, such vagueness does not trouble Ayer. All he need do, he thinks, is to specify that when we speak in the verifiability criterion about experiential propositions, or observation-statements, being entailed by factual propositions we mean one or other of a set of such statements which all refer to sense contents falling within a certain range.[30]

A much more troublesome objection to Ayer's weaker

129

criterion was raised by Sir Isaiah Berlin. Ayer recognised its force sufficiently to reformulate his criterion yet again. Berlin pointed out that Ayer's criterion is such that it allows meaning to *any* statement whatsoever. Given any statement, S, and any experiential proposition, or observation-statement, O, then O follows from the premises (i) S, and (ii) If S then O, without following from (ii) alone.[31] A statement such as 'God governs the world' can pass this test:

God governs the world
If God governs the world, then this rose is red.

This rose is red

In admitting this, Ayer points out that, if we express the criterion in terms of falsifiability the same objection would apply; that is, if we say that a statement is meaningful, if some observation-statement is incompatible with it in conjunction with some other premise, which would not be incompatible with this other premise alone. 'This rose is red' would be incompatible with (i) 'God governs the world' and (ii) 'If God governs the world, then this rose is not red', as it would not be incompatible with (ii) alone. So 'God governs the world' would be meaningful by this criterion.

Ayer emends his criterion to meet such objections in the following way. He introduces the expressions 'direct' and 'indirect' verifiability and then goes on:

I propose to say that a statement is indirectly verifiable if it satisfies the following conditions: first, that in conjunction with certain other premises it entails one or more directly verifiable statements which are not deducible from these other premises alone; and secondly, that these other premises do not include any statement that is not either analytic, or directly verifiable, or capable of being independently established as indirectly verifiable. And I can now reformulate the principle of verification as requiring of a literally meaningful statement, which is not analytic, that it should be either directly or indirectly verifiable, in the foregoing sense.[32]

130

The second condition of indirect verifiability is the important new feature of this reformulation. It protects the criterion against premises of the form 'If God governs the world, then this rose is red' which furtively import empirically unverifiable statements into the relevant premises. This premise could not have been established as (indirectly) verifiable 'independently' of 'God governs the world' which was the statement under test in the above example.

But even this reformulation will not serve, as Ayer has to recognise in his most recent discussion of the verifiability criterion.[33] Professor Alonzo Church reviewing the second edition of *Language, Truth and Logic*[34] pointed out that, even as emended there, Ayer's criterion still allows meaning to any statement whatever. Let O_1, O_2 and O_3 be three observation-statements (or experiential propositions) such that no one of the three taken alone entails any of the others, and S be any statement whatever. Not-O_1 stands for the negation of O_1 and not-S for the negation of S. Church introduces the complex formula:

Either (Not-O_1 and O_2) or (O_3 and not-S)

This, he says, is directly verifiable according to Ayer's emended criterion because when put together with O_1 it yields the conclusion O_3, where this conclusion is not entailed by O_1 alone:

Either (Not-O_1 and O_2) or (O_3 and not-S)
But O_1

Therefore O_3

If Church's directly verifiable formula is now put together with S it entails O_2

Either (Not-O_1 and O_2) or (O_3 and not-S)
But S

Therefore O_2

So S is indirectly verifiable according to Ayer's emended

131

criterion. (Unless, Church adds, it happens that his own formula alone entails O_2 in which case not-S and O_3 together entail O_2 so that not-S is directly verifiable). So, S i.e. any statement whatever, can be shown to be verifiable by Ayer's present criterion.

In conceding that this objection is fatal, Ayer remarks that it not-O_3 is substituted for O_3 in Church's formula so that it becomes: Either (Not-O_1 and O_2) or (not-O_3 and not-S), then Church's argument would be as fatal against a criterion in terms of falsifiability as it has been against his own verifiability criterion. It would show that any statement whatever is falsifiable.[35] Ayer thinks that no successful way of further emending his criterion to evade Church's objection has so far been found.[36]

The Meaning of Factual Statements

The third question concerning the logical positivists' criterion of meaning which I posed above[37] was: does it misrepresent the meaning of factual statements?

One way in which such misrepresentation can be effected is by reducing one sort of factual statement to another. This is what some logical positivists have certainly done. The Vienna Circle, or some of them, took all factual statements to be logically reducible to statements about sense-experience. Statements about physical objects, historical events, the consciousness of other minds, etc. were thought to be reducible to statements consisting exclusively of logical connectives and expressions which can be defined ostensively by the content of immediate sense-experience. 'There is a table under the window', for instance, is equivalent in meaning to some set of statements describing sense-experience such as 'Anyone coming into this room will see brownness, feel hardness, . . . etc.'; 'Caesar crossed the Rubicon' means something like 'Anyone who looks into such-and-such archives or other sources will see such-and-such things'; 'My brother John is feeling sad' is equivalent to some description of John's observable behaviour. Such reductionism is, of course, mistaken: its programme cannot be carried through. There is no statement, or set of statements, describing sense-experience, the truth of which is the necessary or sufficient condition of the truth of any statement about a physical object. It is always logically possible that the sense-experience statements are true and the physical object statement false, or *vice versa*; people may always be suffering the illusion that there is a table under the window when there is not, or that there is not when there is. By the same token, historical events cannot be reduced to the sense-experience of present-day historians, nor mental events to bodily movements. Latter-day positivists, such as Ayer, were, of course, aware of these objections to phenomenalism. Ayer accordingly differentiated[38] his verifiability criterion, as a procedure for determining *whether* a statement is meaningful or not, from Schlick's verification principle, which had been a procedure for determining *what* meaning a statement has. This difference is important, says Ayer, because, on his own version, it is possible to hold that the propositions of a scientific theory must be testable by observation without holding that their content is reducible to that of the propositions in which these observations are recorded.

Phenomenalism was not, of course, an essential element in Logical Positivism. The essence of the latter was the doctrine that putative statements of other-than-logical fact have literal, or cognitive, meaning, if and only if they are empirically verifiable.

One obvious objection to this doctrine is that a sentence must (logically) have meaning before we can know whether what it states is verifiable. If we do not know what a statement means, how can we possibly decide whether what it says can be verified or not? Verifiability implies, but is not identical with, meaningfulness.

Another objection, as we have already noted (see above pp. 117–18) is that truth conditions must be clearly distinguished from verification-conditions. The meaning of a proposition can be identified with its truth-conditions. To recall Wittgenstein's example, I do not know what 'He has angina' means if I do not know that its truth-condition is his having bacillus so-and-so in his blood. But I may well know what this statement means and not know that its verification-condition is his having a sore throat, or whatever.

To these two objections Ayer would presumably not demur. What he evidently wishes to argue is that verifiability is a criterion of meaningfulness in the sense that knowing the verification-conditions of a statement is a *necessary condition* of knowing its truth-conditions. If I know the truth-conditions, which give the meaning of the statement, then I must know the verification-conditions; and, by contra-position, if I do not know the latter I cannot know the former. To know the truth-conditions of a statement, says Ayer, is to know what kind of experiences we should have, if the statement were true, or probably true, and what kind we would have if it were false or probably false.[39] It is, for instance, to know what it would be like to observe, or fail to observe, bacillus so-and-so in someone's blood. But if we know this, then in principle we know how to verify the statement under consideration. We have some conception, that is to say, of what it would be like to observe that the relevant truth-conditions are fulfilled, or not fulfilled. But in the absence of any such conception − i.e. if we did not know even in principle how to verify the statement − then how could we be said to know its truth-conditions? And if we do not know the latter, we do not know the meaning of the statement in question.

This line of argument is open to the following objection. If I know the truth-conditions of a statement, then it may be that I can infer its verification-conditions; indeed, it may be that unless I can infer the verification-conditions I do not know its truth-conditions. But in either case the fact remains that the verification-conditions are a matter of *inference*. A cognitive statement *states* its truth-conditions; it does not *state* its verification-conditions. Therefore, while the former may be taken for its meaning, the latter may not. 'He has angina' *says* that he has bacillus so-and-so in his blood. It does *not say* that any observer will observe bacillus such-and-such in his blood under certain given conditions.[40] Good ground is found here, then, for concluding that verification-ism misrepresents the meaning of factual statements.

There is a further problem which has to do with the fact that it is *empirical* verification which is in question. The theory which we are examining is that statements of fact are meaningful if they are *empirically* verifiable. This implies that statements of fact are such that they could conceivably be shown to be true or false by appeal to sense-experience alone. The problem which this raises is that many, if not all, statements of fact appear to contain elements which in the nature of the case could not be verified by sense-experience alone. In his most recent writings about scientific statements of fact, for instance, Ayer recognises how difficult, if not impossible, it is to be sure that a statement of fact is a record of sense-experience unalloyed by any theoretical elements. All scientific statements are theory-laden. Ayer draws a distinction between the meaning of a theory, i.e. the meaning of the sentences in which the theory is formulated, and what he calls its 'factual content', i.e. the account which is derivable from it of what is actually observable.[41] The sum total of such purely factual propositions, whether true or false, he calls, following F. P. Ramsey, a 'primary system', The 'secondary system', or set of systems, consists of sentences formulating the relevant theory or theories which legislate for possible as well as actual cases and can contain terms which are not directly related to anything observable. All scientific statements contain both elements. Suppose, for example, I say that an Asian 'flu epidemic has been caused by the spread westward of a certain virus. In saying this I am saying that certain empirically observable events have occurred — such-and-such people sneezing, running a temperature, coughing, suffering from pain or depression in such-and-such places in such-and-such a sequence and so on. But I am also, in effect, offering an explanation of these phenomena as caused by infection, which is caused by the generation and spread of viruses of certain strains, and so on. The principle of causality is not empirically observable but is invoked to explain what is.

Any idea that all theory-laden statements of fact can be analysed into non-theory laden ones is mistaken. As Ayer recognises in a discussion entitled 'On What There Is': 'what is counted a fact depends in part upon our conceptual scheme'.[42] (For the moment we take the point without troubling over the qualification 'in part'). Any statement of fact, or putative fact, belongs within some conceptual scheme — that of common sense, science, morality, or religion, etc. *None* of the following statements 'It is raining', 'Water boils at $100°C$', 'Love is better than hate', 'God is our Father', can be analysed *without loss or change of meaning*, into what Ayer calls 'a factual content' alone.

135

The notion that there is non-theory-laden experience, to which appeal might conceivably be made, is also mistaken. As Sir Karl Popper has remarked[43] we 'make' our experiences by the questions which we put to nature. Such questions always arise within conceptual schemes and are 'loaded' with the presuppositions of their scheme. How, for instance, could the experience we call remorse, or that which is described as a sense of the numinous, be conceived in non-moral or non-religious terms respectively?

In so far as logical positivists have overlooked what may be called the theoretical element in both facts and experiences, their empiricist verificationism misrepresents the meaning of factual statements. I am not suggesting, of course, that positivists such as Ayer have done so. Ayer does not hold that facts or experiences come, so to speak, unburdened with theory. He even concedes that there may be specifically religious experiences which one needs to have had in order to understand specifically religious propositions, and simply insists that in such case the factual content of these propositions will have to be determined by these experiences.[44]

Ayer's position, in the end, seems to be that statements of fact, of whatever sort they may be, are unlike statements of scientific fact, if their truth or falsity is not a matter of something *within our experience* being different or being differently arranged or explained, if they are true from what it would be, if they were false. All that is left of the logical positivist attack on metaphysics when we come to Ayer's *The Central Questions of Philosophy* (London, 1973) is the minimal demand that if a metaphysical statement aspires to truth ' . . . there should be some way of deciding whether it attains it. Even if it has no factual content, in the sense which I am giving to the term, it should contribute something to the arrangements of facts. Otherwise we have no criterion by which to determine whether it is acceptable'.[45] We shall see in the next section how religion faces vis-à-vis this demand. For the moment it suffices to note that the vaunted verification principle is no longer the devastating razor which it appeared to its proponents to be in the 1920s and 30s.

136

IV. VERIFICATIONISM AND RELIGIOUS BELIEF
Wittgenstein and the Logical Positivist Critique of Religion

Recapitulating, the logical positivists' definitive opinions about religious belief may be summarised as follows. If expressions of such belief purport to be, or to imply, statements of fact, then they are meaningless because they are neither analytically nor empirically testable. In order to understand a statement of logical fact we must be able to show that it is true or false from the definitions of the terms used in it. In order to understand a statement of other-than-logical fact we must be able to indicate what sort of experiences we should have if it were true, or probably true, as distinct from what we should have if it were false, or probably false. Nothing can (logically) be a statement of fact which is not understandable in one or other of these ways. Religious beliefs do not purport to be statements of logical fact: as normally held they concern a being, God, and not simply the implications in use of a certain definition of the word 'God'. They do purport to be statements of other-than-logical fact, but according to logical positivists they necessarily fail to qualify as such for two related reasons. One is that God is, by definition, transcendent and so statements concerning his existence or activity cannot (logically) be confirmed by human experience alone. The other is that religious belief is, by definition, belief which nothing in human experience is, or at any rate ought to be, allowed to disconfirm.

Did Wittgenstein share these grounds for rejecting religion as meaningless, during the late 1920s and early 30s? He evidently took the view that if nothing empirically observable is allowed to falsify a proposition, then it has no explanatory power: 'A proposition, an hypothesis, is coupled with reality — with varying degrees of freedom. In the limit case there's no longer any connection, reality can do anything it likes without coming into conflict with the proposition: in which case the proposition (hypothesis) is senseless!' (PR p.282). The demand for significant negatibility in the *Tractatus* (see above p. 32) becomes in *Philosophical Remarks* a demand for empirical falsifiability. On the same page as the last quotation, Wittgenstein emphasises that it is 'immediate experience' which couples propositions with reality. If there

137

is nothing in immediate experience which would be incompatible with the proposition, then the proposition is senseless. We may safely infer that Wittgenstein would have said that religious beliefs are a case in point.

However, Wittgenstein's attitude to religion, even in this period of his life should not be identified with that of the logical positivists. He continued to hold the views about the mystical or transcendental expressed in the *Tractatus*, especially the opinion that religion cannot be talked about. In some remarks on religion, dated 17 December 1930 and recorded by Waismann (see WWK pp. 117-8), Wittgenstein claimed that the essence of religion has nothing to do with talk. He says that he can conceive of a religion in which there are no doctrinal principles. If I understand him rightly, he differentiates here between talk *about* religion and talk *as a constituent part of* some religious activity. By the latter he presumably meant speach-acts in the course of the liturgy, such as prayer or exhortation. He says, evidently referring to such speech-acts, that it is not at all a matter of whether the words are true, or false, or nonsensical. But he will not allow that such talk in religion is metaphorical: one would have to cash the metaphors in literal terms and that cannot be done. Wittgenstein says that the facts are for him unimportant: presumably this means the particular conditions prevailing in the world. He is concerned with what people mean when they say that 'the world is there'. This is reminiscent of the *Tractatus* remark: 'It is not *how* things are in the world that is mystical, but that it exists' (6.44). Asked by Waismann if the existence of the world relates to the ethical, Wittgenstein replied that people have felt that there is a connexion. They have expressed this by saying that God the Father created the world whereas God the Son (or the Word that proceeds from the Father) is the ethical. That men should have thus divided the Godhead and then reconceived of it as a unity implies that there is some connexion between the world and the ethical, said Wittgenstein. This is a dark saying but whatever it means, it can hardly be taken to express contempt for religion. Indeed, Wittgenstein is explicit that he feels no contempt for the tendency in man to seek some way of expressing religion. He is not making fun of it. He 'takes his hat off' to it (*ich ziehe den Hut davor*). And

138

that remark, he says, must be understood, not as a sociological description, but as expressing his own personal attitude to it.

These latter remarks indicate clearly that whilst perhaps standing on the same philosophical ground as the logical positivists, Wittgenstein's attitude, even at this time, to religious belief was different from theirs. And we also have Carnap's word for that. In his 'Intellectual Biography' he writes of a conversation between Wittgenstein and Schlick to which he was a party:

> Once when Wittgenstein talked about religion, the contrast between his and Schlick's positions became strikingly apparent. Both agreed of course in the view that the doctrines of religion in their various forms had no theoretical content. But Wittgenstein rejected Schlick's view that religion belonged to the childhood phase of humanity and would slowly disappear in the course of cultural development. When Schlick, on another occasion, made a critical remark about a metaphysical statement by a classical philosopher (I think it was Schopenhauer), Wittgenstein surprisingly turned against Schlick and defended the philosopher and his work.
>
> These and similar occurrences in our conversations showed that there was a strong inner conflict in Wittgenstein between his emotional life and his intellectual thinking. His intellect, working with great intensity and penetrating power, had recognised that many statements in the field of religion and metaphysics did not, strictly speaking, say anything. In his characteristic absolute honesty with himself, he did not try to shut his eyes to this insight. But this result was extremely painful for him emotionally, as if he were compelled to admit a weakness in a beloved person. Schlick, and I, by contrast, had no love for metaphysics or metaphysical theology, and therefore could abandon them without inner conflict or regret. Earlier when we were reading Wittgenstein's book in the Circle, I had erroneously believed that his attitude toward metaphysics was similar to ours. I had not paid sufficient attention to the statements in his book about the mystical, because his feelings and thoughts in this area were too diver-

gent from mine. Only personal contact with him helped me to see more clearly his attitude at this point.[46]

Transcendence

I noted above that logical positivists evidently assumed theists as such to be committed on two points: that God is (a) transcendent in the sense of absolutely incomprehensible to mortals, and (b) the object of faith which nothing in experience should be allowed to destroy. This assumption is, to say the least, open to question. In this sub-section I will deal with (a) and in the next with (b).

Some philosophical theologians such as Rudolf Otto and Paul Tillich, have indeed taken God's transcendence to consist in his absolute incomprehensibility. The former speaks of the object to which the numinous state of mind refers as inaccessible to the most concentrated attention of the conceptual understanding; and the latter speaks of the word 'God' as transcending its own conceptual content, whatever that may mean.[47] But it is arguable that theistic necessity is served when the transcendence of God is interpreted differently. It can be interpreted as the possession in a surpassing degree of such characteristics as wisdom, goodness, or power. So interpreted, it does not state, or imply, that God is incomprehensible. To say that God has more wisdom than any being of whom we ever heard is to say something perfectly comprehensible. To affirm that he has all the wisdom we could imagine and more besides is also quite intelligible. We know what the meanings of the words 'wisdom' 'all' 'more' 'besides' are; and we can therefore form some idea of what it would be like to encounter a greater wisdom than we had hitherto encountered and to go on encountering greater and greater wisdom without limit. To speak of God as *surpassingly* wise in this sense is quite different from saying that his wisdom is incomprehensible. The claim that a being is transcendent in the sense of surpassingly wise is verifiable in principle. It is perfectly possible to imagine ourselves discovering a wisdom greater than we had discovered before, and to imagine this process of discovery going on and on. The claim that a being is transcendent in the sense of *incomprehensibly* wise is, by contrast, one which we could never, even in principle, test.

140

Corresponding moves can be made with the other qualities, goodness, power, etc. attributed to God.

It is sometimes said that unless God were transcendent in the sense of utterly incomprehensible to men, there would not be religiously adequate grounds for worshipping him. But I find this unintelligible. I can see some point in worshipping a being who is surpassingly wise, etc. But what significance or value could there be in worshipping that which was incomprehensible? Would it even make sense to say that one was doing so?

There is, however, a further sense in which God is transcendent. There are conditions to which God does not have to conform though men would have to in similar case. I am not thinking of the practical limitations which human ignorance and weakness may impose, but of certain logical conditions to which, so to speak, God evidently sits lightly. For example, to say that any being is wise is to say that he is disposed to do wise things; and to do wise things requires a physical body. Wise thoughts need a brain as their occasion, wise words a voice, wise moves a hand, wise steps a foot, and so on. God does not possess a physical body so how (logically) does he manage to be wise? There is perhaps an even more fundamental problem. Human agents are identified by a body which can be located in time and space, but since God is not a temporal or spatial being, how do we identify this divine agent? God is evidently not identified as men are, nor does it mean the same thing entirely to say that he acts as it does, that they act. Does transcendence in this sense, amount to incomprehensibility? That is, as I see it, the most pressing of philosophical problems where religion is concerned; and I have discussed it at some length in my *A Philosophical Approach to Religion* (London, 1974).[48] Conceivably, what it means to say that God acts could differ so completely from what it would mean to say that a man had acted that there would be no apparent reason why we should use the word 'acts' in the former case at all. This is that 'death by a thousand qualifications' of which, as we shall see in the next sub-section, Professor Anthony Flew speaks.[49] Language in religion is, one must admit, sometimes strained to breaking point: so much licence is allowed in its use, as applied to God, that the result is incomprehensibility. But does this *have* to happen? If it does then the consequence is not that God has a remarkable characteristic called transcendence, but that religion is necessarily nonsensical. If, however, we can make out a case that the use of language in religion, though sometimes peculiar to it, is not unintelligible, then we may say that God is transcendent in the sense that he must not be taken for other than he is. I endeavour to make out such a case in the book to which I have just referred.

Faith and Falsifiability

I turn now to the assumption that God is ideally the object of faith which nothing can destroy; and the inference that statements concerning him are therefore meaningless.

Attempts are sometimes made, like that of Mr. David Cox in his article 'The Significance of Christianity' which was published in *Mind* 1950, to treat religious belief as consisting of a set of empirically testable hypotheses. Cox proposed that the use of the word 'God' should be restricted to contexts which describe the human experiences called 'meeting' or 'knowing', God, etc. The belief that God exists can then be treated as a hypothesis equivalent in meaning to 'Some men and women have had, and all may have, experiences called "meeting God" etc.' He claimed that, so far from being destructive of traditional Christianity, this proposal is not even revolutionary. Christian doctrines, such as 'God created the world' or 'God loves men', were all framed in the first instance simply to give expression to certain religious experiences which members of the Church had undergone; and later on, when controversies arose on points of doctrine in the course of Church history, the issue was always settled in the end by an appeal to experience. But if belief in God is to be compared to a scientific hypothesis, or set of such, then it must be possible to predict under exactly what circumstances these experiences called 'meeting God', etc. are expected to occur, so that the hypotheses into which they enter can be experimentally tested. If they do occur, belief in God is confirmed, if not, it is discredited. Some sophisticated advocates of religion have ventured to suggest that this can be done, but I think the facts are against them.

142

Theism enjoins its adherents not to abandon belief in God, however strong the reasons for doing so may appear to be. 'Though he slay me, yet will I trust in him' (*Job* xiii.15) is held up as a paradigm of faith. It was this feature of theism on which Professor Antony Flew fastened in his oft-quoted essay 'Theology and Falsification'.[50] He had evidently observed how religious believers, when confronted by some circumstance which seems to falsify their belief in God, are wont to cast about for some saving explanation of the apparently contrary evidence; and that, if necessary, they preserve their belief by qualifying it in various ways. Up to a point it is, of course, legitimate for them to do so, but believers go far beyond that point. They stop at nothing to hold onto their belief. In the end it 'dies by a thousand qualifications'; and they themselves are left in a state of Orwellian 'doublethink'. An example might be the attempt to solve the problem of evil by claiming that God's goodness is infinite and therefore a logical oddity such that the evil in the world is not inconsistent with it:[51] a move which evacuates God's 'goodness' of meaning and licenses assent, on the part of believers in it, to contrary or contradictory propositions. Flew borrowed John Wisdom's parable[52] of the overgrown garden and likened religious believers to those who insist that a gardener comes secretly to tend it, even though it looks very overgrown and no device, such as bloodhounds, electric wires or whatever, can detect a trace of a gardener. God is as elusive as the gardener and the evidence of his activity as ambivalent; yet theists persist in their beliefs. Flew evidently sees in this fact ground on which the meaninglessness of theistic beliefs can be exposed. He points out that 'to assert that such and such is the case is necessarily equivalent to denying that such and such is not the case' (p is materially equivalent to not not-p). Therefore 'if there is nothing which a putative assertion denies then there is nothing which it asserts either: and so it is not really an assertion'. These remarks simply express an analytic truth about assertion, so cannot be rejected without self-contradiction. In the light of them, Flew puts to religious believers his now famous question: 'What would have to occur, or to have occurred, to constitute for you a disproof of the love, or of the existence, of God?' As a secular propagandist, he is moving in on his assurance that religious believers, when their faith is wholehearted and sincere, can only reply 'Nothing'. If that is their answer, there will be nothing which religious beliefs deny and so nothing which they assert. Therefore they cannot be taken to have cognitive meaning.

Flew infers from the fact that religious believers refuse to let anything count against their beliefs the conclusion that these beliefs have no literal, or cognitive, meaning. Is he entitled to do so?

Just before answering, it will be useful, if once again I define precisely some relevant terms which have already been used in this chapter. *Evidence* I take to be verification- (or falsification-) conditions, arrived at by verification- (or falsification-) procedures. *Meaning*, i.e. the cognitive meaning of indicative sentences, I take to be identifiable with the truth conditions of statements which these indicative sentences make. I define '*truth-condition*' thus: T is a truth-condition of any statement S, if T is a necessary and sufficient condition of the truth of S. For example, having bacillus so-and-so in one's blood is a truth-condition of the statement that one has quinsy. '*Verification-condition*' (or *mutatis mutandis* 'falsification-condition') I define thus: V is a verification-condition of any statement S, if V is a sufficient condition of there being reason to believe that S is true. One's having an inflamed throat is, in the example used by Wittgeinstein, a verification-condition of one's having quinsy. (I use the expressions 'necessary condition' and 'sufficient condition' in accordance with their normal meanings. If E is that of which C is the condition, then C is a *necessary condition* of E when: if E then C (or if not C then not E); and C is a *sufficient condition* of E when: if C then E (or if not E then not C)).

The crucial question for our purposes is as follows: Is knowing that a statement has a verification-condition a necessary or sufficient condition of knowing that it has a truth-condition? In other words, is the possibility of evidence a necessary or sufficient condition of meaning? If S has a truth-condition, it does not follow that it has a verification-condition. It is perfectly conceivable that there should be known to exist a condition of a statement's being *true* without there being known to exist a condition of its being

144

verified. The truth-condition(s) of any statement would normally suggest some verification-condition(s) of it: but the truth-condition does not *state* or *logically imply* the verification-condition. 'He has bacillus so-and-so in his blood' does not *say* 'He has an inflamed throat' nor imply it necessarily. So knowing that a statement has a verification-condition *is not a necessary* condition of knowing that it has a truth-condition. But it *is a sufficient* condition. If I know that there exists a condition which would provide reason to believe that a statement is true or false, then by implication I know that there exists a condition which would constitute that statement's being true or false. If I know, for instance, that there is a verification-condition of having quinsy, then I know that there must be something, the truth-condition, which is what having quinsy is. All I have been saying here holds good, incidentally, whether or not I know the content of the verification-condition and the truth-condition concerned.

The point, now, to take about Flew's argument outlined above is that it assumes falsifiability, i.e. having a falsification-condition, to be, *not a sufficient condition* of cognitive significance which it undoubtedly *is, but a necessary condition* which it is *not*. Flew's position is the inadmissible one that if there is cognitive meaning, i.e. a truth-condition, then there must be the possibility of evidence against i.e. a falsification-condition, and if there is no such possibility, there is no conceivable meaning. He interprets his main point — viz. if there is nothing which a putative assertion denies, then there is nothing which it asserts either — to mean: if nothing is allowed to count as evidence against a statement, that statement is no statement.

This was a mistake, as he now concedes in a paper called 'Theology and Falsification in Retrospect'.[53] He made it through identifying *'counting against'* with *'being incompatible with'*. Between his two remarks on assertion and denial, quoted above (p. 143), we find him saying that he is asking the believer 'what he would regard as counting against, or as being incompatible with' the truth of his religious assertion. And again, that 'anything which would count against the assertion, or which would induce the speaker to withdraw it and to admit that it had been mistaken, must be

145

part of (or the whole of) the meaning of the negation of that assertion. And to know the meaning of the negation of an assertion, is as near as makes no matter to know the meaning of that assertion.' It is clear that Flew is conflating 'counting against' with 'being incompatible with'. This, as he himself says, was 'a serious offence'.

To identify 'counting against' and 'being incompatible with' is to confuse a falsification-condition with a falsity-condition. Two statements are (semantically) *incompatible* if and only if they cannot both be true because their meanings are what they are. So a statement's incompatibles (like its entailments) serve to reveal and clarify its meaning. They fulfil the same purpose as 'criteria' i.e. they state falsity-conditions and thereby contribute to the definition of meaning. If a statement has no incompatibles, it has no meaning. What, on the other hand, is 'counting against'? Anything which counts against the truth of a statement is a result obtained by falsification-procedures. It constitutes a falsification-condition as distinct from a falsity-condition.

Two criticisms, then, can be levelled at Flew. (i) He was confused in his argument. He supposed religious beliefs to have no incompatibles simply because, as he took it, believers cannot say what counts against their beliefs. (ii) He was mistaken on the point at issue. Religious beliefs do have incompatibles and believers can say what these are; for instance, 'God abandons us in our pain or loss' is incompatible with 'God loves us'.

Flew, I think, would now yield to both criticisms. But he argues that the heart of the matter still remains: it concerns the price which religious believers are prepared to pay for their assertions. Saving hypotheses can always be introduced to protect religious assertions from evidence which counts against them, without these assertions thereby becoming meaningless. But they may, in the process, become just silly, as Flew, following Basil Mitchell, remarks. Death by a thousand qualifications is still a possibility, but it is the death of irrelevance, obscurantism or otherworldliness, rather than of cognitive insignificance. What is left of Flew's question to religious believers then, is this: How far along this road are you prepared to go? To what extent, that is to say, are you willing to save your beliefs, by qualification, from that which

146

counts against them? You say, for instance, that God, who is all-powerful and good, exists and loves us. How does this tally with human pain and loss? How far are you prepared to go in making it tally by qualifying what you mean by 'good' or 'all-powerful', or by conjectures concerning our life here or hereafter? To the point of silliness?

Eschatology

But what constitutes silliness? Let us consider a particular case. Believers frequently protect their belief in God by some kind of eschatology. Broadly speaking there are two kinds: what might be called 'hereafter-eschatology', as found for instance in the last book of the Bible, and the 'here-and-now' kind, which is found, for example, in the *Gospel of John*. The former looks to a world to come in which we shall stand before God; the latter concerns our experience of confrontation by God in this life. The evil experiences which count against belief in God are counterbalanced, or so it is claimed, by eschatological experiences of God's companionship in the here and now, or will be counterbalanced by such experiences in the hereafter. We must, as the saying goes, 'let God finish his sentences' and then we shall see that all things work together for good to them that love God.

Is the saving hypothesis that religious beliefs are eschatologically verifiable, or falsifiable, silly? Two distinct descriptions may, I think, be covered by the adjective 'silly' in a context such as this. A belief may be silly in the sense that it is unsophisticated or off-beat. On the other hand, it may be silly in the sense of self-contradictory or unintelligible. In the former case, it offends against fashion; in the latter, against reason. Eschatological beliefs of either kind might be thought silly in the former sense because, in our secular age, they run counter to the atheistic presuppositions on which most of our thinking is based; or silly in the latter sense because either they are self-stultifying or strain the meanings of words to breaking point. I have discussed elsewhere,[54] with reference to religious belief in general, both the challenge to it of secularisation and the question of its rationality or otherwise. Here it suffices to make one or two remarks with particular reference to eschatological beliefs.

As for silliness in the former sense, hereafter-eschatological

147

beliefs are thought silly nowadays even by some believers: they are so out of fashion that it is only from very conservative pulpits that one hears sermons on life after death and not often even from there. Here-and-now eschatology, though still with us, has been markedly secularised in some quarters; the believer is exhorted to mean by 'God' none other than his gracious neighbour. But these assessments of the situation, if true, are only of sociological interest. It would not necessarily discredit eschatological belief, if it were thought so silly in this sense that a mere handful of men subscribed to it.

Of far more importance for our purposes is the question whether eschatological beliefs are silly in the sense of self-contradictory or unintelligible. If we subscribe to hereafter-eschatology, then we have on our hands the problem of how we are to conceive of experience in a context which is non-spatial, non-temporal and immaterial. What could it be like to have experiences in such a world? If we adopt here-and-now eschatological beliefs, then we have to face the problems of (a) how experiences of meeting God are to be identified as experiences *of God*, and (b) how we are to show that they cannot be reduced to experiences describable in non-theistic terms. It would be beyond the scope of this section to pursue such questions. Discussions of them abound elsewhere.[55] All I wish to say here is that, as a demand for answers to this kind of question, in its recast form, Flew's challenge to believers remains. But it is important to see how radical its recasting has been. It is not empirical falsifiability which is now demanded but intelligibility. The two are not to be confused.

Religious Statements of Fact

This whole discussion of religious belief and verificationism has been concerned with whether or not expressions of religious belief can be regarded as statements of fact or, which amounts to the same thing, as having cognitive meaning. We have reached the conclusion that being verifiable, or falsifiable, is not a necessary condition of cognitive meaning. Having entailments and incompatibles, on the other hand, is. If religious beliefs do not have verification- (or falsification-) procedures or conditions, it does not follow

148

that they are cognitively insignificant. But if they have no entailments or incompatibles — if there is nothing which a statement of religious belief implies to be, or not to be, the case — then religious belief is meaningless. Despite the foolish assertion 'God is above logic' which one sometimes hears, no religious believer, in practice, takes his beliefs to be without entailments or incompatibles.

Nevertheless, there is some force in two closely related points made by Ayer and Flew respectively. The former, as we have already noted (see p. 136 above) held that if a metaphysical belief aspires to truth, then 'there should be some way of deciding whether it attains it'. Unless it has, at least in principle, some empirically observable verification- (or falsification-) condition, no way of deciding will be open to us. To say that 'there should be some way of deciding' is, of course, to say no more than that it is unreasonable to concern oneself with issues concerning which one has no way of deciding one way or the other. Flew's point is to the same effect. He says in 'Theology and Falsification in Retrospect': 'Immunity against even the theoretical possibility of falsif- ication in this our world would have been achieved only and precisely at the cost of a complete and necessary irrelevance to it'. And he points out that religion's advocates usually claim that it is 'supremely relevant' to life.

A set of metaphysical or religious beliefs to which everything that occurred, or might occur, in this world was irrelevant would not necessarily be meaningless: but if religion purports to take up the time and attention of reasonable men, then it must have some bearing upon that which they experience. To echo Ayer's words, it must have some relation to the facts or at least the arrangement of the facts (see above p. 136). That is to say, our experience itself, or our understanding of that experience, must be stateably different, supposing religious beliefs to be true from what it would be if they were false. It is possible to conceive of religious, or at least metaphysical, beliefs to the truth or falsity of which nothing in our world or our life is in any way relevant: nothing counts as evidence for or against them and our understanding of the world and our life within it is precisely the same whether those beliefs are true or false. Ayer and Flew are saying that no reason would exist why men should concern themselves with beliefs which fit this description. And of course they are right: their point is tautological. But I know of no religious beliefs, past or present, actually held by men which do fit this description. Even the most otherworldly of religions always in practice posit some connexion, albeit minimal, between what happens in this world and what happens in the world to come.

5 Lectures on Religious Belief

In the last two chapters we have considered critically how religion appeared to Wittgenstein in the light firstly of the *Tractatus*, which was published in 1921, and secondly of the empiricist verificationism with which he seems to have sympathised during the late 1920s and early 1930s. Now we must turn to such evidence as we have concerning the views on religion which he held in the light of his late philosophy. This evidence consists mainly of notes taken by students who attended lectures on religious belief which he gave in Cambridge during 1938. Cyril Barrett, who compiled and published them in a volume entitled *Lectures and Conversations on Aesthetics, Psychology and Religious Belief* (Oxford, 1966), is careful to emphasise in his preface that they are not Wittgenstein's own lecture notes, that he neither saw nor checked them, and that he might not have approved of their publication in the present form. However, those who took them down were amongst Wittgenstein's most ardent disciples and we may safely assume that they have provided a faithful record of his teaching.

My opening remarks in the last paragraph may have given the impression that I assume Wittgenstein to have passed through three clearly distinguishable phases in his thinking about religious belief. If so, I must correct that impression. We simply do not know what phases Wittgenstein's thought on this subject passed through; nor can we say how he would have related to each other the various ideas about religion which we know him to have expressed at one time or another. How, for instance, is the *Tractatus* doctrine of the mystical as inexpressible related to the contention in the *Lectures* that religion uses a picture? Would Wittgenstein have said that the latter is a development or a rejection of the former? Would he have told us that he was moving away from the contention that the mystical cannot be put into

151

words, when he took up the idea that religion is using a picture; or that he was simply carrying that conviction to its logical conclusion by treating all religious language as 'uncashable' metaphor? His published work on religious belief is too fragmentary to provide clear answers to questions like that. All one can do is take the fragments as they are; see how they are grounded in Wittgenstein's wider philosophical thinking at their appropriate time; and consider what light, if any, they shed upon the philosophical problems generated by religion.

In the two previous chapters I have endeavoured to do something of this sort with Wittgenstein's *Tractatus* doctrine that the mystical shows itself, and with such indications as we have that he once subscribed to a verificationist critique of religion. Now I must do the same with the *Lectures on Religious Belief*, which offer the fullest treatment of their subject to come down to us from Wittgenstein and which approach it in the light of some of the leading ideas of his late philosophy.

I. THE PHILISOPHICAL BACKGROUND OF THE LECTURES ON RELIGIOUS BELIEF

We have already considered this late philosophy in detail in chapter 2. In particular I tried there to get clear how Wittgenstein thought that the *meaning of language* must be discovered, and its *relation to reality* understood. The essence of the matter concerning the meaning of language, we found to lie in the instruction; ' . . . look at its use and learn from that' (PI 340); and, concerning the relation of language to reality, in the remark 'grammar tells what kind of object anything is' (PI 373). Wittgenstein's treatment of religious belief in the *Lectures* provides a paradigm case of his late method of philosophising. He looks carefully at one or two examples of the language used to express religious beliefs in order to learn how that language is used and what, if anything, it is about. His views about the meaning of language and its relation to reality, expressed elsewhere in general terms, are here given a particular application.

The Meaning of Religious Language
So far as the meaning of religious language is concerned,
152

Wittgenstein quite clearly considers it of the first importance to recognise points which he makes elsewhere in general terms about language-games or forms of life. I quoted above his injunction: 'One must always ask oneself: is this word ever actually used in this way in the language-game which is its original home?' (PI 116; cf. above p. 60). In the *Lectures* he was at great pains to place expressions of religious belief in their native habitat and expressly condemned any assimilation of them to other kinds of utterance such as scientific statements. We found above that he implicitly took discovering the meaning of language to be like understanding a game by watching it being played and inferring the rules inductively. It was precisely this exercise in which he engaged in the *Lectures*. He looked at what religious believers do with language and sought to learn from that. His approach was guided by the kind of insights which had led him away from the *Tractatus* theory of meaning to the doctrine of language-games or forms of life, developed in *The Blue and Brown Books* and the *Investigations*. Amongst such insights two which I mentioned above were first, the recognition that, in order to understand an utterance, one must place it within the language-system to which it belongs, and second that one must be alive to the modal component or the functional, as distinct from the radical, element, in language (see pp. 36–41 above). We find both kinds of insight guiding Wittgenstein's approach to religious belief.

As regards the former, he was intent upon showing that utterances within religion must be understood as moves within a distinctive system of thought and language, otherwise they make no sense. What counts as evidence here would hardly do so elsewhere and what are intelligible as expressions of emotion, given certain religious beliefs, would be incomprehensible apart from them. As for the modal or functional component in religious language, one of his central ideas in the *Lectures* is that in religion we 'use a picture'. This is reminiscent of his allusion above to how the picture of a boxer in a particular stance can be used either to describe or admonish. (PI p.11n; cf. p. 44 above). The use to which a picture (or pictures) is put in religion is a complicated matter, and Wittgenstein is fully alive to this. Among the elements combined within an expression of religious belief there may

153

be assertion, decision, commitment, emotion, and no doubt other things as well. Any adequate account of the meaning of an expression of belief must take account of all the illocutionary elements compounded within it and of their relationships to one another. Fragmentary and brief as our records of Wittgenstein's lectures are, they shed light on the complexity in the modal component of religious language; and on the kind of question which may arise from it. Examples of the kind of questions which arise would be: if religious beliefs are commissive, are they by implication also constative?; In so far as they are constative, how do they compare with other kinds of factual statement?; Given the complexity of religious language, how should the difference between believers and unbelievers be understood? Such questions were in the forefront of Wittgenstein's mind when he lectured on religious belief.

The Relation between Language and Reality

What Wittgenstein had to say about the relation between language and reality in religion was in line with what he said in his late philosophy about this relation with more general application. We saw that, as early as his conversations with the Vienna Circle in 1930, he held that objects, in the technical sense of the *Tractatus*, should be thought of as whatever must necessarily exist, given a particular proposition-system (see p. 38 above). The conception of reality as constituted, to some degree at any rate, by language, is developed in the course of his later work until, as we saw, it appears in the doctrine that 'grammar tells what kind of object anything is' (PI 373; see pp. 62–7 above). Grammar, according to Wittgenstein's use of that expression, is concerned with the rules of usage of linguistic signs, and it is attention to these which tells us the nature of the object or objects, which they signify. But we noted Wittgenstein's warning in *The Blue Book* that we should not consider these objects to be objects of various kinds in the way, say, that different sorts of apples or automobiles are various kinds of object (cf. above p. 65). The 'objects' about which we speak in our language-games may be much more radically different from each other than that. To the same effect Professor Gilbert Ryle has warned against 'smothering' the differences between theology and science by supposing them to be offering different pictures, reports or explanations of some common reality. He writes: 'If the seeming feuds between science and theology ... are to be dissolved at all, their dissolution can come not from making the polite compromise that both parties are really artists of a sort working from different points of view and with different sketching materials, but only from drawing uncompromising contrasts between their businesses ... Indeed, this smothering effect of using notions like *depicting, describing, explaining*, and others to cover highly disparate things reinforces other tendencies to assimilate the dissimilar and unsuspiciously to impute just those parities of reasoning, the unreality of which engenders dilemmas'.[1] Wittgenstein's *Lectures* certainly draw uncompromising contrasts between religious beliefs and scientific hypotheses and make it clear, albeit implicitly, that if we are dealing with a reality in religious belief, it is of a radically different kind from the physical world which science investigates. Where Ryle speaks of dilemmas or 'wrongly imputed parities of reasoning',[2] Wittgenstein warns against 'the bewitchment of our intelligence by means of language'. (PI 109: see pp. 59–62 above). It is the same sort of confusion which each had in mind: a confusion of one sort of discourse and what it is about with another sort and what it is about. Wittgenstein obviously thought that the way to avoid such confusion lies through an analysis of the grammar of religious language. He said, it will be recalled (see pp. 57–9 above), that 'what we do in a language-game always rests on a tacit presupposition' (PI p.179e). In the *Lectures*, he is evidently starting an inquiry the goal of which, if it can be attained, will be to expose the ultimate presupposition of religious belief. What, in the last analysis, makes religious language religious? If we can discover that, we shall discover what religion is about, i.e. so to say, what kind of 'object' God is.

Intelligibility, Justification and the Religious Form of Life
I referred above (see pp. 54–7) to the fact that Wittgenstein spoke of 'forms of life' as 'the given' and 'what has to be accepted' (PI p.226); and I endeavoured to explain these remarks as the attribution to forms of life of a certain

155

ultimacy of intelligibility and justification. There comes a point, that is to say, when the only reply to 'Why do you say that?' or 'Why do you argue like that?' must be, 'This is simply what I do' (PI 217) This does not mean, of course, that the individual speaker has the right to claim that when he uses a word it signifies whatever he wants it to signify. The point is rather that we could have, to recall Wittgenstein's examples, no concept of nature apart from the uniformity of nature, or of human beings without souls. So if asked 'Why do you think, speak, or act, on the tacit presupposition that nature is uniform, or that human beings have souls?', the answer is simply that this is what we do. There is no higher logical order to which we can take the questions 'Does it make sense to speak of them in that way?' or 'Are we justified in arguing as if nature is uniform, or human beings have souls?' We must speak and argue in these ways, in the sense that unless we do, it is not nature or human beings of which we shall be speaking, or about which we shall be arguing. Having doubts as to whether we are entitled to talk of nature as uniform, or of human beings as having souls, is an example of the kind of scepticism which, as we noted above, P.F. Strawson has exposed as self-defeating (see above p. 58).

Now, there are grounds for claiming that religious belief is one such 'given' form of life. There is, so to speak, an ultimacy of intelligibility and justification in religious utterances. There comes a point at which to the questions 'Why do you say this?' or 'Why do you argue in this way?' the only reply which the religious believer can give is 'This is what we do'. Attempts to make sense of religion, or to validate its claims, in non-religious terms are self-defeating. They destroy the very thing which they purport to save. To put religious beliefs into non-religious terms is inevitably to take away their meaning. To base religious claims on non-religious grounds is inevitably to surrender them.

Religious belief is, then, in some sense, a logically self-contained universe of discourse. But it is important to be clear in what sense. Religious believers do not use a totally idiosyncratic language, peculiar to them and them alone. The language they use is ordinary language given a particular application. Men thank each other as well as the Deity; they

156

make requests of each other as well as of Providence; they offer things to each other as well as to God: the language of liturgy is not a language unheard in the street, the market or the home. Nor is the language of catechism: men, as well as God, may be said to create things, to act justly, to love mercy, and so on. To understand what religious believers say in their worship or in their attempts to give belief formulation, we have to learn how they modify ordinary language and not to learn a new language altogether. The sense of their utterances, and the justification of their claims, is therefore contingent, to some degree, upon what it makes sense to say or to claim in other contexts. For instance, to say that God is good, or acts in the world, will be pointless if 'good' or 'acts' mean something here which is *altogether different* from what they mean in other contexts. There would in such case be no point in using the words 'good' or 'acts' of God, rather than any other words.

The ultimacy of intelligibility and justification, as I have chosen to describe it, which belongs to religion, consists in the fact that religious beliefs and claims cannot, without loss or change of meaning, be replaced by non-religious ones. To substantiate this contention we must show that the 'grammar' of religious belief is such that the 'object' with which it has to do is ultimately different from that with which other universes of discourse have to do. God is not a physical thing, not a moral obligation, not an aesthetic emotion, not anything other than God.

II. THE CONTENT OF THE LECTURES ON RELIGIOUS BELIEF

The content of the *Lectures on Religious Belief* can, I think, be usefully organised under three main headings, viz. (i) The logical distinctiveness of religious belief, (ii) Religious belief as 'using a picture', and (iii) The essential difference between religious believers and unbelievers. These three subjects are closely connected and there will inevitably be some overlapping of the material arranged under them. My division of the content of the lecture notes under three such heads may seem somewhat arbitrary, but I hope that it will help to bring Wittgenstein's views into clearer focus, especially for those who are not very familiar with this material.

157

Wittgenstein remarks upon the fact that we learn to speak in a religious way very early in life — 'the word "God" is amongst the earliest learnt' (LRB p.59). Although, this word is used 'like a word representing a person', he says, 'if the question arises as to the existence of a god or God it plays an entirely different role to that of the existence of any person or object I ever heard of' (ibid.). Two particular differences in the way we speak of God's existence as distinct from that of persons or things occur to him. First, if one does not believe in the existence of something, this is not normally considered reprehensible, but as a child, 'one said, had to say, that one *believed* in the existence (*sc.* of God), and if one did not believe, this was regarded as something bad' (ibid). Secondly, if one believes in the existence of something, as opposed to knowing that it exists, people might naturally say 'You only believe — oh well . . .'; but one does not invite that comment if one says that one believes in God. Believing in God's existence is not some state of mind which it would be better to replace by knowing for sure; yet it is not synonymous with knowing for sure (LRB pp. 59—60)

What, then, is believing in God? Wittgenstein recalls that we are taught that it must be accepted on trust: 'If I even vaguely remember what I was taught about God, I might say: "Whatever believing in God may be, it can't be believing in something we can test, or find means of testing." ' (LRB p.60). But he has to recognise that someone could raise the objection that religious people often claim that their beliefs *are* based on evidence, e.g. that of religious experiences, and this seems to imply that such beliefs can be put to a test. So Wittgenstein has to look more closely at the connexion between religious beliefs and the evidence sometimes offered for them. Is it the same as the connexion between scientific hypotheses and empirical evidence?

'The mere fact that someone says they believe on evidence doesn't tell me enough for me to be able to say now whether I can say of a sentence "God exists" that your evidence is unsatisfactory or insufficient' (ibid.). Wittgenstein's point here is that evidence must not be thought of as some kind of homogeneous commodity a certain amount of which has to be offered to validate any or every belief. He remarks that where someone makes a claim which 'sounds a bit absurd' one might well say that there is not enough evidence for it, but where the claim is 'altogether absurd' one might feel it inappropriate to say that the evidence is insufficient. If, for instance, we had a fair amount of evidence that Smith had been killed in the war and then someone claimed to have seen him in the street, even though he was never heard of again after that, Wittgenstein would say 'This isn't sufficient evidence' and that would be the end of the matter. But suppose someone claimed that he knew what the Last Judgment would be like because he had seen it all in a dream, and someone else said 'This is poor evidence'. Wittgenstein would say that if you want to compare this evidence with, say, the evidence that it will rain tomorrow, 'it is no evidence at all' (ibid.), but he would wonder why you should want to make that comparison. Why should you regard belief in a Last Judgment as comparable to belief in a weather forecast? Says Wittgenstein: 'If you compare it with anything in Science which we call evidence, you can't credit that anyone could soberly argue "Well, I had this dream ., . therefore . . . Last Judgment." ' But that might not be the end of the matter. You might well be constrained to add: ' "For a blunder, that's too big." ' (LRB pp.61–2).

This last remark is very important. Wittgenstein expands it thus: if someone wrote on a blackboard 2 + 21 = 13, 'I'd say: "This is no blunder" ' (LRB p.62). Of course the person who wrote this might be mad or making fun, but ' . . . there might be cases where I look for an entirely different interpretation altogether. In order to see what the explanation is I should have to see the sum, to see in what way it is done, what he makes follow from it, what are the different circumstances under which he does it, etc.' (ibid.). The explanation might turn out to be that he has written a correct equation in some 'queer' arithmetic, not a mistaken one in ordinary arithmetic. Similarly, argues Wittgenstein, when people say things about their religious beliefs we should be open to the realisation that they are not doing the same thing as scientists are doing when they talk about their hypotheses. Belief in a Last Judgment is not the same kind of thing as belief in rain tomorrow. If I said that I felt sure it would rain tomorrow because I had dreamed that it would, this would be 'a bit absurd' because in our society we do not base weather forecasts on the evidence of dreams. But it is 'altogether absurd' to assume that religious beliefs are like weather forecasts and that anyone who bases belief in, say, a Last Judgment on dreams is making the same kind of blunder as a weather forecaster would be who told us that it will rain tomorrow because he has seen it doing so in a dream. 'Whether a thing is a blunder or not - it is a blunder in a particular system. Just as something is a blunder in a particular game and not in another' (LRB p.59). We need to know the rules of the game in order to know whether a move is permissible within it or not; we need to watch how someone is operating with numbers before we can tell whether $2 + 21 = 13$ is a blunder or not. In just the same way, says Wittgenstein, we need to look at the things which religious believers say about their beliefs, and the ways in which they react to them, before we can decide whether 'I had this dream . . . therefore . . . Last Judgment' makes any sort of sense or not. If, for instance, someone was interested only in the *date* of the Last Judgement - in whether it will happen in 2000 years from now - and said that he had dreamed that this would be the date, then we should say his evidence was insufficient. Dreams are not a reliable guide to the dates of future events. But we might well add that if it is the date of the Last Judgment which interests him - if he is thinking of it as, or simply as, a future spatio-temporal event, comparable say, to an eclipse of the sun - his is not a *religious* belief at all. On the other hand, asks Wittgenstein, 'In the case where there is hope, terror, etc., would I say there is insufficient evidence if he says, "I believe ,. . .""? I can't treat these words as I normally treat "I believe so and so" ' (LRB p.62). Wittgenstein's point appears to be that if someone was filled with hope, terror, etc., at the thought of a Last Judgment because he had seen it all in a dream, this, whatever it might be, could hardly be called a case of having insufficient evidence. That sort of belief in a Last Judgment — holding it in the mind as a thought which inspires one with hope, terror, pity, or whatever and not simply as the dispassionate thought of some future spatio-temporal event — is not the sort of belief about which one would say 'You only believe — oh well'. (LRB p.60, cf. above p. 158). Religious

160

beliefs are not graded according to their probable truth in the
light of the available evidence. You don't get people saying
'Well, possibly there will be a Last Judgment' as you do
people saying 'Well, possibly there will be a war'. As
Wittgenstein has it:

> Those who said: "Well, possibly it may happen and
> possibly not" would be on an entirely different plane.
> This is partly why one would be reluctant to say:
> "These people rigorously hold the opinion (or view) that
> there is a Last Judgment." "Opinion" sounds queer.
> It is for this reason that different words are used:
> 'dogma', 'faith'.
> We don't talk about hypothesis, or about high pro-
> bability. Nor about knowing.
> In a religious discourse we use such expressions as: "I
> believe that so and so will happen", and use them
> differently to the way in which we use them in science.
> Although, there is a great temptation to think we do.
> Because we do talk of evidence, and do talk of evidence by
> experience. (LRB pp.56–7).

If we make religious belief a matter of evidence in the way
that science is a matter of evidence, says Wittgenstein, then
'this would in fact destroy the whole business.' (LRB p.56).
It would reduce religion to superstition. Wittgenstein does
not consider religious believers to be, as such, superstitious,
but only so if they treat their religious beliefs as though they
were the same kind of thing as scientific ones. He refers to
Father O'Hara who, in a symposium on *Science and Religion*
'makes it (*sc.* religion) a question of science' and says 'I
would definitely call O'Hara unreasonable. I would say, if
this is religious belief, then it's all superstition'. (LRB pp.57
& 59).

What then is the difference between religion and science?
Two people may disagree as to whether someone is dead or
not and if they mean the same by 'dead' we can understand
the nature of this disagreement; it is a matter of whether they
believe that a certain kind of evidence exists or not. But a
religious believer could agree entirely with an unbeliever
about the evidence for concluding that a certain person is

161

dead, and yet claim that this person is not really dead at all. It seems that he both does and does not mean the same by 'dead' as the unbeliever. 'What is the criterion for meaning something different?', asks Wittgenstein and answers, 'Not only what he (sc. a believer) takes as evidence for it (sc. his belief), but also how he reacts, that he is in terror, etc.' (LRB p.62). But he recognises that this matter of the criteria of meaning something different is a complicated one. In a passage such as the following one we find him trying to clarify it. He says:

If an atheist says: "There won't be a Judgement Day," and another person says there will, do they mean the same? - Not clear what criterion of meaning the same is. They might describe the same things. You might say, this already shows that they mean the same.

We come to an island and we find beliefs there, and certain beliefs we are inclined to call religious. What I'm driving at is, that religious beliefs will not . . . (*sic.*) They have sentences, and these are also religious statements.

These statements would not just differ in respect to what they are about. Entirely different *connections* would make them into religious beliefs, and there can easily be imagined transitions where we wouldn't know for our life whether to call them religious beliefs or scientific beliefs.' (LRB pp.58, italics mine)

The point to fasten on here is the reference to the 'connections' of religious beliefs as compared with scientific ones. Wittgenstein has made out a case for investigating the possibility that religious beliefs are beliefs of a logically distinct kind and not just bad, superstitious, blundering pseudo-scientific ones. What he now has to provide is some account of the nature of the 'connections' referred to in the last quoted passage.

Religious Belief as 'Using a Picture'
Religious believers might say that a man is not really dead, even though by ordinary criteria he is. That is to say they think of him as really alive even though he is what we all call dead. They speak of him as a disembodied spirit. What

162

Wittgenstein wants to know is whether or not one can 'connect (anything) with these words' (LRB p.65). There is a 'technique of usage' for the word 'dead' considered as 'a public instrument' (cf. LRB pp.68–9); one aspect of this technique being that if people are said to be dead they must have ceased to exist. If religious believers want to say that the dead have not ceased to exist but are really 'disembodied spirits', they must tell us 'what to do with these words', 'what consequences (they) will draw', 'what (they) oppose this to' (LRB p.69). Until they do that, we have no clear idea what it is they believe.

> Suppose someone said: "What do you believe, Wittgenstein? Are you a sceptic? Do you know whether you will survive death?" I would really, this is a fact, say "I can't say. I don't know," because I haven't any clear idea what I'm saying when I'm saying "I don't cease to exist, etc.(LRB p.70)

What clarifies this idea of not ceasing to exist, of the dead as disembodied spirits? Wittgenstein offers two examples of 'connections' which might do so. A spiritualist talks of 'apparitions'of the dead. Says Wittgenstein, 'Although he gives me a picture I don't like, I do get a clear idea. I know that much, that some people connect this phrase (sc. 'I don't cease to exist') with a particular kind of verification. I know that some people don't — religious people e.g. — they don't refer to a verification, but have entirely different ideas' (ibid.). It is interesting that Wittgenstein contrasts spiritualists with religious people here. It gives us some indication of what he meant by superstition, as distinct from religion (see above p. 161). But, at the moment, he is concerned only to discover some connexions which will clarify the idea of the dead not ceasing to exist. Another such 'connection' is the idea of responsibility from which not even death could absolve one. Wittgenstein cites 'a great writer' who said that as a boy he had been given a task by his father and had suddenly felt that not even death could eliminate his duty to perform it; this experience the writer concerned took to be proof of the immortality of the soul. 'Well, if this is the idea (all right)' (LRB p.70) is the comment which the lecture

163

notes attribute to Wittgenstein. Once we know such connexions, then, we see that there is a use for talk of
disembodied spirits or of the survival of the dead.

Wittgenstein goes on to say that, given such connexions, if
someone from whom he was parting perhaps never to meet
again, said 'We might see one another after death', he would
not necessarily fail to understand the speaker; he thinks it
possible that he would understand perfectly. Faced with the
objection that all one could take these words to be is the
expression of an attitude, say of lasting affection or courage
at the parting, Wittgenstein replies, 'No, it isn't the same as
saying, "I'm very fond of you" — and it may not be the same
as saying anything else. It says what it says. Why should you
be able to substitute anything else?' (LRB p.71). This
remark, I think, should disturb those Wittgensteinians who
interpret religious beliefs as the expression of attitudes: who
say, for example, that when a religious mother prays that the
Virgin Mary will protect her child all she is really doing is
expressing her wonder and respect at the Virgin's holiness,[3]
Wittgenstein himself would evidently reject that sort of
reductionism.

I have spoken hitherto as if understanding those who say
that we do not cease to exist at death were simply a matter
of familiarising oneself with the 'connections' of this belief in
the sense of taking note of what religious believers do with it
in their own distinctive kind of discourse. But there is at least
one remark in the lecture notes which raises the question
whether Wittgenstein took this to be the whole story. It is
this: 'If what he (*sc*. the believer in disembodied spirits) calls
his "idea of death" is to become relevant, it must become
part of our game' (LRB p.69). Wittgenstein has just defined
'our game' as "the game played with 'death' which we all
know and understand." (ibid.). Does he mean no more than
that we must learn to play the believer's language-game with
'death' if we are to understand him? That we must take his
game into ours, so to speak? Or does he mean that the
believer's 'game' must to some degree at any rate, conform to
the rules of that 'game played with "death" which all know
and understand', if what he says is to make any sense? That
he must take our game into his, so to speak? In talking about
'surviving death' that is to say, must a believer mean by

164

'death' what we normally mean by it *and* be able to show that, even so, his talk of surviving it is not self-contradictory? On this latter view, although the believer does not wish to say the same things about death as the unbeliever, what he does wish to say must be something which can *logically* be said about death. As Wittgenstein points out at the beginning of the passages which we are considering in this sub-section (see LRB p.65), unless the believer is restricted in this way there is no reason why he should use the word 'death' rather than any other word for what he is talking about. So the question which the remark in the lecture notes, on which I have just been commenting, raises is this: Did Wittgenstein think of religious belief as a logically self-contained language-game or form of life, or as a member of a family of logically interdependent ones? And, more important than the question as to Wittgenstein's view is the question as to which is the correct view. I shall deal with this latter question in the sequel. As for Wittgenstein's view, this will perhaps become clear if we follow him a little further in his discussion of religious belief.

At this point he introduces the notion of 'using a picture'. With reference to the man whom he has supposed, on parting, to say, 'We might see one another after death', Wittgenstein remarks, 'Suppose I say: "This man used a picture"' (LRB p.71). And he goes straight on to offer another example: '"God's eye sees everything" — I want to say of this that it uses a picture' (ibid). No disparagement of religious beliefs is intended by so describing them. Wittgenstein is careful to point out that he is not 'belittling' belief nor wishing to say of it 'anything (the believer) wouldn't say' (LRB p.71). He goes on 'When I say he's using a picture I'm merely making a *grammatical* remark: [What I say] can only be verified by the consequences he does or does not draw.' (LRB p.72). Consequences here evidently means conclusions. 'What conclusions are you going to draw?' Wittgenstein asks those who use the picture 'God's eye sees everything'. Specifically he enquires: 'Are eyebrows going to be talked of, in connection with the Eye of God?' (LRB p.71). What one has to discover is the 'technique' of using the picture. What conclusions does a believer draw from a picture such as 'God's eye sees everything' and what conclusions does he refuse to draw? For instance, believers evidently draw the following conclusion: if God's eye sees everything, then he is aware of everything which goes on, not only in the world, but in our own hearts. But, asks Wittgenstein rhetorically, what about eyebrows? Believers do not draw the conclusion that, since God has an eye, he must have eyebrows. There have not been any theological dogmas or controversies concerning the shape or shagginess of the divine eyebrows. That is not how believers use the picture. To learn what conclusions they do draw, and what they do not, is to understand their 'technique of usage'.

As Wittgenstein suggests, those of us who had a religious upbringing acquired this technique of usage through being shown pictures or learning catechisms when we were children. We learnt that pictures of God are not used like pictures of aunts (LRB pp.59). No one presents you with a picture of God and then shows you what it is a picture of, as they might show you a picture of your aunt in Australia and then take you to see her. We came to know what conclusions it was appropriate to draw from the picture and what not. The catechism taught us not only the right answers but the right questions to ask. If shown a picture of God in majesty, for instance, one did not ask where he got his robes: if told the story of creation one did not ask what God made the world out of. These latter illustrations are mine, not Wittgenstein's, but I think they illuminate what he meant by his remark: '"Being shown all these things, did you understand what this word (sc. 'God') meant?" I'd say: "Yes and no. I did learn what it didn't mean. I made myself understand. I could answer questions, understand questions when they were put in different ways — and in that sense could be said to understand" (LRB p.59). Children's religious 'howlers' — 'But mummy, what *did* God make the world out of?' — are evidence that 'what it didn't mean' is not always easy to learn.

These last remarks shed some light on our question of a moment ago: Did Wittgenstein think of religious belief as a logically autonomous language-game or as a member of a family of interdependent language-games? The language used in religion is ordinary language. 'Eye', for instance, is a word with which the non-religious are as familiar as the religious.

166

The conclusions which can be drawn from statements about eyes are those which this word implies in ordinary use. Of these some are drawn, and some are not drawn, in the case of God's eye. We do not understand about God's eye until we know which are drawn and which are not. Our understanding of 'eye' in this religious sense is, therefore, logically parasitic on our understanding of 'eye' in its wider usage. We must know how God's eye differs from an ordinary human eye but we cannot (logically) know this unless we know what an ordinary human eye is. The language used in religion is qualified ordinary language: it makes no sense unless its peculiarities are explained as modifications of ordinary usage. If we did not know what human eyes were, we could form no idea of God's eye. To understand 'God's eye sees everything' is to understand how God's eye is (a) like, and (b) unlike, eyes in general; and the understanding of both is obviously dependent upon an understanding how eyes are talked about in general. The answer to our question, therefore, is clearly that Wittgenstein thinks of the religious language-game as a member of a logically interdependent family of language-games. His query: 'Are eyebrows going to be talked of, in connection with the Eye of God?' clearly implies this.

The 'connections' which make religious beliefs distinct from scientific beliefs are a matter of the use which is made of certain pictures such as that of God's all-seeing eye. Such pictures when embodied in propositions like 'God's eye sees everything' have certain implications, i.e. certain entailments and incompatibles, (cf. above p. 162), which follow if the words in which the picture is embodied are taken in their ordinary sense. Of these some are ignored, and others seized upon. Some conclusions drawn and some not. It is essential to know these connexions if we are to know the meaning of the relevant 'pictures' within religion.

The Essential Difference between Believers and Unbelievers
Believers use the relevant pictures with the relevant connexions; unbelievers do not. Using a picture, if it is to serve as a definition of religious belief, cannot, however, be simply a matter of accepting, or rejecting, logical implications of propositions such as 'God's eye sees everything'. What more is there to religious belief than this? We must consider now

167

such answers to that question as Wittgenstein's lectures suggest.

He was clearly preoccupied with this question of the difference between believers and unbelievers in religion. At the beginning of the lecture notes he says:

> Suppose that someone believed in the Last Judgment, and I don't, does this mean that I believe the opposite to him, just that there won't be such a thing? I would say: "not at all, or not always." (LRB p.53)

The difference between believers and unbelievers is not as simple as that. It is not just a matter of believing that there will, or will not be, such a thing as a Last Judgment. If someone said that there was a German aeroplane overhead, another man might say 'Possibly. I'm not so sure'; and in such a case we would say that they were fairly near in their beliefs. Wittgenstein contrasts this difference with that between a believer who says 'I believe in a Last Judgment' and someone who might conceivably say 'Well, I'm not so sure. Possibly' (LRB p.53). He points out that, so far from thinking these two fairly near in their beliefs, we should say that there was 'an enormous gulf' between them (ibid.). In religious controversy, you do not get some people being sure of a thing and others saying 'Well, possibly' (LRB p.56). The difference between believers and unbelievers in religion is not just a difference of opinion as to whether certain things are the case or certain events will occur. Believers 'mean something altogether different', are 'on an entirely different plane', from unbelievers. They cannot be conceived to be 'contradicting' one another on some matter of fact, or not simply. So to conceive of them would be 'missing the entire point' (LRB p.53). Wittgenstein goes on:

> Suppose somebody made this guidance for this life: believing in the Last Judgment. Whenever he does anything, this is before his mind. In a way, how are we to know whether to say he believes this will happen or not.

Asking him is not enough. He will probably say he has proof. But he has what you might call an unshakeable belief. It will show, not by reasoning or by appeal to

168

ordinary grounds for belief, but rather by regulating for all in his life.' (LRB pp.53-4)

Religious belief is undoubtedly *more* than the belief that something or other is, was, or will be, the case. A man may be said to believe that the world will come to an end in 2000 years time without this implying that he is in any distinctive way affected by his belief. But if he is said to have a religious belief — in a Last Judgment, say — then it is implied that what he believes affects him deeply. It is 'always before his mind'; it 'regulates for all in his life'. In other words, 'I believe in a Last Judgment' is characteristically a commissive speech-act, not simply a constative one. To believe in a Last Judgment is to be committed (logically) to a certain way of assessing things: like Carlyle who, as he sat in London drawing-rooms listening to the chattering company, was wont to say to himself 'How will this look in the Judgment and before the Creator of man?'

Notice particularly a remark of Wittgenstein's in the passage just quoted: 'In a way, how are we to know whether to say he believes this will happen or not?' I have been pointing out why religious belief is more than the belief that something will happen, but ought one to have said that it is something not only different from, but exclusive of, a belief that something will happen? Wittgenstein evidently sees a problem here. Some recent writers[4] on religion have concerned themselves a good deal with the difference between belief-*in* and belief-*that*. They define belief-in as involving an affective attitude, or as having some commissive force, whereas they take belief-that to be expressible in non-affective, flatly constative terms. Now a religious belief is undoubtedly belief-*in*; but is it not by implication also belief-*that*? Can there, indeed, be belief-*in* without belief-*in*? This is the issue raised by Wittgenstein's remark to which I have just called attention. I will return to it in the next section (see pp. 175–83).

To get back to the lectures, Wittgenstein sees the religious believer as one who risks things on account of his belief which he would not risk on things which are far better established for him (see LRB p.54). By well established he means resting on an adequate amount of the kind of factual

169

evidence on which our ordinary common sense beliefs rest. We can hold beliefs which are very well grounded in that sort of evidence and yet not be prepared to risk anything, or forego anything, for the sake of them. On the other hand, we may be prepared to give up pleasures and hazard our very lives on a belief for which that sort of evidence is slender or non-existent. The firmness of a belief may be conceived in terms of either how much empirical evidence can be adduced for it or of how much the believer is prepared to risk for it. Religious beliefs are firm in the latter sense. Suppose people who could accurately foretell the future predicted some sort of Judgment Day and I believed them. Even if their evidence for saying that it would occur was very sound, even if this event occurred just as they predicted, my belief in their forecast 'wouldn't be at all a religious belief', according to Wittgenstein (LRB p.56). I might even agree with their prediction that 'if I do so and so, someone will put me in fires in a thousand years etc.' and still not 'budge' (ibid.). Mere assent to a prediction of a future event is not religious belief however strong the evidence for it. What am I prepared to risk for my belief? — that is the crucial question where religion is concerned. If you try to make it simply a matter of weighing the evidence for or against certain tenets, 'this would in fact destroy the whole business', says Wittgenstein (LRB p.56). He goes so far as to add, on behalf of the religious believer, 'Anything that I normally call evidence wouldn't in the slightest influence me, . . . a religious belief might in fact fly in the face of such a (sc. well-established) forecast' (LRB p.56). Christianity is said to have a historic basis, to rest on certain putatively historical facts such as the birth, crucifixion, and resurrection of Christ. But, says Wittgenstein, 'here we have a belief in historic facts different from a belief in ordinary historic facts.' (LRB p.57). Statements of these christian facts are not treated by believers simply as empirical propositions for which there is good evidence. Even if the evidence for them were as indubitable as that for the life and activities of Napoleon, 'the indubitability wouldn't be enough to make me change my whole life' (ibid.). And religious belief does imply a willingness to change one's whole life. It is not, or not simply, a matter of assenting to certain propositions for which there is deemed to be good evidence, but of being

170

ready to risk everything for the sake of one's beliefs.

We would usually call a belief reasonable when there is a certain weight of evidence to support it. Wittgenstein wonders, 'When you call it reasonable, is this *only* to say that for it you have such and such evidence . . . ?' (LRB p.57). Religious people base enormous things on evidence which would seem in any other context exceedingly flimsy. 'Am I to say they are unreasonable? (LRB p.58). He goes on:

> I would say, they are certainly not *reasonable*, that's obvious.
> 'Unreasonable' implies, with everyone, rebuke. I want to say: they don't treat this as a matter of reasonability.
> Anyone who reads the Epistles will find it said: not only that it is not reasonable, but that it is folly.
> Not only is it not reasonable, but it doesn't pretend to be.
> What seems to me ludicrous about O'Hara is his making it appear to be *reasonable*. (LRB p.58)

O'Hara, it will be recalled (see above p. 161), thought religious beliefs could be made a question of science. If 'reasonable' here means 'scientific', then all this quotation amounts to is that religion is not science and need not feel ashamed of itself on that account. But, of course, the question of the rationality of religion cannot be dismissed so lightheartedly, as Wittgenstein was well aware. I shall have more to say about rationality and religion in the next section (see pp. 183–7)

Religious belief is not, or not simply, a matter of weighing the evidence for or against certain propositions, and assenting or dissenting accordingly, but of holding a certain picture in mind and being moved by it affectively and conatively. As Wittgenstein said:

> As it were, the belief as formulated on the evidence can only be the last result – in which a number of ways of thinking and acting crystallize and come together.
> A man would fight for his life not to be dragged into the fire. No induction. Terror. That is, as it were part of the substance of the belief . . .
> Here believing obviously plays much more this role:

171

suppose we said that a certain picture might play the role of constantly admonishing me, or I always think of it. Here an enormous difference would be between those people for whom the picture is constantly in the foreground and others who just didn't use it at all. (LRB p.56)

The role which the picture plays may, however, be conceived as psychological, logical, or a combination of the two.

To hold a picture before the mind may be thought of as the way to produce certain psychological effects. Preachers used to hold verbal pictures of Hell fire before the minds of their congregations in order to produce conversion or good conduct; saintly men frequently concentrated their attention on the example of Christ with the intention of strengthening their will to imitate him. Some of the things which Wittgenstein says about using a picture — e.g. that it may constantly admonish one (cf. above) — suggest that he thought of the picture's role as psychological.

Other remarks, however, seem to indicate that he thought of it as logical. For example, he asks rhetorically, 'Why shouldn't one form of life culminate in an utterance of belief in a Last Judgment?' (LRB p.58). Beliefs such as that there will be a Last Judgment may constitute what has been variously described as a 'blik', or 'onlock' or 'end-statement'.[5] That is to say they may determine what counts as a religious explanation, or what characterises a religious experience. Says Wittgenstein:

> Suppose you had two people, and one of them, when he had to decide which course to take, thought of retribution and the other did not. One person might, for instance, be inclined to take everything that happened to him as a reward or punishment and another person doesn't think of this at all.
>
> If he is ill, he may think: "What have I done to deserve this?" This is one way of thinking of retribution. Another way is, he thinks in a general way whenever he is ashamed of himself: "This will be punished." (LRB pp. 54–5)

To say that a man believes that we live under the judgment of God means that when things go well for him he explains them as divine favours; when they go ill, as signs of God's wrath. He does not, for instance, *qua* religious believer, say simply 'This is bankruptcy' but 'This is punishment', or 'This is an unexpected legacy' but 'This is a blessing'. The examples are, of course, grossly simplistic but, however sophisticated we made them, the point would always emerge that a religious believer as such explains what happens in the world or in his own life in terms of the relationship with God in which he believes he and others stand. Moreover, the experiences which he has as a believer have the character which they have because he subscribes to certain beliefs. Wittgenstein's example of someone who, when he feels ashamed says to himself 'This will be punished' is a case in point. As a religious man, he feels not only remorse but alienation from God or sorrow at having offended God, when he reflects on his own misdemeanours. If he had no belief in God, it would be logically impossible for his experience to have this particular character. It is, then, a logical (not merely a psychological) fact that religious explanations and experiences are what they are because of the pictures which the believer uses.

Wittgenstein then, seems clearly to have thought of the role of the picture in both a psychological and a logical way. We have already noted his remark: 'A man would fight for his life not to be dragged into the fire. No induction. Terror. That is as it were, part of the substance of the belief.' (LRB p.56; cf. above p. 171). This describes the psychological effects which keeping a picture of the Last Judgment in mind may have. But then again we find Wittgenstein affirming that the believer and unbeliever cannot contradict one another and this suggests that there is some logical distinction between them; that the picture plays a logical role in the believer's thinking which it does not play in the unbeliever's. He says:

> Take two people one of whom talks of his behaviour and what happens to him in terms of retribution, the other one does not. These people think entirely differently. Yet, so far, you can't say they believe different things.
>
> Suppose someone is ill and he says: "This is a punishment", and I say: "If I'm ill, I don't think of

173

punishment at all." If you say "Do you believe the opposite?" — you can call it believing the opposite, but it is entirely different from what we would normally call believing the opposite.

I think differently, in a different way. I say different things to myself. I have different pictures. (LRB p.55)

In what sense can one *not* say that believers and unbelievers believe different things? Surely that is precisely what they do! No: Wittgenstein points out that the difference between them is not simply a matter of the believers affirming certain propositions and the unbelievers denying them, or *vice versa*. That is what we normally call believing the opposite. But believers and unbelievers, by contrast, think of things in different, rather than opposite, ways. 'If you ask me whether or not I believe in a Judgment Day' says Wittgenstein, 'in the sense in which religious people have belief in it, I wouldn't say: "No I don't believe there will be such a thing." It would seem to me utterly crazy to say this' (LRB p.55). He does not mean, of course, that he would subscribe to the belief. The clue to what he does mean is in the next words: 'And then I give an explanation: "I don't believe in . . . ", but then the religious person never believes what I describe.' (ibid.) The point Wittgenstein appears to be making is that when an unbeliever says what it is that he does not believe, this is never what the believer would say that he does believe. An unbeliever may say, for instance, that he does not believe in an after-life and when asked to explain may say 'I don't believe that we shall go on living to be 200, 300 . . . , and so on, years old.' 'But that's not what I mean by an after-life!' says the believer, 'Eternity is timelessness, not endless duration!' (cf. above p. 94).

We must not say, then, that a believer in, for example, a Last Judgment, simply affirms, whereas an unbeliever denies, the statement, 'There will be a Last Judgment.' Wittgenstein says: 'But I couldn't either say "Yes" or "No" to the statement that there will be such a thing. Nor "Perhaps", nor "I'm not sure." It is a statement which may not allow of any such answer' (LRB p.58). The reason he gave is (as we have already seen) that this utterance may be the culmination of a form of life. Believers and unbelievers cannot contradict one another because they do not share the same 'form of life.' It is not that they disagree about some proposition within a form of life, but that they refuse to say the same kind of things as each other.

Such a refusal is different from contradicting one another. If someone says 'God is wise' we are entitled to presume that he thinks God exists; but, by tne same token, if 'God is not wise' is intended as a contradiction, we are entitled to assume that the speaker also takes God to exist. The essential difference between believers and unbelievers is not that sort of difference. It is that the unbeliever refuses to participate in the believer's form of life at all. Does it follow that because the unbeliever cannot contradict the believer, this means that he does not understand him? Is it necessary, as many have said, to believe in religion in order to understand it? Wittgenstein faces this question but says it is Greek to him — 'My normal technique of language leaves me. I don't know whether to say they understand one another or not' (LRB p.55). To this question of the connexion between belief and understanding I come back below (p. 192).

III. SOME QUESTIONS WHICH ARISE
The Existence of God

Contemporary writers on religious belief, as I remarked above (p. 169) are wont to draw a distinction between believing *in* God and believing *that* God exists. As ordinarily used, the expressions 'believe-in' and 'believe-that' can be differentiated as follows.[6] If I say that I believe in somebody, or something, I may be taken thereby (a) to recognise that the existence of that in which I believe is a matter of some dispute; or (b) to commit myself in trust or loyalty to that in which I believe; or both. For example, if I say 'I believe in Martians', I will normally be taken to mean no more than that I believe such creatures to exist: this illustrates (a). But if I say 'I believe in human beings', I will normally be taken to mean that I am prepared to trust their honesty, good sense, or whatever: this illustrates (b). When a religious believer says 'I believe in God; he is normally taken both (a) to recognise by this form of expression that God's existence is a matter which many not unreasonable people doubt, and (b) either to commit himself thereby, or express the fact that he has already committed

175

himself, in trust to God. No one who professed to believe in God would normally be taken merely to be affirming his belief that God exists, as he would be taken to affirm no more than belief in the existence of Martians if he said that he believed in them; but neither would he be taken merely to be committing himself in trust to a being whose existence is not in doubt, as he would if he said, for instance, 'I believe in my lawyer'.

Religious belief, then, is belief *in* God, and as such is something more than the belief that God exists. An affirmation of religious belief, where the speaker is sincere and knows the meanings of the words which he is using, has what J. L. Austin called performative illocutionary force. *In* affirming this belief the speaker is doing something other than, or more than, simply stating a putative fact. The illocutionary force of his speech-act is, to use Austin's expressions, behabitive, verdictive, commissive, and possibly other things as well. Behabitive, in that it expresses an attitude of gratitude to God;[7] verdictive in that it registers, or re-registers, a decision to embrace religion;[8] commisive, in that it commits the speaker to certain courses of action.[9] The ground for the claim that affirmations of belief have these kinds of illocutionary force is the logical oddness of utterances which implicitly deny it. How strange it would sound if someone said 'I believe in God but I have no feelings towards him'; or 'I believe in God but I am still not sure whether to take up religion'; or 'I believe in God but I am not prepared to serve him'! We should assume that the speaker in such cases either was insincere or did not understand the behabitive, verdictive, or commissive meaning of what he was saying. It should be noted in passing that religious belief is belief in God in the sense which I have just been explaining, whether the affirmation of it occurs as part of some religious ritual, as e.g. when the Creed is recited in a service, or in the course of ordinary conversation, as e.g. when a believer affirms his faith to a friend. Again, it is so whether the performative force of the affirmation is explicit as in the speech-act 'I believe in God's love', or implicit as in the speech-act 'God is love'.[10] Yet again, it is so whether religious belief is expressed in words which purport to be addressed to its object e.g. in a prayer; or to those other than its object,

176

e.g. in preaching or testimony.

What I have been saying so far is that the affirmation of religious belief, whatever else it may or may not be, includes the expression of affective and conative attitudes. Wittgenstein was well aware of this. As for affective attitudes; he speaks of terror as 'part of the substance of the belief' in a Last Judgment (LRB p.56); of religious belief, as 'the case where there is hope, terror, etc.' (LRB p.62); and of 'how he (i.e. the religious believer) reacts, that he is in terror, etc.' (ibid.) as part of the criterion by which we determine what the believer means by his affirmation of belief (cf. above pp. 171–2). As for conative attitudes, Wittgenstein describes the religious believer as 'the man [who] risks things on account of it (sc. his religious belief) which he would not do on things which are by far better established for him' (LRB p.54): and he says that 'the measure for the firmness of a belief' in religion is 'what risks would you take (sc. for the sake of it)?' (ibid.). Wittgenstein, however, recognised that religious belief cannot be equated with the expression of certain attitudes: '"No, it isn't the same as saying 'I'm very fond of you"' – and it may not be the same as saying anything else. It says what it says. Why should you be able to substitute anything else?' (LRB p.71).

The question which this last passage raises is: what is expressed by an affirmation of belief in God *beyond* an affective or conative attitude? As my remarks so far have occasionally implied, at least part of the answer is that it expresses the belief that God exists.

Belief-in normally implies belief-that. If I say that I believe in my lawyer, I shall be taken to imply a belief that he exists and has certain qualities. There are cases where I could believe in something without believing that it exists: for instance, 'I believe in victory', said in the course of some campaign, makes sense as it would not if victory were already gained. But unless we are speaking in terms of highly sophisticated 'life force' or 'process theology' conceptions of God, it is not with such cases that belief in God must be compared. As the words are normally used, it would sound exceedingly odd if anyone said 'I believe in God but I do not believe that he exists or is trustworthy'. Belief that God exists and has certain characteristics is a necessary condition

177

of belief in God.

It has been important to state this clearly because some recent writers seem to think that, because religious belief is belief in God, the troublesome problem of whether or not he exists may be set aside. Professor Norman Malcolm,[11] for example, asks rhetorically: would a belief that God exists, divorced from any affective or conative attitude towards him. be 'anything at all'? He thinks not because it would enter into no form of life, make no difference to anyone, and be of no interest, not even to God. If Malcolm's point were simply that religious belief is more than the belief that God exists, we could have no quarrel with him. But he is expressly making this point against philosophers who think it important to settle the question whether God exists or not, before deciding whether or not to trust him. That question cannot be brushed aside. It may be that one will never know that God exists unless one adopts certain conative or affective attitudes towards him on the assumption that he does. But to say this is not to deny that the question 'Does God exist?' makes perfectly good sense, and is logically distinct from the question 'Shall I trust him?' Indeed, the statement 'You cannot discover whether God exists or not unless you trust him' would not be informative, unless there were a logical distinction between what it is to know that God exists and what it is to trust him. The statement I refer to could, of course, be tautologous. But I do not think that Malcolm would consider it to be so, for he says simply that a belief *that* God exists enters no form of life, etc., *if it is 'logically independent'*[12] of any and all ways of regarding God (i.e. of all conative or affective attitudes towards him), not unless it is synonymous with some such ways.

If belief that God exists is the necessary condition of belief in God, the question which next arises is: what constitutes belief that God exists? It may be that Malcolm took himself to be answering this question; and in so far at least as he indicated that it is not as simple as it appears we can go along with him. Wittgenstein says in his lectures: 'If the question arises as to the existence of a god or God, it plays an entirely different role to that of the existence of any person or object I ever heard of' (LRB p.59). To say that god or God exists is not to say the same kind of thing as that a person or object within the world exists. The reasons which Wittgenstein gives for this contention in the context, it will be recalled (see above p. 158), were that it is considered reprehensible by religious people to disbelieve in the existence of God; and that one does not find people saying in religion 'You only believe – oh well! . . . .' as if there were something better than believing, namely knowing. These reasons call attention to certain differences between religious belief and other forms of discourse. Wittgenstein, to the same effect, goes on to discuss at length the difference between the way 'evidence' is used to support religious belief and the way in which it is used to establish scientific or common sense beliefs (see above pp. 158–62). His lectures are throughout this kind of investigation into the logical syntax of religious belief, i.e. into its 'grammar' (see above p. 63). The aim of such an inquiry is to establish 'what kind of object' (pp. 62–7 above) the object of religious belief is. Wittgenstein's conclusion was that this object is not the same kind of object as any person or thing and whatever it may be for this object to exist, it is not the same kind of thing as for them to exist.

What then is the object of religious belief? My own view, which I have stated in my *A Philosophical Approach to Religion* (London, 1974) is that religious belief is constituted in the last analysis by the concept of transcendent conscious- ✓ ness and agency. I call this the concept of god (with a small 'g'). The word 'transcendent' I define in this connexion as follows: 'By saying that divine consciousness and agency are *transcendent*, I mean, to put it in a nutshell, that there is always more to god's consciousness or activity than to man's. God's understanding is more acute than man's or, at least, more guileful; god's activity is more powerful, or at least more effective. But not only is there, so to speak, more of the same kind of thing to god. Transcendence, as I am thinking of it here, is the special (let us say supernatural) character, which whatever is god is always conceived to have whereby god does not have to conform to all the (logical) conditions to which men have to conform in order to be conscious or active. For instance, the stick or stone within which the animist's god dwells does not need any physical sense, such as sight, hearing, touch, etc., in order to be communicated with; and again, the god of theism does not

179

need a body in order to be active in the world' (op. cit. pp. 14–16). The particular content given to the concept of god within religions varies widely, of course; but anything said within religious belief is said in terms of god. If a belief is religious, then it is a belief which involves transcendent consciousness and agency of some kind. In Wittgenstein's terminology, I think that the concept of god is the 'tacit presupposition' (PI p.179; cf. above pp. 57–9) of religious belief. I would compare it in this regard to the concepts of moral obligation and physical objectivity. Anything said within morality is said in terms of moral obligation. Of course, there is dispute amongst moral philosophers as to the account which must be given of the logic of moral discourse, but that it is moral obligation which they are seeking to understand — i.e. what makes morality morality as distinct from science, or religion, or whatever — is not in dispute. Similarly anything said in physical science is said in terms of physical objectivity; and whilst philosophers of science may disagree about the logic of scientific discovery, they do not dispute that physical science is concerned with spatio-temporally identifiable phenomena and these alone. In a comparable manner, religious belief is constituted by the concept of god and the concern of philosophers of religion is to discover the grammar, or logic, of god.

Now it is important to see that the question of the existence of God may arise on two levels. On the first, to put it summarily, 'Does God exist?' means 'Is God god?' That is to say, it is a question *within* religious belief. There are many different religions and within each, many varieties of belief. Religious people discuss their differing beliefs with one another and sometimes at least recognise ways of resolving differences. If 'God' stands for what any religious believer takes to be the nature of god, then within religion the question can arise as to whether he is correct in his view. This question is a religious one. 'Does God (in this sense) exist?' means simply 'Is God god?' — i.e. 'Is this what we should take god to be?' It may illuminate what I am saying here about religion to compare it with what could be said about morality. Utilitarians and existentialists, for instance, may argue as to whether moral obligation consists in maximising happiness of exercising freedom of choice. Such arguments

180

presuppose the existence of moral obligation and are simply concerned with what it is. Similarly, the question 'Is God god?' presupposes the existence of god, i.e. of transcendent consciousness and agency, and is concerned simply with whether or not there are good religious reasons for giving a particular content, viz. that given to 'God' by theists, to the concept of god.

On what I have chosen to call the second level, the question about the existence of God becomes 'Does god really exist?' That is to say: does talk in terms of god correspond to objective reality? Just as we may say 'Yes, of course men talk about moral obligation, but is there really any such thing?', or 'There is indeed such a thing as physical science but does it describe appearance or reality?', so we could say 'There is undoubtedly a universe of discourse constituted by the concept of god but are those who participate in it merely exercising their imagination or are they speaking of something which really exists?' Philosophical attempts to prove, or disprove, the existence of God have been *au fond* concerned with this question. It is notoriously difficult to answer.

One problem about it is where to go for an answer. It is logically impossible to take this question into religious belief because everything said in that universe of discourse presupposes the existence of god. Moreover, if god is by definition, not a physical object, or a moral obligation, or whatever, then it is also logically impossible to take the question of god's existence into non-religious universes of discourses.

At this impasse, it is tempting to take a short way with the question of god's existence and to equate it with the existence of religious discourse: to say, as Professor D.Z. Phillips for instance, does, 'Discovering that there is a God . . . is to discover that there *is* a universe of discourse we had been unaware of.'[13] There undoubtedly exists a way of *talking* which is constituted by the concept of god, but to take the existence of this universe of discourse as establishing the real existence of god looks like chicanery. When philosophers and others ask whether god exists or not, the last thing they are wondering is whether religious discourse exists or not, since their question can only arise on the

181

assumption that it does. If there is indeed nowhere to go for an answer to the question 'Does god really exist?', then it may be fair to dismiss that question as meaningless. But to regard it — as Phillips seems to do — as answered in the affirmative by the mere existence of talk in terms of god seems singularly unhelpful.

I do not think that the question is meaningless, but I think that there are certain peculiarites about it which must be recognised. If I decide that anything really exists, then I must do so in accordance with certain criteria for the use of 'really exists'. For instance, within physical science the criterion of real existence is, to put it as briefly as possible, actual spatio-temporal identification. But it makes sense to ask 'Do physical objects (i.e. those things which have been actually identified within space and time) really exist?', provided that some coherent criterion of real existence other than actual spatio-temporal identification is proposed. It is not inconceivable that such a criterion should be proposed. Let us call it C. Then the question will mean 'Are physical objects instances of the fulfilment of C?' But then we may ask 'Do what are instances of the fulfilment of C really exist?', provided we propose another coherent criterion of real existence. And so *ad infinitum*. As I have suggested elsewhere,[14] there is an 'indefinability' to 'really exists' which is not unlike the indefinability which G.E. Moore attributed to 'good' (though I do not wish to compare the two expressions in any respect beyond this). It follows that no one can ever say that his view of what really exists is not open to question; but it does *not* follow that questions about what really exists are meaningless (any more than questions about what is good are). Our answer to 'Does god really exist?', if affirmative, will rest in the last analysis upon what may be called an ontological choice, i.e. a decision as to what the criteria of real existence shall be taken to be. Is the same true of a negative answer to this question? It may be; but here I think there is more to be said. In so far as the god to whom our question refers should turn out to be the subject of logically impossible claims, then we may say with finality that he does not exist. That which is logically impossible is not existentially possible. In order to claim that anything can exist, we must be able to form some concept of it, otherwise our claim

182

has no meaning. In so far as god is the subject of logically impossible claims, he is inconceivable. And in so far as he is inconceivable, he cannot be conceived as existing.

Is God, or god, the subject of logically impossible claims? This question of the intelligibility of religious language is one to which we must next turn.

The Intelligibility of Religious Discourse

Religion is often rejected on the ground that it is unintelligible. That is to say, because the language in which it is expressed, seems to be strained to breaking point. Many people, for example, would consider the meaning of the word 'good' to be extended out of existence when the creator of a world as full of pain as this is called good. The Wittgenstein of the *Lectures* would no doubt have replied to such an objection that when religious believers say that God is good they are not entertaining a hypothesis to be proved or disproved by the empirical evidence in the world. If they were it would be 'all superstition' (LRB p.59). To suppose that religious believers have failed to notice how heavily the evidence would weigh against such a hypothesis is to suppose them guilty of a blunder which is just too big (cf. LRB p.62). Some apologists[15] for religion have, of course, attempted to establish religious belief in the way that scientific hypotheses are established, but believers do not use the idea of God as scientists use a hypothesis (LRB p.57). It is not something to test (cf. LRB p.60), to support by empirical evidence (cf. LRB p.56). So to conceive of it is to 'destroy the whole business' (ibid.).

In the spirit of Wittgenstein's *Lectures*, some contemporary philosophers have undertaken to defend religion against the charge of incoherence. D.Z. Phillips, for instance, draws freely and impressively on the *Lectures* in his *Death and Immortality* (London, 1970). He is replying to those who dismiss belief in immortality on the ground that it is self-contradictory to hold that someone can be dead in the ordinary sense of 'dead' and yet meet with others after death. This criticism, according to Phillips, uproots belief in immortality from its natural setting and so misconceives of it. Religious believers would regard as boringly irrelevant questions about how or where those who are dead can meet each other. Their picture of immortality is not meant to be used in that way. It is not a conjecture or prediction about what will happen to men after death; evidence which would ordinarily count for or against conjectures or predictions about the future course of events is ignored here. Believing in life after death has to do with how a man lives now. Phillips cites Wittgenstein's words about having 'the picture constantly in the foreground', and speaks of drawing sustenance from it, judging others by it, being afraid of it, etc.[16] What is important is the religious and ethical role which the picture plays in the believer's life. Phillips, as a variant on Wittgenstein's illustration of the boy who felt that not even death could take away his obligation to complete the task which his father had given him (see above p. 163), supposes a man who pictures certain deceased members of his family reunited in heaven and feels an obligation to do what will be pleasing in their eyes.[17] To get a clear idea of what religious people are saying when they say that we do not cease to exist at death, we must recognise that this is the kind of role which the picture plays. It keeps them mindful of their obligation to treat others 'in the equality which death will reveal'.[18] In so far as they keep the picture in the forefront of their minds, they 'will make decisions and react in ways very unlike the man who holds ideas such as that everyone has his own life to live, that the old have had their chance and should make way for the young, that no one should stand in anyone else's way and so on'.[19] Still drawing on Wittgenstein's lectures, Phillips insists that we must not treat religious pictures as substitutes for something else, in the way that pictures of aunts are substitutes for aunts in the flesh.[20] The truth of these pictures is not figurative, simply because truth can be identified as figurative only when it can be contrasted with truth which would be literal, and in this instance that cannot be done. Interpreted literally belief in life after death does not make sense. The truth of the pictures - the literal truth, if you like - says Phillips is the role they play in changing someone's whole life.[21] It is hard to dispel the feeling that there is some sleight of hand in his argument here: literally they can't be true, so figuratively they can't be true, so literally they must be true! But however that may be, we can sympathise with Phillips on the

184

main point, that religious language, to quote Wittgenstein, 'says what it says' and so 'why should you be able to substitute anything else?'.[22] The logical distinctiveness of religious discourse seems evident to Phillips from the fact that those who use it are not available to the argument that they should cease to do so because it is incoherent. Believers do not give up religion because they are shown that it is self-contradictory to say of anyone that he is both dead and meets with others in heaven, or because it is pointed out to them that what they quote as evidence for a Last Judgment is unlike anything we call evidence in science. When they cease to use their religious pictures it is not for such reasons, or not usually. It is because of personal tragedies in which they find no comfort from the pictures, moral revulsion for the people or the pictures associated with religion, the mere realisation that the pictures have ceased to mean anything to them, etc. Phillips recognises that societies, no less than individuals, interpret their lives in terms of certain pictures and these may become obsolete and get forgotten (cf. PI 23). He contends that, if religious pictures suffer this fate, something irreplaceable dies with them; this point he takes to be the force of Wittgenstein's remark that 'the whole *weight* may be in the picture' (LRB p.72). If, for example, the picture of marriage as made in heaven is replaced by that of marriage as an experiment, then certain ways of acting and reacting go with it. Nothing can substitute for the religious picture of marriage in the sense of saying precisely what it says about marriage.[23]

Religious discourse is certainly distinct from other kinds of discourse. But is it logically self-contained? Its pictures, true enough, are not pictures of something else which can be identified apart from them, like pictures of aunts, but that is hardly the point. In so far as these pictures are expressed in language, the words used are not exclusive to this context. When religious believers speak of the dead meeting in heaven, they must mean by 'dead' what we all mean at least to a degree which justifies their use of this word rather than any other. Some logical limitation is placed on what they may, or may not, say by this fact. It is true, as Phillips observes, that believers do not normally give up religion because of philosophical arguments purporting to show that their use of language breaks too many of the rules for its ordinary use;

185

but the question is, ought they not to do so? I spoke above (pp. 54–7) about the ultimacy of the forms of life in which men participate so far as what they find it intelligible or justifiable to say is concerned. But can *one* form of life isolate itself from the rest and claim such a logical ultimacy *of its own*? Surely not, if the language used to constitute it is common to other forms of life as well, as most, if not all, of the language used to express religious beliefs is. Wittgenstein in the lectures (see above pp. 164–5)differentiated between the public and the private use of 'death' and insisted that any believer who claimed to have his own private idea of death must be told that if this has nothing in common with the public idea, i.e. 'the game played with "death", which we all know and understand' (LRB p.69), then it is of no interest to unbelievers. 'It must' he says 'become part of our game' (ibid., cf. above p. 164). But, once it does so, it must conform, to some degree at least, to the rules of that public game.

Most philosophers of religion would concede the force of this. Phillips himself does so in his paper 'Religious Beliefs and Language Games'.[24] Where there is disagreement among philosophers of religion it has to do with the implications of this concession. The concession has to be made on two closely related levels.

The first level concerns the *subject-matter* of religion, i.e. *what it is about*. In one sense the subject-matter of religion is its own distinctive concern, namely god; but here I am thinking of what it is about in another sense. Anything may form part of the subject-matter of religion though most characteristically religion has to do with personal relationships within the home, the church, the neighbourhood, or private experiences such as a feeling of responsibility, the fear of death, suffering, and so on. In so far as what it says is about these things, what is meant by them in religion must be the same as what is meant elsewhere,[25] otherwise what religion says will be unintelligible and irrelevant. True, it frequently says that something is not what it has been taken to be: e.g. suffering is not just a misery but a discipline; death, not an end but a beginning; and so on. Within religion the relationships and experiences of life are given a new meaning, but it must be a meaning which they will bear. It

186

lights up suffering to say that it is a necessity which may be turned to glorious gain; or death, to claim that it is not a sleep but an awaking. We can all see some point in such remarks whether or not we agree with them. But to say that suffering is a Sunday dinner, or death a ride in a motor-car would be pointless (unless, of course, one's wife was an execrable cook or a frightful driver!). In transforming the meaning of things, religion must understand them to be what they are, not something outrageously removed from that.[26]

The second level at which the concession has to be made concerns the *language in which what religion has to say about its subject-matter is expressed*. When I say, for example, that suffering may bring gain, or death be an awaking, what I mean by 'gain' or 'awaking' must not be so far removed from what I mean when I speak of capital appreciation as a gain, or coming out of sleep when the alarm clock rings as awaking, that there is no reason why I should use the same words - 'gain' and 'awaking' respectively - in each case. The objection which philosophers hostile to religion raise is that it inevitably destroys the significance of the language it uses 'by a thousand qualifications'.[27] I do not think that the only way of dealing with this objection is to agree with it, and then claim that it does not matter because religious believers are not perturbed by it, which seems to be Phillips' way. I think religious beliefs, or some of them, can be expressed in language which is not strained to breaking point in the process. I have, for example, ventured elsewhere[28] to argue that it is possible to take 'omnipotent' and 'good' in senses which do no violence to their ordinary meanings and still say significantly that God is good and omnipotent despite the evil in the world. Whether such attempts to defend religious belief are successful or not is, and has long been, a matter of much debate. And rightly so. For it is the only way of deciding whether or not religious belief can 'become part of our game'. If it cannot, then what follows is not that it is interestingly or significantly different from other universes of discourse, but that it is incoherent and unworthy of the attention of rational men.

The Logical Use of the Picture
Wittgenstein speaks of religious belief as using a picture, or

187

pictures. The pictures concerned are, of course, mental ones. What is meant by using them? As I noted above, (p. 172) the use may be either psychological or logical. To use a picture *psychologically* is to hold it before one's own or someone else's mind for the sake of the mental or spiritual effects which it produces. Wittgenstein, as we saw (above p. 169), said that the picture of the Last Judgement, if kept in the foreground of consciousness, can regulate for all in one's life and constantly admonish one. Very often religious pictures are held in mind by believers for the sake of the strength which they give to the will or the purity which they preserve in the heart. To use a picture *logically*, on the other hand, is something quite different. Wittgenstein spoke of the 'technique' of using a religious picture and said that it consists in learning certain 'connections' (LRB pp. 70–1; cf. above p. 162). These connexions seem, from his illustrations to have been of two distinct kinds. First, there are the arbitrary ones. Spiritualists are said to 'make a connection' with talk of men surviving death by their talk of apparitions (LRB p.70; see above p. 163); and the 'great writer' made one when he put the idea of responsibility together with that of immortality (ibid.). These are logical connexions but of a somewhat arbitrary kind. Disembodied spirits are a logically quite distinct concept from spiritualistic materialisations; moral responsibility is not at all the same kind of thing as living eternally. Such connexions, whilst logical in the sense of providing a use or meaning for the expression, are arbitrary in the sense of idiosyncratic to their religious context. But when Wittgenstein goes on to ask what conclusions are to be drawn from the picture of the Eye of God, and specifically, whether eyebrows are going to be talked of in this connexion (LRB p.71; cf. above p. 165), the case is different. The connexion between eyes and eyebrows is not peculiar to religious contexts. To say that some being has an eye normally creates the presumption that he also has eyebrows. The connexion arises from the ordinary meaning of the word 'eye'. It is a non-arbitrary one.

When Wittgenstein says that believers must learn the technique of using religious pictures, therefore, what he meant could be any of at least four things. It could be learning psychological techniques of concentration so that

188

the picture will stay in the foreground of one's own mind; or of persuasion, so that one can hold it tellingly before the minds of others. Again, it could be learning certain arbitrary logical connexions in accordance with which the picture is used; or recognising which of the ordinary logical implications of the terms employed to express the picture must be drawn out and which not.

In so far as the use of the picture is logical, it must be possible to put it into words. To say, 'This is what the picture means . . .' and supply either a definition or statement. For instance, 'By "life after death" I mean spiritualistic apparitions or absolute moral responsibility'; or 'When I talk about the picture, God's eye, I mean the proposition "God has an eye" '. In so far as religious pictures are expressed in statements, we may ask, on the one hand, whether or not they can be verified, and on the other, what their entailments and incompatibles are (cf. above pp. 165—6). Religious pictures, such as 'There will be a Last Judgment', 'We might see one another after death', 'God has an eye', were taken by Wittgenstein to be either unverifiable or verifiable in ways quite different from those in which scientific or common sense statements are verified, e.g. by dreams. To learn this about them is to learn something about their logical use. As for their entailments and incompatibles, these may follow either from arbitrary stipulative definitions which are given to the statements or from the ordinary meanings of the words employed to make them. Wittgenstein seems to leave room for either kind of implication. If 'I shall survive death' means 'I cannot evade this responsibility' (cf. LRB p.70), then its entailments and incompatibles will be different from what they would be if it had its normal meaning, viz. 'I shall go on living after my heart stops beating'. But, by contrast, the question whether we should deduce from 'God has an eye' that he also has eyebrows (cf. LRB p.71) is a question about the implications of the word 'eye' as ordinarily used. Learning the logical use of a picture is learning what conclusions to draw, and what not to draw, from either the stipulative or the ordinary definitions of the words used to express it. The technique of using religious pictures, in a logical sense of 'using', has, therefore, something to do with reasoning.

189

√ When Wittgenstein says that he would not call religious beliefs either reasonable or unreasonable (LRB p.58, cf. above p. 171) he can hardly have been denying what I have called their logical use. Or if he was, this denial is at variance with other things he plainly says. To use the picture is, on the one hand, to adduce the kind of evidence which is taken to be evidence of its appropriateness; and, on the other, to make inferences from it which are appropriate to the occasion. Both these activities can be described as reasoning in a perfectly ordinary sense of the word. Though not, of course, as scientific or common sense reasoning because these latter descriptions refer to universes of discourse which are clearly distinct from religion. Religion does not pretend to fit into either of them. That I take to be the point which Wittgenstein was making in his remarks about reasonability.

So far as drawing out the entailments and incompatibles of religious pictures is concerned, it is useful to differentiate, as I have done elsewhere,[29] between the use of a picture which is given in, or definitive of, a religion on the one hand, and the use to which adherents of a religion may put a picture in their reflections or disagreements, on the other. For example, within Christianity it is taken for granted that at the Last Judgment the Judge will be just. Is injustice going to be talked of in connexion with the judgment of God? Of course not: the question makes no sense because God's justice is part of the use of the picture of God which is given in, definitive of, Christianity. Sophisticated believers can be found arguing, however, about such matters as what conclusion should, or should not, be drawn from the 'last' in 'Last Judgment'. Should we take this picture to imply simply that human history will reach some temporal dénouement; or that the judgment of God on human beings takes place here and now but is final in the sense simply that it cannot be gainsaid? Neither conclusion is definitive of Christianity in the way that the justice of God is.Individually and collectively, religious believers use pictures in this latter sense of trying to infer from them the conclusions which shed most light on their own conditions or problems. That is how religious doctrine develops and religious devotion deepens.

What is it to be a Religious Believer?

Wittgenstein was intent upon pointing out the difference between religious believers and unbelievers. The main point which emerges from his treatment of this subject, I think, is that the difference is constituted by belief itself and is not a heterogeneous consequence of it. Mr. Rush Rhees[30] compares it in this respect to the difference which being in love makes. It would be stupid to ask a young man what he had got out of being in love as though it needed to be justified by certain effects. One might ask of other things, psychiatry say, what good they do, but it would hardly be taken as the same kind of inquiry, if someone asked what good being in love does. As Wittgenstein said of the happy man in the *Tractatus*, his world waxes and wanes as a whole (6.43). The world of the religious man does so too in the sense that the whole difference between believers and unbelievers lies in being in it or not being in it. So, what does it mean to be in it?

The answer which emerges from the *Lectures* is, I think, threefold. (i) The believer's use of certain pictures is *explanatory*. These can give a significance to everything in his life - set it so to speak in the dimension of God - which is totally lacking in the unbeliever's life. (ii) The believer's use of his pictures is *commissive*. He risks things for the sake of them. In so far as he does this sincerely they change not only his understanding of life, but the value judgments he forms, the decisions he makes, and the deeds he does. (iii) The believer's use of his pictures is *affective*. Pity, terror, awe, etc. are part of the substance of his beliefs. In saying these things to himself he not only explains, or commits, his life, but he gives it a distinctive feeling-tone. From all three of these characteristics the unbeliever is excluded.

Can the unbeliever contradict the believer? Wittgenstein evidently thought not. Speaking for the unbeliever he says:

In one sense, I understand all he says — the English words "God", "separate", etc. I understand I could say: "I don't believe in this," and this would be true, meaning I haven't got these thoughts or anything that hangs together with them. But not that I could contradict the thing.

You might say: "Well, if you can't contradict him, that means you don't understand him. If you did understand

191

him, then you might." That again is Greek to me. My normal technique of language leaves me. I don't know whether to say they understand one another or not. (LRB p.55)

The unbeliever could understand what it is for the three characteristics of the believer, which I have listed above, to be fulfilled. If this were not possible, then none but believers could understand my way of differentiating believers from unbelievers, and that seems absurd. But the unbeliever does not *share in* the believer's explanatory, commissive, affective use of the relevant pictures; and in that sense, these pictures do not have the meaning for him which they have for the believer. The point to take is that the unbeliever does not *use* the pictures as the believer does and this is not a matter of the one contradicting the other.

The sense in which the unbeliever cannot contradict the believer may be illuminated by recalling the ground on which Professor P.F. Strawson attempted to dispose of Russell's Theory of Descriptions. Russell had propounded this theory to rebut what seemed to him the absurd argument that because a significant statement such as 'The king of France is wise' must be either true or false, *and* because it can only be true or false, if there is a king of France who is either wise or not wise, *therefore* there must (in some sense or some world) be something which is the king of France. Against this, Russell maintained that 'The king of France is wise' is a complex existential proposition of which the elements are three: (i) 'There is a king of France', (ii) 'There is not more than one king of France', (iii) 'There is nothing which is king of France and is not wise'. Assertion (i) is false and this is enough to render the complex existential proposition as a whole false. The sentence 'The king of France is wise' is thus shown to be significant but false, and so there is no need to postulate something which is the king of France in order to save its significance. Strawson's criticism,[31] invites us to think what we would do if someone, having said 'The king of France is wise', asked us whether we considered what he had said to be true or false. We should say that we did not consider it to be either because, since there is no king of France, the question whether or not he is wise simply does

192

not arise. Strawson argues that, whilst anyone who said 'The king of France is wise', would normally be taken to believe that there is a king of France, his statement *does not logically entail* that there is, as Russell supposed, because if in reply to it we said 'But there is no king of France', we should *not* consider ourselves, or be considered by others, to have *contradicted* the speaker. We should not be saying that what he had said is false. We should be saying that the question of its truth or falsity simply does not arise. Russell found unacceptable the implication of this argument, viz. that statements can be significant even though they are neither true nor false. He said: 'Suppose, for example, that in some country there was a law that no person could hold public office if he considered it false that the Ruler of the Universe is wise. I think an avowed atheist who took advantage of Mr. Strawson's doctrine to say that he did not hold this proposition false, would be regarded as a somewhat shifty character.'[32] Well, he might be so regarded by the unsophisticated. But it does not require a great deal of sophistication to recognise that an unbeliever is someone who rejects the believer's whole form of life rather than contradicts his beliefs. Russell regarded all significant statements as either true or false. Strawson[33] appears to think that one cannot say whether a sentence is true or false until one knows the 'form of life' to which it belongs and to know this one must understand its use in the sense just defined (cf. PI 241). Applying this to religious belief we should say that an unbeliever is someone who rejects the whole religious 'form of life' rather than someone who can participate in it to the extent of calling the believer's assertions false. Strictly speaking, to contradict another person is to utter the negation of what he has asserted. Unbelief is not accurately described if it is defined as the contradiction, in this strict sense, of belief.

Notes and References

Chapter 1

1. The biographical material used in this chapter has been gleaned from the following sources: B. Russell, 'Ludwig Wittgenstein', *Mind*, 1951; G. Ryle, 'Ludwig Wittgenstein', *Analysis*, 1951–2; G.E.M. Anscombe, 'What Wittgenstein really said', *Tablet*, 17 April 1954; B. Russell, 'Philosophers and Idiots', *Listener*, 1955; K. Britton, 'Portrait of a Philosopher', *Listener*, 1955; Letter from G.D. Arnold, *Listener*, 1955; N. Malcolm, *Ludwig Wittgenstein : a Memoir* (with a biographical sketch by G.H. von Wright) (London, 1958); E. Heller, M.O'C. Drury, N. Malcolm, R. Rhees, 'Ludwig Wittgenstein : a Symposium', *Listener*, 1960; G. Pitcher,*The Philosophy of Wittgenstein* (Englewood Cliffs, N.J., 1964); P. Engelmann, *Letters from Ludwig Wittgenstein* (with a Memoir) (Oxford, 1967); F.R. Leavis, 'Memories of Wittgenstein', *The Human World*, 1973; W.W. Bartley, *Wittgenstein* (London, 1973); A. Janik and S. Toulmin, *Wittgenstein's Vienna* (London, 1973).

Chapter 2

1. T p.5.
2. PI p.x.
3. E.g. A. Kenny, *Wittgenstein* (1973) chapter 12.
4. E.g. D.F. Pears, *Wittgenstein* (London, 1971) p.95.
5. T p.3.
6. 'Notes on Logic', Appendix I to *Notebooks 1914–16* (Oxford, 1961) p.93.
7. Ibid., p.79.
8. L. Wittgenstein, *Letters to C.K. Ogden* (Oxford, 1973) p.20.

9. Ibid., p.86
10. 'Biographical Sketch', *Phil. Rev.* 1955, reprinted in N. Malcolm, *Ludwig Wittgenstein* (London, 1958) pp. 7—8.
11. *Notebooks 1914—16*, p.7
12. Ibid., p.7n.
13. *A Companion to Wittgenstein's Tractatus* (Cambridge, 1964) p.79
14. Letter dated Cassino, 19 August 1919, quoted in J. Griffin, *Wittgenstein's Logical Atomism* (Oxford, 1964) p.88.
15. *A Companion to Wittgenstein's Tractatus*, pp.80—81.
16. Cf. W.W. Bartley, *Wittgenstein* (London, 1973) pp. 85—86.
17. See G. Pitcher, *The Philosophy of Wittgenstein* (Engelwood Cliffs, N.J. 1964) p.8n.
18. *Proceedings of the Aristotelian Society, Suppl. Vol. 1929*; reprinted in *Essays on Wittgenstein's Tractatus*, edited by I.M. Copi and R.W. Beard (London, 1966) pp.31—37.
19. Edited by R. Rhees (Oxford, 1965) English translation, Oxford, 1975.
20. Edited by R. Rhees (Oxford, 1969) English translation, Oxford, 1974.
21. Edited by G.E.M. Anscombe and R. Rhees (Oxford, 1967).
22. Edited by G.H. von Wright, R. Rhees and G.E.M. Anscombe (Oxford, 1967).
23. Edited by R. Rhees (Oxford, 1969).
24. Edited by R. Rhees (Oxford, 1969).
25. Edited by B.F. McGuinness (Oxford, 1967).
26. Edited by C. Barrett (Oxford, 1966).
27. Edited by G.E.M. Anscombe and G.H. von Wright (Oxford, 1967).
28. Edited by G.E.M. Anscombe and G.H. von Wright (Oxford, 1969).
29. 'Some Remarks on Logical Form' in Copi and Beard, op.cit. (note 18) p.35.
30. F. Waismann, *Wittgenstein und der Wiener Kreis* (Oxford, 1967) pp.63—64. Kenny's translation in op.cit., pp.106—107.
31. Ibid.
32. Waismann, op.cit.,p.81; Kenny, op.cit. (note 3) p. 114.

33. E. Stenius, *Wittgenstein's Tractatus* (Oxford, 1964) chapter ix.

34. After Wittgenstein: cf.PI p.11n.

35. R.M. Hare, 'Imperative Sentences', *Mind* 1949 and *The Language of Morals* (Oxford, 1952).

36. Cf. below p.46.

37. PI p.11.

38., Op.cit. (note 33), p.159.

39. Ibid., pp.159f.

40. Ibid., p.160.

41. Cf.Wittgenstein's list in PI 23.

42. E.g. Kenny, op.cit., pp.167–68.

43. See *How To Do Things With Words* (Oxford, 1962).

44. Op.cit. (note 17), p.243.

45. 'Is Understanding Religion compatible with Believing?' in *Faith and the Philosophers*, edited by J.H. Hick (London, 1964).

46. *Individuals* (London, 1959) p.35.

47. Cf. my *Ethical Intuitionism* (London, 1967).

48. *The Foundations of Wittgenstein's Late Philosophy* (English translation, Manchester, 1969) p.25.

49. Ibid., p.146.

50. Ibid., p.148.

51. Cf. Specht, ibid., p.157; T 6.3751; and 'Some Remarks on Logical Form', in op.cit. (note 18).

52. P. 37.

53. See his 'Verifiability', *Proceedings of the Aristotelian Society, Suppl. Vol.* XIX, reprinted in *Logic and Language* (First Series) edited by A. Flew (Oxford, 1955) p.137.

54. Op.cit. (note 48), p.160.

Chapter 3

1. References in brackets are to Wittgenstein's *Tractatus Logico-Philosophicus* translated by Pears and McGuinness (London, 1961).

2. Cf. M. Black, *A Companion to Wittgenstein's Tractatus* (Cambridge, 1964) p.190.

3. *Grundgesetze der Arithmetik*, II.56; cf. J. Griffin, *Wittgenstein's Logical Atomism* (London, 1964) p.9.

4. T p.xxi.

5. Ibid.

6. 'Ethics', pp. 9—10.

7. Ibid., pp.11—12.

8. I discuss Logical Positivism and religious belief in my *A Philosophical Approach to Religious Belief* (London, 1974) chapter 5, and my *Modern Moral Philosophy* (London, 1970) chapter 2.

9. Quoted in P. Engelmann, *Letters from Ludwig Wittgenstein with a Memoir* (Oxford, 1967) p.143.

10. Engelmann, op.cit.,p.47 footnote.

11. R. Carnap, 'Intellectual Autobiography' in *The Philosophy of Rudolf Carnap* edited by P.A. Schilpp (London, 1963) pp.26—7.

12. Engelmann, op.cit., p.97.

13. See his letter to Ficker, op.cit., Frederich Waismann, *Philosophical Review*, January 1965, p.13, and A. Janik and S. Toulmin, *Wittgenstein's Vienna* (London, 1973) p.194.

14. WWK p.118; N. Malcolm, *Ludwig Wittgenstein: a Memoir*, p.71.

15. T p.3.

16. *Werke* III p.341, quoted in Engelmann, op.cit. (note 9), p.129 and Janik and Toulmin, op.cit.(note 13), p.89.

17. Engelmann, op.cit., p.123.

18. Englemann, op.cit., p.127.

19. Cf. his *Principles of Mechanics*, quoted in Janik and Toulmin, op.cit., p. 140

20. Ibid., quoted in Janik and Toulmin, op.cit., p.141.

21. Englemann, op.cit., p.7.

22. Ibid., p.82

23. Ibid., pp.83—4, footnote.

24. Ibid., p.85.

25. Janik and Toulmin, op.cit., p.196.

26. W.W. Bartley, *Wittgenstein* (Philadelphia and New York, 1973); see also his *Theory of Language and Philosophy of Science as Instruments of Educational Reform: Wittgenstein and Popper as Austrian Schoolteachers* (reprinted from *Method and Metaphysics*, edited by R.S. Cohen and M.W. Wartofsky) (Boston, 1974).

27. Cf. Bartley's letter in *Times Literary Suppl.*, 11 January 1974.

28. Cf. Letters in *Times Literary Suppl.*, from Anscombe and Koder, 16 November 1973, 4 January 1974, 8 February 1974, and Bartley, *Wittgenstein*, p.149.

29. B. Russell, *Autobiography*, vol.ii, pp.167—68.

30. Ibid., p.100.

31. Bartley, op.cit., p.83.

32. Ibid., p.117.

33. See e.g. Englemann op.cit., pp.109—10.

34. Ibid., pp.133—6.

35. Quoted in Engelmann, op.cit.,p.143 footnote, and Janik and Toulmin, op.cit., p.192.

36. *Matthew* vi.7.

37. *Matthew* xxi.30.

38. Engelmann, op.cit., p.135.

39. Ibid.

40. Ibid.

Chapter 4

1. Cf. above p.86.

2. Reprinted in *Logical Positivism*, edited by A.J. Ayer (Glencoe, Ill., 1959).

3. Ibid., p.54.

4. Ibid., p.56.

5. Ibid.

6. Ibid., p.57.

7. Ibid., p.58.

8. Ibid., pp.58—9.

9. Ibid., p.56.

10. Ibid.

11. Ibid.

12. Cf. PI 354.

13. Even in PI 353, Wittgenstein says: 'Asking whether and how a proposition can be verified is only a particular way of asking "How do you mean?" The answer is a contribution to the grammar of the proposition.' The identification of *how you verify* with *how you mean* in this late passage is the more surprising because in the next paragraph of PI, Wittgenstein remarks on the fact that 'the fluctuation in grammar between criteria and symptoms makes it look as if

there were nothing at all but symptoms'. It is just this fluctuation of which he seems guilty in PI 353.

14. I am indebted to Mr Keith Dickson for advice in translations of WWK.

15. Cf. R.S. Heimbeck, *Theology and Meaning* (London, 1969) p.57.

16. A. Kenny, *Wittgenstein* (London, 1973) pp.134—5.

17. Moore, *Philosophical Papers*, p.266.

18. Op.cit., second edition (London 1946), in which the first edition of 1936 is reprinted with a long corrective introduction, p.35.

19. Ibid., p.9.

20. Ibid., pp.8, 15—16.

21. Ibid., p.41.

22. Ibid., p.41.

23. Ibid., pp.15, 114—20.

24. *Language, Truth and Logic* (second edition) pp. 15—16; *Logical Positivism*, p.15.

25. *Language, Truth and Logic* (second edition) p.16.

26. *Langauge, Truth and Logic* (second edition) pp.37—8.

27. Ibid., p.39.

28. Ibid., pp.38—9.

29. Cf. F. Waismann, 'Verifiability' in *Logic and Language*: first series, edited A. Flew (Oxford, 1955).

30. Ayer, op. cit. pp.12—13.

31. Berlin, 'Verifiability in Principle.' *Proceedings of Aristotelian Society*, 1938—39; cf. Ayer, op. cit., pp.11—12.

32. Ayer, op.cit., p.13.

33. A.J. Ayer, *The Central Questions of Philisophy* (London, 1973) p.27.

34. *Journal of Symbolic Logic*, 1949, pp.52—3.

35. Op. cit. (note 33), p.28.

36. Ibid., p.27.

37. See p.127.

38. *The Central Questions of Philosophy*, pp.23—4.

39. *Language, Truth & Logic* (second edition) p.15.

40. Cf. Heimbeck, op. cit. (note 15), pp.67—8.

41. *The Central Questions of Philosophy*, p.33.

42. 'On What There Is' in A.J. Ayer, *Philosophical Essays* (London, 1954) p.229, (reprinted from *Proceedings of the Aristotelian Society*, suppl. vol. 1951).

43. *The Logic of Scientific Discovery* (London, 1959) p.280.

44. *A Modern Introduction to Philosophy*, second edition, edited by P. Edwards & A. Pap (New York, 1965) p.743; cf. *Language, Truth and Logic*, p.15.

45. Op.cit., p.34.

46. *The Philosophy of Rudolf Carnap*, edited by P.A. Schilpp (London, 1963) pp. 26—7.

47. See e.g. R. Otto, *The Idea of the Holy* (Pelican edition, London, 1959) p.74; and P. Tillich, 'The Meaning and Justification of Religious Symbols' in *Religious Experience and Truth*, edited by S. Hook (London, 1962) p.315.

48. See especially pp.161—76.

49. See below p. 143.

50. First published in *University*; reprinted in *New Essays in Philosophical Theology* (London, 1955) edited by A. Flew and A.C. MacIntyre, and many other collections.

51. Cf. I.T. Ramsey, *Religious Language* (London, 1957) p.68.

52. 'Gods'. *Proceedings of the Aristotelian Society*, 1944; reprinted in *Logic and Language* (first series), edited by A. Flew; and *Philosophy and Psycho-Analysis* (Oxford, 1957).

53. 'Theology and Falsification in Retrospect' an as yet unpublished paper which Professor Flew has kindly allowed me to see. My criticism of Flew owes much to R.S. Heimbeck, op.cit. (note 15).

54. See my *A Philosophical Approach to Religion* (London, 1974) chapters V & VI.

55. Cf. e.g. J. Hick, *Faith and Knowledge* (New York, 1957) and K. Nielsen, *Contemporary Critiques of Religion* (London, 1971) chapter 4.

Chapter 5

1. *Dilemmas* (London, 1954) p.81.

2. Op. cit. p.67.

3. Cf. D.Z. Phillips, 'Religious Beliefs and Language-Games' in *Faith and Philosophical Inquiry* (London, 1970) pp.104—5 (reprinted from *Ratio*, 1970.)

4. See e.g. H.H. Price, *Belief* (London, 1969), Lecture 9; N. Malcolm, 'Is it a Religious Belief that God exists?' in *Faith and the Philosophers*, edited by J. Hick (London, 1964), and my *A Philosophical Approach to Religion* (London, 1974) pp.90—94.

5. See R.M. Hare, 'Theology and Falsification, B' in A. Flew and A. MacIntyre, *New Essays in Philosophical Theology* (London, 1955); D.D. Evans, *The Logic of Self-Involvement* (London, 1963); P. van Buren, *The Secular Meaning of the Gospel* (London, 1963).

6. Cf. J.J. MacIntosh, *'Belief-in'*, *Mind*, 1970.

7. See J.L. Austin's, *How To Do Things with Words* (Oxford, 1962) p.159.

8. Ibid., p.152.

9. Ibid., p.156.

10. On explicit and implicit performatives cf. Austin, ibid., pp.32—3.

11. Malcolm, op.cit. (note 4).

12. Ibid., p.108.

13. 'Faith, Scepticism and Religious Understanding.' in *Religion and Understanding* (Oxford, 1967), edited by D.Z. Phillips, p.69.

14. *A Philosophical Approach to Religion* (London, 1974) pp.97—105.

15. Wittgenstein cites one, LRB p.57.

16. Death and Immortality, p.68.

17. Ibid., pp.68—9

18. Ibid., p.66.

19. Ibid., p.71.

20. Ibid., p.64.

21. Ibid., p.65—6.

22. Ibid., p.70. (cf. LRB p.71).

23. Ibid., pp.76—7.

24. See note 3.

25. Cf. Phillips, op. cit. p.98.

26. Cf. S.C. Brown, *Do Religious Claims Make Sense?* (London, 1969) p.178.

27. Cf. A. Flew, 'Theology and Falsification' A. Flew and A. MacIntyre, op.cit.

28. See 'An Attempt to Defend Theism', *Philosophy*, 1964.

29. 'Some Remarks on Wittgenstein's Account of Religious Belief' in *Talk of God*, edited by G.N.A. Vesey (London, 1969) p.38; see also W.D. Hudson '"Using a picture" and religious belief', *Sophia*, 1973.

30. 'Religion and Language' in *Without Answers* (London, 1969) pp.123—4.

31. 'On Referring', *Essays in Conceptual Analysis* (London, 1956) edited by A.G.N. Flew (reprinted from *Mind*, 1950).

32. 'Some Replies to Criticism' in *My Philosophical Development*, (London, 1959) pp.243—4.

33. Op.cit. pp.30—1.

Index